GETTING
UNSTUCK

GETTING UNSTUCK

by

LINDA MINTLE

GETTING UNSTUCK by Linda Mintle
Published by Creation House
A division of Strang Communications Company
600 Rinehart Road
Lake Mary, Florida 32746
www.creationhouse.com
www.charismalife.com

Unless otherwise noted, all Scripture quotations are from the New King James Version of the Bible. Copyright © 1979, 1980, 1982 by Thomas Nelson, Inc., publishers. Used by permission.

Scripture quotations marked TLB are from The Living Bible. Copyright © 1971. Used by permission of Tyndale House Publishers, Inc., Wheaton, IL 60189. All rights reserved.

AUTHOR'S NOTE: All of the stories in this book come from my clinical and personal experience with people over the past twenty years. I have lived and worked in various states and settings around the country. Names, places and any identifying details have been changed and altered to protect the privacy and anonymity of the individuals to whom they refer. People referenced are actually composites of a number of people who share similar issues and are equally protected with names and information changes to remain confidential. Any similarity between the names and stories of individuals described in this book and individuals known to readers is purely coincidental and not intentioned.

Copyright © 1999 by Linda Mintle
All rights reserved

Library of Congress Catalog Card Number: 99-76012
International Standard Book Number: 0-88419-652-6

9 0 1 2 3 4 5 VERSA 8 7 6 5 4 3 2 1
Printed in the United States of America

DEDICATION

This book is dedicated to all the women who have graciously allowed me to be part of their lives and the healing process. Over the years, our journey together has taught me much. We've laughed; we've cried; we've persevered; but most of all we have overcome.

To my mother and father, William and Esther Marquardt, who have suffered multiple losses but have come through the pain to the other side. You have laid a godly foundation.

To my mother-in-law, Bea Mintle, who has lived the godly example of a woman who has the joy of the Lord despite her circumstances. You have lived out your faith quietly but as a daily witness of the healing power of God.

ACKNOWLEDGMENTS

As a woman, wife, mother, daughter, professor, therapist and friend, I can only write books because of the love and support from so many people. Thank you:

To God who is the ultimate transformer
of loss to new life.

To my husband, Norm, who has been my
partner for twenty-five years and is still adored.

To my children, Matt and Katie, who allowed
me to work on my book this summer.
You are my gifts from God.

To my parents for sacrificing their time
to give me peace of mind while I wrote.

To my pastor, Rev. Greg Dickow, for his
uncompromising teaching of the Word.

To my new "good mother" and encourager,
Charlotte Hale.

To my friends with whom I process my
"stuff," Bunny, Diane and Jan.

To Rick Nash and Dave Welday at Creation House
for their faith in me and this project.

To all the wonderful people at Creation House
for being a part of the team—especially
Connie Gamb, Sandy Hill and Peg deAlminana.
It was these women who got the job finished!

CONTENTS

1

Woman to Woman

This is a book for women. There are too many books written by men that talk about women—you know, Mars explains Venus. Don't you think it's time to have Venus write about Venus? Well, Venus is here to talk planet to planet. OK, enough about planets; I can't keep them straight anyway. Men can hear our pain but can't live it and intimately know the reactions we share. That's OK. We don't have to wave our feminist flag and declare men incompetent. But understanding ourselves is simply one reason I am writing to you—woman to woman.

For the past twenty years I have devoted my life to helping people get unstuck—first as a therapist, and now also through teaching, speaking and writing. My motivation in telling you these stories of triumph is to encourage you to be courageous, face your problems and get unstuck from depression, anxiety and eating disorders.

GETTING UNSTUCK

Getting unstuck is far from easy. But astonishing change is possible. But you have to decide to do the hard work and trust God to help you move from stuck to unstuck.

You will undoubtedly find yourself in these stories. You will come to understand a way to think about your life when you are stuck, figure out what is keeping you there and learn new strategies to move you forward.

But before we go further, we have to dispel a few crazy myths about change. Compiled at the home office in Chicago, Illinois, here is today's top seven list. (OK, so it's shorter than Dave Letterman's.) Anyway, the category is—"Seven questions I feel too stupid to ask but am really thinking." (I am now tearing open the envelope.)

Question # 1: Am I doomed by my dysfunctional family?

Show me a family that is not dysfunctional, and we will all move to that planet! (We are back to planets again!) And when we do move to that planet, there are no guarantees that people won't become dysfunctional. You can't blame your family for your problems, even if they are aliens! Family may contribute to your problems, but you are ultimately responsible for fixing them.

Question #2: Do we always talk about our mothers?

Only if they are not in the room! Actually, moms have a bad rap. Being a mom is the hardest job I have ever undertaken. We *should* talk about moms, but in kinder, more empathetic ways, and stop blaming them for the ills of the world. They did not cause famines in our land, riots in our streets or wars among nations.

Question #3: Am I having problems because I wasn't breast fed?

You are having problems if you even ask this question. How can someone's breasts cause you to have problems? I mean, think about it. Freud just needed to blame his mother. (See Question 2.)

Question #4: Do I have to lie down on the couch and get in touch with my inner child?

Inner child, outer child—get in touch with your *grown up* child! I am not dismissing the wounds of childhood. They deeply affect us, but we can get so stuck in the childhood pain that we don't change our current adult behavior.

Question #5: If I help people am I codependent?

By today's definition of codependency, Jesus was codependent. Helping others and showing concern for them is not pathological. It's called *Christlike*. It's part of who we are as women. The problem comes when help isn't helpful—when you do for others what they can do for themselves.

Question #6 : I am a victim, aren't I?

(See Question 1.) If you were raised in the 1950s, you suffer from the repression of women. If you were raised in the 1960s, then the "devil made you do it" and is to blame. If you were raised in the 1970s, free love and drugs led you astray. If you were raised in the 1980s, you got caught up in materialism and greed. If you were raised in the 1990s, Bill Clinton's mother and grandmother are to blame. (See Question #2.)

The truth is . . . everything can influence you, but you are ultimately responsible for who you are before God. On the Day of Judgment, I can't imagine God allowing us to parade a long line of people who prevented us from taking responsibility. Somehow I think we face the big Guy alone.

Question #7: Will I have to seek counseling for the rest of my life?

If you do, you're not seeing a counselor. You are seeing a crook. The purpose of counseling, or any help for that matter, is to get you standing on your own two feet. The idea is to get the problem resolved and move on with life. A good counselor, especially one who understands the transforming power of God, doesn't give you a life sentence.

WHO NEEDS HELP?

Here's another problem related to getting help today. If you are my mother, you probably think people who admit to problems foam at the mouth, have plundered and murdered, shave their heads and only communicate through primal screams. To be honest, I've seen a few of those types in my twenty years of practice, but by and large, I see you. That's right—the woman next door, the guy in the pew, the kid at the movie theater. Sorry it's not more dramatic, but people who seek help are, as my six-year-old says, "reg'lar people." They are nice people whom I usually like a lot.

Ideally we could all do without extra help if we lived right, knew and believed God loves us and loved each other the way God outlines. I know this sounds very elementary; sometimes I'm going to bring you back to very basic points. Why? Because we go brain dead on these simple but inescapable truths. Most of us (myself included) need lots of reminders to go back to the elementary education of our Christian faith. We need help discovering who God intended us to be. We get caught up with people's opinions about God rather than God's opinions about us.

But talking to a therapist, is that really necessary? Time out. I may need to revise the top seven list. Are we now at number eight? Of course it's necessary or people wouldn't do it. People don't come to see me to talk about the latest trend in fashion (although I'm always interested to hear it). They have better ways to spend their hard-earned money than on me! They come because they are stuck. By the time they've come to me, they've talked to everyone else and are still stuck. They want answers. Sometimes my answers are very simple and to the point; sometimes they are complex. You will get a little of both in this book.

ALL WE ARE INTENDED TO BE

The sixty-four-million-dollar question then is, how do we become all we were intended to be? It's a simple answer, so hand over the money. Get ready. I warned you this was coming:

1. *Think* what you are supposed to think.
2. *Behave* in the way you are supposed to behave.
3. Be a *loving person* in all your relationships.

Common sense says this is simple but not easy. Right! It takes work, hard work, work that goes against your nature and the messages of today's culture. You have to fight your nature and society to be the way God intended you to be. It is only possible with God's help.

Why is it so hard to change? You have seen the desk plaque, "If it were simple, everybody would do it." Why don't they? I have a theory.

FACING LOSS

As soon as we are born we start to die. I know that's a depressing thought that may put some of you in therapy right now! But stay with me because it's true. Living is about dying and facing losses in our lives. Not only do we all ultimately face the death of this body, but we face loss continuously throughout our lives. We just do not always recognize loss.

As Emeril, my favorite TV cooking-lite guy says, "Let me kick it up a notch." Loss is not just about the death of someone, although that obviously qualifies as loss. As we move through life, losses come in many ways. We face loss in relationships because they are constantly changing. For example, when we are children, we leave the safety of Mom and Dad and go off to school—that's a loss. When we marry, we leave our home and cleave (do you have weird associations to this word as I do?) to another—that's a loss. Once married, we try not to lose ourselves. Some of us face separation, divorce. We lose our exclusivity with our partner when children enter the picture. Then our children slowly leave us. We age and face losing our youth. And so on.

We also face the loss of *things*—jobs, money, power, status, our identities to name a few. Things come and go, and some of us do better with this than others because the loss of "things" may not be in our control. Losing control is not an easy thing. How we respond to the loss of things is important to our mental health. We can respond with bitterness, anger, envy and other negative emotions that bring on depression, anxiety and eating disorders. Or we can learn not to hold on too tightly to anything that does not have eternal value. In the end, things do not matter.

And we face the loss of dreams, visions and ideals. Life is never quite the way we, or Hollywood, depict it. We carry an elusive ideal about the way things should be that slowly erodes with time. Idealism gives way to real life. Upset that life isn't what we imagined it to be, we can develop anxiety, depression and eating disorders.

The way we think about loss is so important. When loss is viewed as bad or negative, we can get stuck. Loss is not going from *having* to *not having*. If it was, I would be depressed! Loss is going from one thing to a *new* thing—it's change, letting go and watching the new thing emerge. It's growth. It's the power of God making something new out of the ashes.

Spiritually, our growth depends on our ability to lose ourselves and find Christ. Paul, who had everything going "right" prior to his conversion, understood, when he was transformed, that he had to lose everything to gain Christ. (See Philippians 3:7–8.) He could no longer trust in people, things or his own ideals but had to put his trust in God. His willingness to lose himself transformed him from Saul to Paul.

LOSS AND TRANSFORMATION

You are a bona-fide grownup when you face the fact that loss is an ongoing, constant part of life. For those of you struggling to grow up, there is good news, so don't get depressed on me and say, "This woman is a real downer." Here's what we need to do.

We must recognize loss, confront it by grieving and move on to the new thing. Loss can be transformed to new life. This should ring a spiritual bell. Jesus transformed death (loss) into new life. It's the model He gave us—embrace loss; don't avoid or deny it. When we try to avoid or deny loss, we get stuck.

The recognition of loss begins early in life. Listen to the recognition of loss by my six-year-old daughter, Katie. "What's with that Adam and Eve? Why did they have to go wreck things for the rest of us? Now we can get sick and get shots in the arm." Katie understands that when Adam and Eve ate the fruit, they lost their perfect communion with God. Sin and disease were brought into the world. That was mankind's beginning of experienced loss.

What Katie struggles with at the age of six, is what we all struggle with throughout life—"Why do problems have to come into our lives?" We live in a fallen world, and like Adam and Eve we have choices to make in our lives. But instead of getting stuck on the *whys,* we need to focus on what we can do *when* losses come. Because losses will come, and we will be faced with grieving over things we wished never happened.

Ever since the Fall we have been trying to get up. We are trying to get back to the Garden. We long for that perfect place of rest, peace and intimate connection with God and each other. Thankfully, Jesus came to show us how to find that connection. What does He tell us to do?—lose our life to find it.

He tells us we can save our life by losing it. This is radical thinking and certainly goes against the thinking of our culture. So the challenge is not to fear loss but to embrace it so you can find the new thing. That way you will not be dependent on people, things or your ideals to meet the needs of your soul. Be dependent on God. We can't lose Him. He's never been lost. Only we have.

WHAT TO KNOW AND BELIEVE

We must learn to be dependent on God and nothing else. That is where our hope lies. The problem is, many of us don't know and understand the love God has for us, so it's hard for us to be completely dependent on Him. First John 4:16 says, "And we have known and believed the love God has for us. God is love, and he who abides in love abides in God, and God in him." This scripture is telling us to *know* and *believe* God loves us.

How do we know God loves us? He tells us so. (It's that simple stuff again!) We also know by God's action. He sent His only Son to suffer and die in order to take away our sins and provide us with eternal life so we could be with Him forever. What a sign of love—to lay down His life for us while we were yet sinners! If you aren't sure God loves you, get out your Bible and start reading about His love.

We are told to *believe* He loves us. Many of us *intellectually* know that God loves us. We've repeated it a hundred times in Sunday school. We've sung the song, "Jesus loves me. This I know." But do we really *believe* He loves us? As adults, do we say, "Jesus loves me" and claim all that He has for us? No we don't, and that's the problem. Knowing and believing are two separate things.

If we believe God loves us, we have no cause to worry about anything. Like a child in Daddy's arms, the world feels safe and protected in the middle of the storm. God's love is even greater. He is the only one who will never let us down no matter what. There is no one else like Him.

Many times we feel we don't deserve God's love, and that's OK because we don't. It's not about what we do to earn His love. It's about what He did for us—He gave. We can't go by how we feel, what we do or how important we are. None of that matters to God. What matters is that we learn to accept His love as freely given. The love of God makes it possible for us to work through any loss that comes our way.

POWERFUL PROMISES

Here are four of the many promises God gave to show He loves us. We need to know these, believe these and remind ourselves of them regularly. They are at the root of conquering and moving on from any problem in life. They are simple promises that take too many of us a lifetime to own:

- God will *never* break His covenant with us (Judg. 2:1).
- God will never leave us (Heb. 13:5).
- God will never forsake us (Heb. 13:5).
- God will never remember our sins (Micah 7:19).

As we wrestle with life's losses, we can get stuck. We can get really stuck! Why? Because, like six-year-old Katie, we don't want to face all the

8

emotional complications of an imperfect world that can't give us everything we need. We think, *If only…* rather than thinking loss is inevitable. Instead of grieving and moving on, we lose our dependence on a loving God who is waiting to help us. We forget the promises because at the moment, things don't look so good.

Necessary Emotions

When we face loss, we often get stuck in the accompanying emotions—shock, denial, anger, depression, sorrow and confusion. These emotions must be felt, managed and accepted or problems can develop.

For example, Liz was a teenager who finally realized that her parents' divorce was unavoidable. But when the divorce actually occurred, Liz was overwhelmed with grief and sadness. She didn't know how to handle the intensity of the loss she felt and got stuck. Liz developed bulimia and for years reacted with feelings of sadness and grief by bingeing and purging. Liz was stuck.

Intellectually, Liz knew her parents were divorced but didn't want to think about it and certainly didn't want to feel the pain. Others deny loss or pretend it doesn't exist at all. How do they do this? By numbing the pain though food, alcohol, drugs, work or any other obsession. When we do this, we sidestep the pain and its accompanying growth. Depression, anxiety and eating disorders are rooted in losses that are avoided, denied or numbed.

Excuses, Excuses, Excuses!

So, if facing loss is best, why don't we do it? I thought you would never ask. Here is the tough stuff. This is where the work begins. "You have gotta," as my pastor says, "get a hold of this." We are stuck because of these six excuses:

1. I don't want to do what it takes to get better.

As a therapist, I can help you identify the problem, relate it to loss, help you grieve and then give you ideas about what to do to move on with your life. What I can't do is *make* you do it. Well, I could, but that would be unethical. *You* have to act. If you don't, nothing changes.

Too often I see people unwilling to change. Frankly, I've told people not to waste their money seeing me in therapy because it is clear to me they do not want to change. People complain about their not-so-perfect lives, I offer help, and then they do not act on it. In therapy, this is called *resistance*. Spiritually, we cannot wait for our desire to catch up to our obedience. We should try to act on God's truth whether we want to or not.

2. It doesn't feel good.

You know the saying, (I'm paraphrasing here) "If it doesn't feel good don't do it." Excuse me, but since when are we ruled by our feelings? Apparently since the 1960s. The problem with feelings is we can't always rely on them. They get us in trouble. Ask any three-year-old what happens when she only does what feels good. Or try asking a hormonal teenager the same question. A major part of growing up is learning to override our emotions. Some of us are still stuck in adolescence trying to do this.

So we have a lot of stuck people. Change doesn't feel good. Initially it usually feels lousy, and I often remind my clients of this. "How was your week," I ask. "Lousy, all kinds of tough issues were coming at me, and I felt horrible." "Good," I reply. "Then we are probably getting some-where." If you feel good at the beginning of change, you probably aren't changing. You are in your comfort zone. We do what we do because it's familiar, comfortable. Change is uncomfortable, uneasy and provokes a motivating kind of anxiety.

3. It's too hard.

We've become a bunch of lazy people who only want to do what's easy and effortless. At times, we feel it is too hard to face the pain in life. Obviously, ignoring the pain doesn't work either. As I said, change is hard work. It's not for the fainthearted. We can wallow in our problems, be the eternal victim or do something to change our lives. It's up to us. We can stay stuck, or do the hard work and get unstuck.

4. I am too afraid.

Well, join the rest of us. We may be afraid, but we do what we have to do anyway. For example, when I'm the only grownup in the house in the middle of the night and I hear a noise, I can lie in my bed terrified, or I can get up terrified and protect my kids. Facing loss or pain is scary. But we have to get out of bed and face it.

When we let fear guide our decisions, we stay stuck. Fear takes us nowhere. It only builds on itself and paralyzes us. I remember the time we were at Disney World facing one of those fun but scary-looking rides. Now I know the difference between fun and terrifying when it comes to rides, and I never push anyone to do *terrifying*. But *fun* is another story.

I knew my son, Matt, would love the fun ride. Once he conquered his fear, his confidence would be built. So we talked about not letting fear take over and keep us stuck on the ground, never to experience a joy or a thrill. The ground is safe but there is so much more above it. Fear keeps us on the ground, getting by with life but never really experiencing life's thrills and joy. Matt conquered his fear and got on that ride. He discovered the thrills above the ground. Now you can't keep him on the ground. There is too much fun above it.

5. I do not believe I can do it.

This could be the national anthem of women. We've bought the lie that says we can't do things, that we should be dependent, victims, that we have no talents or special abilities. We can't, 'cause we haven't tried. When we do try, we fall prey to the excuses above. We all need to scream out our windows, "I'm sick and tired of this, and I'm not going to take it anymore." Let's stop putting ourselves down and doubting our talents and abilities. We can do it. We can change. We can get better. But we have to believe it and stop doubting.

6. I don't want to depend on God.

We don't know God, and we think of Him like any other human—flawed and likely to let us down. Instead of understanding the true nature of God and His undying love for us, we attribute human tendencies to

11

Him, making Him weak, uncaring and uninvolved in our lives. Like the music videos on MTV, we've reduced Jesus to a religious figure with no power.

We have to know God intimately in order to live in His love and experience His perfect peace. When we understand who Jesus really is, there is no way we could depend on anyone else. No one is able to come through and love us like He can.

UNBELIEF

Unbelief keeps us stuck. Even Jesus experienced this as He tried to help others. Remember when He returned to His boyhood home, Nazareth, and taught in the synagogue? The people were amazed at His wisdom and mighty works but couldn't believe He was that carpenter's son. They must have stared at Him and said, "That's Jesus? The kid who ran around our tent? Who does He think He is?" They became offended at Him. Because of their unbelief, Jesus did not do mighty miracles in Nazareth.

Unbelief—first in God, then ourselves—keeps us from having the power of God flowing significantly in our lives and keeps us from being all God intended us to be. Just as people doubted Jesus' abilities, we doubt our own. For example, when someone says to me, "Oh, that's just Linda. She's no big deal. Who does she think she is?", I can say I am a daughter of a King! I am valuable, because I was bought with a price. I am God's child and that makes me pretty special. So don't let anyone tell you, you can't! With God, you can do all things.

My experience and faith in God lead me to believe we can move out of our inertia and into a fuller, freer life. Read on, and learn how to get unstuck from the top three mental health problems for women—depression, anxiety and eating disorders.

SECTION
ONE

DEPRESSION

Stuck in Depression

Moms are great, aren't they? I mean, they tell you all this wonderful stuff that may or may not be true. But because it comes from Mom, you can believe it. You know the mom classics: cover your ears so you don't catch cold, wear clean underwear in case you are in an accident and have to go to the hospital, don't drink anything cold because it will give you a cold. Please feel free to send me your favorite. I'm keeping a list for my daughter. My favorite one, though, is the one about toilet seats. Don't sit on the public ones because you'll catch all kinds of diseases. Well, depression is like toilet seats! We have a lot of crazy ideas about how we "catch" it—some accurate and some off base.

IT DOESN'T COME FROM TOILET SEATS!

Depression is a *response* to life's constant losses and challenges. It's more than just feeling sad or down. It's a persistent sadness that affects most aspects of all our lives—sleeping, eating, working, socializing and enjoying life.

You may face big losses like a father diagnosed with cancer, the death of a spouse, a child in chronic physical pain, a tornado demolishing your house, a deadbeat dad not paying child support or a love turned sour.

Or, you can sweat the smaller but significant stuff, such as a husband who won't pay attention to you, a critical boss, a mother-in-law who meddles (not mine thank goodness), a friend who is rejecting, that woman who can't count and is ahead of me with a full cart of groceries in the ten-item express line or a teenager who wants to look like Marilyn Manson. The list could go on forever, but I have a book to finish here.

Put simply, depression can result from not dealing well with people, things and expectations. In most cases, we bring on depression by the way we respond to living. I'm sorry. I know more of you wanted me to say that depression is simply biochemical. So, let's talk about that. Depression is and is not biochemical. How's that for waffling?

Here's the scoop. Some people are more prone to depression because of their biological and genetic makeup. There are some forms of depression like bipolar disorder, for example, that have a strong genetic component and respond well to medication. Other forms of depression are caused by genetic or biological factors such as a lack of sleep, poor diet, PMS, postpartum delivery of a baby, menopause, side effects of medications and disease.

We really are not certain whether changes in brain chemistry cause depression or are a *result* of stress over time. We do know that when someone is depressed, a chemical imbalance can result. That's why antidepressants are so effective in stabilizing mood.

So what does this mean for the average depressed person? It means that there are times when antidepressants help you on the road to healing. Do we trust in the medication to heal us? No—we trust in God, and expect Him to fully heal us. But there are times when we feel so hopeless, so deep in that "black hole" of depression, we need help getting to a place where we can think more clearly and take action. That's when medication can help.

Not everyone needs medication or has even to consider using it. On the other hand, we should be careful not to condemn those who are truly helped by medication. There is nothing wrong with using what is available to help you out of that stuck place.

Now that you have heard my two-second speech on medication, I want to emphasize that most depressions are related to the way we approach and handle life. They are caused by psychological, social and spiritual issues like family experiences, unresolved hurts and anger, negative thinking, loss, social problems, a vicious cycle of thinking depressed thoughts then acting in depressed ways and viewing the world from a negative lens.

HEAR NO EVIL, SEE NO EVIL, DO NO EVIL— THOSE MONKEYS WERE FIGHTING DEPRESSION!

Can you picture those monkeys with their hands over their heads, covering their eyes and ears? They were doing something right. They were blocking out evil. Now negative thoughts and acts are not exactly evil. Don't misunderstand me, but you get the point. For those who don't, the point is, do not dwell on negative thoughts, don't talk negatively and expect bad things to happen and don't act in negative ways. I know this sounds simple, but it isn't. We are more complicated than those monkeys!

When we are depressed we believe crazy notions like "people *shouldn't* act a certain way" even though they do, or "life *shouldn't* go this way" even though it does. Your thoughts are incredibly powerful in affecting your moods. So take the time and think about your thoughts! Are they generally negative? Do you believe thoughts like, *I can't get out of my situation* or *I am a failure* or *Nothing ever works?* Are you listening to all the negative and depressing voices of the day and expecting the worst? If you are, and negative thinking has become a way of life, you need to change.

"But Dr. Mintle, I can't change my thoughts. They just happen!" You *can* change your thoughts. *We have control over what we think!* You may not *take* control, but you have it. Often our thoughts are so automatic that we do not pay attention to them. When we do pay attention, we can learn to stop negative thoughts and change them.

For example, one of the common thoughts of a depressed woman is, *The situation is hopeless. I'm going to be miserable.* With God, is any situation hopeless? No. So stop thinking "wrong." Yes I said *"wrong."* Contrary to popular opinion, and the opinion of my own profession, there is a wrong and right way to think. Any thought that does not line up with the Word of God is wrong. Wrong thoughts lead you to feel more depressed and defeated, and that's right where the enemy wants you. Instead, stop and correct your thought like this, *This situation looks pretty bad but with God, all things are possible.* When you challenge your thoughts with God's promises, you won't feel depressed. You will be encouraged.

Sounds easy, but it's not easy to do. It takes awareness of your thinking patterns and practice to think differently. You have learned to think negatively, now you have to unlearn those thoughts. Philippians 4:8–9 tells us to think about things that are true, good, right, pure, lovely and praiseworthy. If you think about all God has done for you, you can come up with a reason to be glad. In case you are searching for a place to start, here's a good one—God made a covenant with you. He sent His Son, Jesus, to die for you and to forgive you of your sins. That's got to get you a little excited. And nothing changes what He did for you, so you can always meditate on that good thought.

Ann learned the importance of changing her thoughts. Ann's life was chronically unhappy. She faced numerous relationship losses. Her father died when she was young, and her family drifted apart. Her brother married and moved out of the country. Her sister married an international banker and traveled the world. Ann felt alone and abandoned. Ann was married at one time, but had chosen a man whom she hardly knew. He turned out to be a cocaine addict and only worked occasionally. Eventually he divorced Ann and moved in with another drug addict. Disillusioned with marriage, Ann spent her days working hard and caring for her aging uncle. When Ann came to see me, she had nothing good to say about anyone. Her siblings were self-centered, her uncle demanding, and men required too much care and gave little in return. All of her thoughts about living were negative.

Ann was moody and depressed. She was competent on her job as an accountant but losing interest in it. She felt hopeless and annoyed with people. The more she complained, the worse she felt. But she could see no reason to be positive about her life. "Look at my life; would you be happy?" she asked. *People only care about themselves. There is no one who loves me, who will stay around—they either die or take off. I must be undesirable, uninteresting and unable to attract healthy men. No one bothers with me. Life is a pain, and I'm tired, real tired.* These were Ann's constant thoughts.

Ann's mind needed renewing. Her thoughts were only negative. We began by finding anything or anyone who contradicted her negative experience. We focused on one person or one event. For example, one of her coworkers was friendly and reliable. I asked Ann to tell me about this woman. Were there other women, or possibly men, who treated her well and with respect? Yes, she could think of a few. So we concentrated on those relationships. You see, when you are depressed you only focus on the negative experiences, the ones that reinforce your depression.

I purposely stopped Ann from complaining about people and told her to report positive events about her week. She hated this and often got mad at me because it wasn't what she was used to doing. However, she managed to report one or two good moments in her day. After a number of weeks, more of her life was reported as positive. Not much had changed in her day-to-day life, but her attention to positive moments began to change her thinking. When I required her to report positive events in her week, she had to look for them. These events and interactions were evidence that not all of her life was negative. This evidence began slowly to change her thinking.

Another problem with depressed women is that they hang out with other depressed people or isolate themselves. You know the saying, misery loves company. So get around people who can build you up, and talk about things that are hopeful and uplifting. I am not saying dump all your current friends or isolate yourself from anyone who has a problem. I am saying that when you are stuck in negative thinking, one way to help yourself change is to be around people who see life with the glass half full. When you associate with positive, hopeful people, their outlook on life will be contagious.

Again, this doesn't mean you never acknowledge difficulties. It means you deal with difficulty from a much more positive framework. What is that framework? Go back to Jesus, what He did for you, and all the promises of God. Read your Bible. Start with the Psalms—try Psalm 91 for example. When you read Scripture, you can't help but be encouraged. God's promises are powerful. That's why hanging out with people who constantly reference the promises of God is helpful. Get some good friends who will encourage you. If you don't know anyone who knows God's promises, at least find someone who is a positive thinker.

After you work on your thoughts (remember the monkeys—hear no evil), associate with those who give hope (see no evil) and work on your behavior (do no evil). We can quote Scripture until we are blue in the face and hang out with positive people, but if we continue to *act* depressed, we will stay depressed.

Mary was a terrific single parent who became more and more depressed over the behavior of her twin teenaged sons. The two fair-haired blondes were fraternal twins, with one son significantly taller than his brother. The shorter son dropped out of high school and began betting on horses at a local racetrack. The taller one was on his way to the same life plan—not a plan Mary dreamed for either of her boys. They were hanging out with kids who partied and got high, who didn't have paying jobs and were disrespectful and annoying to Mary. As the younger son continued to act up in school and at home, Mary became increasingly depressed.

Mary believed in her sons. Like most moms, she knew they had the potential to be good boys despite their current choices. But Mary had sunk like a rock on the ocean floor. Nothing I said moved her to action. She wouldn't get up out of bed in the morning. She set no rules, because she felt powerless to enforce them. Her depression immobilized her. She and her sons were going nowhere fast. Mary was waiting to *feel* better in order to take a step of action. I was telling Mary to take the step, and eventually she would feel better. Action had to happen, regardless of how she felt.

I had Mary identify one small change she could begin to make—not a lot of big changes—but something small that wouldn't take a lot of energy, because when you are depressed, you don't have a lot of energy. She decided she could make herself eat when she got out of bed. So that's where we started. I know it doesn't sound like much and isn't directly related to parenting her sons, but we always start with something you feel you can do successfully.

The next week I had her add another change. She wanted to get out of bed before her sons left for school. And so it went—small changes each week. As Mary found success making small changes, she started to feel better. When her mood improved, we tackled the tough stuff—setting limits with the boys, working with the school, enforcing rules and the like. Mary still wasn't feeling great, but knew what she had to do. Dealing with conflict is hard work—it can be emotionally exhausting. But Mary knew action was moving her forward. The depressed feelings were improving slowly as she committed to taking steps to help her boys.

I know what you are thinking. When you are depressed, you can't do anything. That's what Mary said. The truth is you don't *feel* like doing anything—you still can—even if it is a small step in the right direction. Each time you take a step, you build confidence and see progress. That reinforces you and gives you more energy to move forward.

So action is important. But the way you act makes a difference. There are those of you whose actions don't line up with God's Word, and you wonder why you feel depressed.

Lynne's life is a good example. Lynne had been through a messy divorce after five years of marriage. Her husband had a homosexual affair and decided he preferred his newfound lifestyle. He left the marriage to live with the other man, his lover. Lynne was devastated. Lynne had no children but a great job as an artist. She threw herself into her work, but after a while she became lonely for male companionship. She had a strong support network of women friends and a family who loved her and saw her often, but she missed the attention of a man. Lynne continued to go to church and joined a home Bible study group.

When I first saw Lynne she was quite depressed. She was grieving her divorce, had good support and was active in her church, but she was stuck in the depression. Something wasn't right. I asked Lynne if she was sexually active with the man she dated from the Bible study. Embarrassed, she admitted she was having sex, "We both know we're not supposed to have sex, but both of us were married before, and it just happened."

My response to Lynne was, "It doesn't just happen. I don't even allow my teenagers to get away with that excuse! The fact that you continue to have a sexual relationship is a decision to break God's rules. You can't just pick the parts of the Bible you like and ignore the other parts and expect no consequences when you profess Christ as your Savior. It must be incredibly tough to have had a sexual relationship for years and suddenly be cut off. But you can't disobey God just because it's tough. Come on, Lynne, you know this."

Obviously, I told Lynne to stop having sex with her boyfriend. I know this sounds really basic, and people do pay me for this kind of brilliant advice, but when Lynne stopped breaking God's law, she started feeling less depressed. It's not always so easy to get unstuck, but obeying God will get you moving.

So let's review (this is the graduate professor in me speaking now). Loss is a part of life. Depression is a response to life's losses. Some depressions are more biochemical than others, but all involve thinking negatively, hanging out with negative people and acting depressed. The challenge then is to learn to think in hopeful ways, associate with people who will encourage you and take action to get out of your depression. You have the basic ideas. Now let's get more specific and apply what we know to everyday living.

3

Losses Come in Threes

I keep mentioning life's losses and have given a few examples. But what kinds of losses am I specifically talking about? When I say loss, most of you think of death. Death is a major loss, and many people get stuck in the normal grieving process because they don't work through the emotional reactions of grief. When someone dies, you experience a wide range of emotions. One of those emotions is depression. I'll deal specifically with the loss experienced by a loved one's death in chapter four. But there are other kinds of losses that keep us stuck—ones we aren't always aware of or don't think about consciously.

If you are having trouble identifying these losses, let me help. Start thinking about ways you encounter loss just by living your life. For example, when you wake up with a great outdoor plan for the day, and it's raining like a hurricane, how do you respond? Or when you go to the parent-teacher conference, and the teacher tells you your daughter is lagging behind the others, what do you do? Or when you get everyone ready for church on time, and the baby throws up going out the door, how do you behave? Or when you have planned the perfect dinner party, and the guests arrive an hour late, how do you act?

These seem like little things that don't mean much, but they do. Your responses to these everyday events are important. You can actually get stuck dealing with even the simplest things. Why? Because the way you respond to simple things is like watching a small frame in the movie of your life. It tells you how you respond to loss.

Please understand that I am not saying loss has to be a bad thing. Facing loss doesn't have to be problematic. For example, when we age, we face the loss of physical function, but we don't need to view this negatively. Loss only means change. Most people think of loss as going from *having* to *not having*. That does sound depressing. But don't think of loss like that. Instead, think of loss as going from one thing to a new thing—think of loss as change, letting go and accepting the new way. Growth can result.

If we really think about it, we can't view loss as bad because nothing that happens to us is out of the sight of God. God's not in heaven saying, "Oh, man, I missed that breast cancer invading Julie's body," or "I should have been more aware that a car could hit Ann's car and hurt her. Next time I'll pay attention."

To think God doesn't see, know and control all is absurd. He does. We may not understand events in our lives. I know I don't. But the promise is that He will work all things for our good if we love Him and are called according to His purpose (Rom. 8:28). Notice the scripture says *all* things—even our wrong decisions—not just *some* things. So when God allows loss (because He could stop it), it must be for a reason. Sometimes it's because He allows us to learn from our wrong decisions. We must take responsibility for our actions and the natural consequences that follow. Other times, loss happens for reasons we don't understand and are beyond our control. So we have to trust Him.

So your job isn't to sit around and wonder *why* loss happens, even though some of us like to speculate. You might have ideas, and you might even figure it out sometimes. But your job is to face loss, deal with it and grow from it. You are to discover the new thing that can come from loss.

So let's get started working on you. Try to think of all the losses you encounter in a day. Then organize these losses into categories. You can put loss in three main categories that make sense. At least they make sense to me!

THREE CATEGORIES OF LOSS

I still don't have a top ten list, do I? I'm working on it but three is a good number. So what are the three categories of loss? You have given them to me in my twenty years of therapy practice. Here they are—not in any particular order, although some occupy more of our life than others:

1. Loss of relationships.

This is a big and significant category of loss because it covers so much of our lives. It includes not having the parents you wanted, not being the kid they wanted, being rejected, abandoned, ignored, losing friendships, losing marriage partners and losing people by death. Unless you are part of the perfect relationship, which is the Triune God—Father, Son Jesus and the Holy Spirit—you probably have experienced relationship losses on several levels.

Women are very relational people. We often define our happiness by the success of our relationships. So when we encounter problems in this area, we feel it intensely and get stuck here more than any other area listed.

The most important relationship loss we suffer, though, is our intimate connection with God. God hasn't gone anywhere, but we do move away from Him. We don't know Him like we should, and consequently He's not an intimate part of our lives. This loss really keeps us stuck!

2. Situational loss.

There is so much of living over which we have no control. We do the best we can, but often situations change. We may make a major move like I recently did when we came from Virginia to Chicago. The move involved numerous losses. Just because of a situation, a move, I lost my friends, my job, my church, my teaching appointments, my house, my neighborhood, my community and my doctors to name a few. Wow, I should be depressed! And we are only talking about me, not the rest of my family. Needless to say, the stress of moving is significant because of the multiple losses involved.

Does this mean I should never move? Well if I wanted to avoid loss, theoretically I could live in the same place all my life, but realistically that's not an option today. But even if I could stay in the same place all my life, loss would still happen. No, instead, I need to be aware of all the losses involved in my current situation and make sure I face them in a sound and healthy way. Otherwise, I can get stuck in the loss part and become depressed. Or I can grieve and move on to the new challenges the change presents to me.

A change in health, finances, status or influence are all other examples of situational loss. Any time your situation changes, whether for great or not so great reasons, you experience situational loss.

Again, think about who is in control of situations. We try to be, but God is ultimately in control. When we finally accept the loss of control over circumstances, we get unstuck.

3. Loss of an ideal, a dream, a vision.

In many ways, this has to do with your expectations, the "shoulds" of life, and the way you think your life should go. When you don't accomplish what you set out to do, or take an unplanned turn in your life, you face the loss of ideals. Many of you feel lost and without purpose in your life. Chronic feelings of unhappiness can stay with you because you don't know your purpose or direction.

Again, I want to be clear that all of these losses are not negative. The point is, they exist and have to be contended with on some level. You can fare well with life's losses, or you can get stuck. Depression is one way to get stuck. Anxiety and eating disorders are two other ways (see sections two and three) and will be dealt with later in this book.

Coping with loss is the key. Coping involves having realistic expectations, unconditional love and support, having routines but not becoming rigid, working through feelings and all sorts of reactions to living. Coping is how we get through to the other side. Stuck is not coping. But more on this later.

WOMEN GO INTERNAL

Now that we have identified three categories of loss, the next step is to look at how you face loss. Do you accept it or deny it, avoid it and/or numb yourself from it? Do you work through the emotions that come with loss or stuff them way down inside? Do you persevere through the tough times or throw in the towel? If you give up and give in, you get stuck. Stuck means a problem develops. Depression hits. So ask yourself two questions: Do I acknowledge life's disappointments and hurts? Do I face pain or give in to it?

Raise your hand if you are one of the twenty million people who get depressed. I see that hand, now put it down, and we'll try to figure out why this is happening.

As women, we don't physically beat each other up when we are frustrated. Generally speaking, we're not the ones shooting each other in the streets or beating up our husbands (I know some women do, and most of us have had thoughts of violence!). But as a group, we've been taught not to lash out at others, not to be aggressive. No, our pain is more polite. We beat up on ourselves. We push our upsets, disappointments, hurts and anger deep inside. They rumble around in our innards, taking on a life of their own, and over time, we get depressed.

Then we begin having problems concentrating, sleeping and eating. We lose interest in fun things and lack the energy to do most things. We feel down, tearful, tired, irritable and worthless. A few think about dying as a way out of feeling bad. Have you figured it out? These are signs of depression.

And as if pain in childbirth wasn't enough to lay on us (thank you, Eve), we also win the contest for getting more depressed then men. That's right, hormones, changes associated with menstruation, puberty and pregnancy are unique to us and may put us more at risk. Now don't get depressed over this or wave your feminine flag, because men have their own set of mental health problems and suffer from depression, too.

But we women struggle more with depression. We live in a culture in which our roles are changing and not always defined. Even more, we are often expected to perform multiple roles with little support. As I write this book I am author, mother, wife, carpool driver, speaker, college professor, friend and therapist. When school starts the roles shift again. No wonder I never have time to bake that homemade bread in the bread machine! No wonder I can't even find the bread machine! No wonder I never bought the bread machine!

We also face the challenge of having less power, money and influence than men, which doesn't exactly make us happy campers. In fact, inequities of power can lead to abuse, poverty and depression. Now, I'm not blaming men for all the ills of women, but the imbalance of power in our society and relationships does affect us. Please understand, I like men. I particularly like my husband, but despite all the cries for equality, men still have the edge.

If you are a woman of color, you have even more injustices in your life. Being a woman is not the only issue—being African American, Hispanic, Asian or any other race or ethnicity carries its own set of issues that can play into depression as well.

So what am I saying? I'm saying that women go internal. Coupled with our unique biology, multiple roles and inequality, we get stuck in depression more so than men. So it's time to get a grip on this problem. Let's drop out of the twenty-million club. Let's tackle loss associated with depression and move on with our lives.

4

Facing the Loss of Relationships

W hen I become a big-time TV star and Barbara Walters begs to interview me on television for huge ratings, she'll ask, "If you could be a tree, what tree would you be?" After carefully thinking through my answer, I'll say, "Barbara, why on earth would I think of myself as a tree? I don't think trees—I think people. Barbara, women define themselves by relationships, not by oaks, maples or willows!" So much for my fifteen minutes of fame! It's true. Women are highly relational—a trait that is not always valued in a male world. Men are raised to be independent, to move away from Mom as soon as possible.

Women, on the other hand, are encouraged to stay connected to Mom, to find identity through relationship, not autonomy. Thus, our relationships, whether we like it or not, are core to who we are. And if you think about that, people can hold a lot of power in our lives if we let them.

FIND ME A FUNCTIONAL FAMILY

Don't you get a little annoyed when people talk about a situation and then say, "Oh, she came from a dysfunctional family." Everyone gets quiet and then nods with an all-knowing expression of sympathy. I'm the loudmouth who won't let it pass so easily. "Name one person who doesn't come from a dysfunctional family, and how is that an excuse for anything anyway?" Sorry, I had a momentary lapse of compassion.

The fact is that no family measures up to our expectations or wishes. We all have a degree of disappointment about the way we grew up. That's why, in our youth and naiveté, we make crazy vows that we'll never do what our mothers did to us. Of course, we usually repeat the patterns.

Parents are products of their parents. Patterns of behavior pass down from generations—kind of like the telephone game. You know, the game in which you start a secret, whisper to the next person and by the time the message reaches the end of the line it's totally wrong because there is no correction along the way. Well, families are like that. Without (godly) correction they keep passing that same mixed-up message down the line. By the time you are born, who knows what's going to happen. Unfortunately, a lot can and does happen.

When we understand how our parents were affected by their parents, we can be more empathetic to the ways they behave. For instance, it's not unusual for a young-adult woman to be angry with her mother for being overly critical. When the young adult finds out that Mom's Mom was also critical, somehow that softens the blow. It doesn't make living with a critical mom any easier, but it makes it understandable. It gives the daughter a measure of empathy for her mother.

In the normal process of developing and separating from your parents, you are becoming your own person. Part of the journey is to find the good parts of your parents along with the problematic ones. No one is all good or all bad. If you can find the good parts and acknowledge them, the relationship with parents strengthens. The section on eating disorders will discuss more about girls who get stuck when they try to separate developmentally.

Then there is a period of dating, testing your way in the world and firming up your identity, which can be challenging as well. Most of you will move along the family life cycle to marriage, parenting, launching children and on to later life. This ebb and flow of life involves constant loss and change. Your ability to manage the losses moves you forward or keeps you stuck.

Add to this other life cycle disruptions such as divorce, unexpected death, mental illness, addiction, abuse and unresolved conflict, and you have women who call me for therapy. How do these problems relate to loss and getting stuck? Let's see.

STUCK IN GRIEF—DEATH

Obviously, death is the most difficult loss of all because you are permanently removed from the person on this earth. The good news for Christians is that death is not permanent. We have the hope of seeing each other again in eternity, because Jesus triumphed over death. Even so, losing the physical, emotional and spiritual presence of a person is traumatic. At times, we don't even recognize the impact of death on us and get stuck in adjusting to the loss.

One of the stuck points in dealing with death is not allowing the natural feelings associated with grief to be expressed. What are those feelings—numbness, shock, denial, sorrow, pain, anger, confusion, loneliness, emptiness, depression, guilt, fear, abandonment, isolation, physical symptoms, irritability, fantasy, restlessness, disorganization and hopelessness. These feelings come and go during the grief process. If they are held in, pushed down and stuffed away, depression can result.

Amelia is a good example of this. Amelia was a quick-witted woman who married Tom. Amelia was content with her marriage but had the usual complaints about her husband—he didn't communicate enough, he worked too much and he seemed cut off from his emotional feelings. But then Amelia admitted she had a few problems from her past as well.

Several years of marriage passed, and Amelia and Tom, her athletic, thirty-five-year-old husband, decided to open a restaurant—a dream Amelia had since childhood. Food was an expression of love and a way she could make a living and give something good to others. After a great deal of apprehension, the restaurant opened. One of the pleasant surprises for the couple was how well they functioned as a business team. Amelia ran the day-to-day operation of the restaurant while Tom handled the business end. Life was good—busy but calm.

Amelia and Tom were happy with each other and the restaurant. Customers were steady, and the restaurant's reputation in the community was growing. Things were going as planned when one day Amelia arrived home and found Tom lying in the back yard.

She panicked. He didn't seem to be moving. She went over to check him. He wasn't breathing, and she could hear no heart beat. She began CPR but got no response. She dialed 911 and after several more attempts to revive Tom, the paramedics arrived and pronounced Tom dead. At thirty-five, Tom was gone.

Three years later, Amelia sat in my office, depressed and anxious about life. She had no desire to live herself, couldn't get the picture out of her mind of Tom lying dead in the back yard where he had been raking leaves. She couldn't cry. She walked around the restaurant in a daze, and several of her employees were afraid she was suicidal. Amelia was stuck in the grieving process of losing Tom. His sudden and unexpected death left a huge hole in her life, and she couldn't move on.

When we began to talk about Tom's death, Amelia was emotionless. She could not allow herself to go to that grieving place. She feared it would be too painful, too overwhelming, and she would fall apart. She had a business to run and no one to help her. For Tom's sake, she had to keep it together.

The problem was that Amelia needed to grieve. She couldn't sleep at night and relied on pills from her doctor to give rest. She was overeating and gaining weight. She never went out and had no interest in anything other than work. Only her one friend, Jan, cheered her up. Jan broke the news one night that her husband accepted a promotion in another state, and she would be moving soon.

Amelia, now even more distressed, became fearful and sought comfort in food. When I asked Amelia about her visits to Tom's grave, she told me she never went to the cemetery. She avoided the gravesite because she was afraid she might lose control emotionally.

In order to get Amelia more in touch with her unresolved grief, I had her write a letter to Tom, recounting the day she found him unconscious and telling him the emotional pain she kept locked away in her heart. Initially she resisted the assignment but eventually mustered up the courage to do it. When she did, the tears began to flow. She had much to tell Tom and was relieved to finally get it out.

Next I sent Amelia to the gravesite. She was to park her car and go to his gravesite behind the little white church. There were no expectations. She was to allow whatever feeling emerged to be expressed. She agreed to go, worried that she would feel nothing. Seeing the grave months after the death made the death more final. This time at the cemetery, she sobbed uncontrollably.

We then set aside periods of her day in which she would allow herself to think about Tom's death. As she gave herself permission to grieve for set periods of time, she felt less depressed. Her repressed grief was released in a more controlled manner making it possible for her to function the rest of the day.

But there was more to do before Amelia could fully move on with her life. Amelia was raised an atheist. She didn't believe in an afterlife or in God. As a result, she was struggling to let go of Tom because there seemed to be no meaning in his death. "You live, die and that's it? Somehow that doesn't make me want to go on living either." Then Amelia asked, "Do you personally feel there is more to living than simply dying?" "If I didn't," I replied, "I would be on the couch, stuck where you are."

So Amelia asked for my opinion of death and the meaning of life. I gave a simple answer to a woman who expected a complicated philosophical answer, "For God so loved…" I began. God's incredible love for Amelia and me resulted in the gift of His Son. Jesus went to the cross. He faced death and for a moment experienced what Amelia has felt so many times—God forsakenness. But God did not forsake Jesus or Amelia. Jesus faced death and then transformed it. Death couldn't hold Him, and out of it came His resurrection. Only Jesus could take a loss and transform it into our rebirth.

Amelia was crying again. She was moved by the love of God. Anyone who would send His only Son to die for her when she didn't even acknowledge Him was pretty amazing. "Why would God do such a thing?" she asked. "Only because of His love for you. No other reason. No deals. No expectations. He wanted you to have a little bit of Him so you could feel alive again," I replied.

Amelia was dead inside. When Tom died she went with him, losing all will to continue and looking for something, anything to give her life meaning. "Could Jesus be the One?" she asked. "What do I have to lose? Nothing," she whispered. "Arrange a meeting."

Stuck in the grieving and ultimately stuck with no one to love or depend on, Amelia was ready to meet a loving God. Death has a way of bringing us to the true meaning of life. When we face death, we have the comfort of knowing we are facing something that even the Son of God had to process. Knowing He had to die, Jesus anguished in the garden. "Take this cup from me," He pleaded. But He knew He had to face death to live again. He knew the cup could not be removed for us to live eternally with Him. It was His love for us that propelled Him to the cross. He moved through the grief and submitted to the will of the Father. Love was stronger than death.

Don't allow death to keep you depressed and hopeless. We are never without hope when we know God.

There are times when we find it hard to stay hopeful and feel God's love. Terry knew God but she still felt hopeless. Why? She couldn't get past the rejection she felt when her father committed suicide.

SUICIDE

Terry was raised in a religious home. The family attended church and was known as an upstanding family in the community. Terry's father was a judge and well respected at the courthouse. People loved her father and commented on what a fair and wise man he was when it came to dealing with matters of the law.

At home, Dad was always sad. As the youngest of seven siblings and an only daughter, Terry spent the most time with her father and felt closest to him. She sensed his sadness and felt responsible for his happiness. Dad confided in her and shared his sense of despair about living. Terry tried to cheer Dad up but never really succeeded. Oh, he would laugh at her jokes and temporarily be lighthearted, but then a black veil would overcome him, and he'd sit alone in his chair and drink.

Drinking caused a lot of tension between Mom and Dad. Mom pleaded with Dad to get help, saying over and over he had a problem and needed to talk to someone about it. But Dad wouldn't go see anyone. Instead he sat quietly in his chair night after night drinking himself to sleep.

Terry's brothers tried to stay away from Dad during the evening hours. For some reason, Dad picked on them. So Terry tried to intervene and pull Dad's attention away from the others. Why did he treat them so mean? What was he so sad about that he didn't participate in the family? Why did he drink so much? Terry understood none of this but felt Dad's incredible sadness. And there were days when Dad told Terry he was so sad that he wasn't sure he wanted to live. "But, Dad, you have me and the family," Terry would say. "Yes, and you are a bright spot in my life. But there is more you don't understand, and I'm not sure I can take it much longer."

Terry continued to try to make Dad happy. She got good grades at school and checked on Dad every night. Not much changed, and Terry was worried. So was Mom, who was now getting angry at Dad's refusal to get help. The tension in the house was thick. Terry's brothers had left home, and Terry was about to leave for college.

Terry will never forget the day Dad dropped her off at the college dorm at Stanford University in California. He cried, but not in a way that was sad about Terry's leaving. Terry felt his sadness was different. He was crying over his own pain, and Terry felt sick inside. She kissed him goodbye, knowing his heart ached.

A year later, a dreadful telephone call came in the middle of the night. Terry was roused from her bed in the dorm, and her brother's shaky voice said only, "You need to come home now. I'll tell you more when you get here." Terry's heart sank. Something was dreadfully wrong. She was scared as her friend picked her up outside her dorm to drive her to the airport for her flight back to Connecticut.

When she entered the house, everyone was crying except her oldest brother, Bob, who was upstairs yelling and pounding his fists on the wall. Mom sat motionless. Terry looked around and nobody spoke, "What happened?" she managed to get out.

Her brother Tim was crying, and Mom began to cry. The silence was killing her because she sensed whatever it was, it was dreadful. Finally her mother spoke, "You know how unhappy your father has been and how for years I have begged him to get help? This afternoon I found him dead in the guesthouse study. He shot himself in the head."

Terry fainted. She couldn't believe what she was hearing.

Moments later she got up and went to her room. Curled up in a ball, she rocked herself and cried, "He told me he didn't want to live." The guilt was overwhelming, "I should have stopped him. I should have been here. I should have seen it coming."

Years passed and Terry's depression worsened. She dated but always broke off relationships before they became close. Although very talented, Terry was in and out of jobs because of the depression. Frequently she fought thoughts of killing herself. Twice she had taken pills as an attempt to overdose but was found by a friend. Terry wanted to die and be with her dad. Only he understood her pain, and she his. No one else could relate.

Terry dropped out of the prelaw program at Stanford, and eventually her mom convinced her to see someone for help. When I first met Terry she was very depressed. Again fighting thoughts of killing herself, Terry was planning another overdose.

Terry's mom had remarried, and Terry hated the stockbroker who was her stepdad. Her biggest complaint? He didn't confide in her and rejected her constantly. He wanted her to get a steady job and stop being so moody and depressed. Terry felt he wanted to get rid of her and resented her presence.

The real issue wasn't the stepdad. It was the terrible rejection Terry felt from her dad's suicide. Terry believed she failed to keep her dad alive. She felt responsible for his death, and experienced the shame associated with having to tell people that her dad shot himself. Her father, an upstanding community judge, couldn't find a reason to live. Terry couldn't face the rejection, so instead she found other men to be mad at and reject—her dates, her bosses and now the stepdad.

In a weird way, Terry's depression made her feel close to her dad. She could identify with his pain and hopelessness about life. What was the point of living? You try your best and people leave you. No one can really be trusted. They may say they care, have tender moments with you, but ultimately they leave you. They bail out, give up.

The depression also kept Terry from facing the anger she had over Dad leaving her. Terry was stuck in the sadness, the hopelessness. Her brothers had no trouble being angry at Dad. In fact, that's where they got stuck—angry and unable to move on. Terry would not allow herself to go there. Anger meant betrayal—not understanding Dad's pain. But she was angry inside, and I knew it. She was mad that he left, didn't say goodbye and couldn't work on his pain in a better way. What hope did that give her?

Terry had to forgive her dad for leaving her. Her immense sense of rejection affected all areas of her life. But how could she forgive Dad? How could she be mad at him and not betray him? She didn't want to be mad at him, she wanted to join him in death.

Terry was deceived. The dark veil that covered her father was covering her eyes as well. The enemy's purpose is to deceive and destroy, and the hopelessness of suicide is a deception. If the enemy could be successful at convincing Terry that there was no hope, he would succeed with yet another member of the family. So I had Terry, her mother and a group of intercessors pray against the deception. We prayed for Terry to open her eyes to the truth.

Every time Terry had a thought of ending her life, I had her stop that thought and speak to it. She was to say to the thought, "You are a lie. I won't listen to the voice of the enemy. I am covered by the blood of Jesus, and He that is in me is greater than he that is in the world." Terry had to fight the enemy as Jesus did in the desert—with the Word.

Terry was also deceived into thinking that no one could relate to her pain of rejection.

Terry had to be reminded that Jesus was rejected and suffered unto death—Isaiah 53:3–5: "We despised him and rejected him—a man of sorrows, acquainted with bitterest grief. We turned our backs on him and looked the other way when he went by. He was despised and we didn't care. Yet it was our grief he bore, our sorrows that weighed him down. And we thought his troubles were a punishment from God, for his own sins! But he was wounded and bruised for our sins. He was chastised that we might have peace; he was lashed—and we were healed!" (TLB). He suffered so Terry could live and have hope. All Terry had to do was accept what Jesus did for her.

Terry had to take authority over the darkness, the voice of hopelessness and defeat. Terry had to work through her anger over her dad's death. She had to stop rejecting men before they could reject her. But the root of her depression was facing the rejection of her father's suicide. Once she believed Jesus could identify with her rejection, she moved from that stuck place.

Not even death has the power to defeat us because of what Jesus did on the cross. His abiding love allowed Him to face every rejection for us so that we can always be accepted by Him. People may let us down. They may even die on us. But Jesus is always there and intimately knows our rejection. He took it so we could give it up.

THE *D* WORD—DIVORCE

Divorce is a traumatic disruption in the life cycle of any woman. Even though divorce is common, it's not expected. You don't go into marriage thinking, *Divorce is so common, I can just expect to get divorced, so I might as well plan for it now.* Other than Hollywood types, most of us enter marriage with the idea that we'll be in it for life. If we are Christians, we know how Jesus feels about divorce—He hates it.

When divorce occurs, it is a breaking of the covenant between two people before God. That loss runs deep. So deep that people rate divorce on a leading stress scale second only to death as a stressful life event.[1] Because divorce involves multiple loss, there are many points along the way for you to get stuck.

Divorce involves a grief process similar to death, only the person is still walking around. In some ways that makes divorce even more difficult. There is no terminal end to the relationship as there is in death. The person lives but the circumstances change. If you have had children with the divorced spouse, you are linked with that person for much longer than the divorce proceedings. You are linked for life. Working through the grief process of divorce usually takes about two to three years before you adjust to the losses. Along the way, the journey can be troublesome with several transitions that can leave you stuck. According to one researcher, divorce is a transitional crisis with stages of adjustment.[2]

First, there is a period of conflict before divorce is ever mentioned. Stress builds. Problems are not getting resolved. Unhappiness and dissatisfaction are mounting. One or both spouses are becoming restless in the marriage and ready to make a change. Usually there is fighting, anger, depression, put-downs, blame and, if an affair has occurred, betrayal. This is a rocky time filled with intense emotions that can continue for months or years.

The next transition is when one person reveals his or her desire to leave the marriage. Most decisions to divorce are not mutual—one partner thinks about it for a while, and the other is devastated by the decision. The one who wants to stay in the marriage usually feels powerless, humiliated and suffers from low self-esteem. That person wants to defend against such rejection. Promises of change are offered. Efforts to reconcile may be given one last shot in an attempt to avoid the divorce.

If divorce is pursued, there is a time of separation. Separation is the most difficult time for the family, and there are feelings of ambivalence that surround the leaving. For the person left, so many feelings surface—loneliness, powerlessness, anger, resentment, frustration, identity problems relating to feeling incomplete, dependency, frustration and wishing he or she had tried harder to work out problems while married. Most do not like their newfound singleness and long to be married despite the anger and conflict that led to the separation.

The person who leaves often has feelings of regret, loss and guilt. He or she is breaking the family unit and the covenant before God. But the person has convinced himself or herself that leaving is the only solution for future happiness. In cases of abuse, physical separation may be necessary in order to stop violence or to bring the person to a place of remorse and need for change. In other cases, divorce occurs because of someone's unhappiness, infidelity or refusal to try and work out differences. The process of divorcing is like a roller coaster ride. Just when you think you have worked through one issue or feeling, another arises and throws you into turmoil again. It's an up-and-down ride, which can leave you exhausted, depressed and unable to work, eat, sleep. Moving in and out of depression and anger is normal. It's when you become stuck in one of those reactions that problems occur.

Women tend to be angrier than men at the beginning of divorce.[3] We want to deal with divorce head on. Men, on the other hand, throw themselves into work and experience unhappiness later in the process.[4] But both partners go through a tremendous period of upheaval that results in loss after loss.

Women usually face a decline in their finances, a loss of friends who are couples, the loss of an intimate and sexual partner, the loss of a full-time coparent, the loss of status and more. Divorce is a crisis; it puts both men and women in new life positions. Crises can be points of "stuckness" or opportunities for change.

Other than in cases of abuse, addiction and incest in which family members are unsafe and violated, divorce is a concession to the hardness of our hearts. (See Matthew 19:8.) During the time of Moses, divorce was widespread but never encouraged by God. (See Leviticus 21:7, 14; Malachi 2:16.) Moses permitted divorce as an act of grace to protect innocent ill-treated women. When the Pharisees confronted Jesus with this fact, they tried to take what was an act of grace and permission and make it a law. Jesus resisted. He avoided the debate about infidelity or just cause for divorce. Instead, Jesus referred to the first marriage, God's plan for covenant.

Covenant is a foreign idea to most of us today, including many Christians. We've bought into the modern view of marriage, which is based on *contract* not *covenant*. The two ideas are very different.

In a marriage contract, each partner is expected to meet the agreements of the other—be an intimate partner, a good listener, someone who shares similar interests and values. If one person breaks the contract, the contract can be dissolved. If I don't feel like I'm getting as much as I give, I can get out. If I'm not happy, and my partner is not meeting my needs, I can get out. If I don't feel like I love my partner anymore, I can get out. And so it goes. You know the reasons people give for ending marriage contracts.

The problem is, we don't enter marriage as a contract. We enter it as a covenant before the Lord. How do we understand covenant? We look to the Bible to see how God established His covenant with His people. (See Genesis 15.) On the day God established His covenant with Abram, He divided the animal sacrifice in two, symbolic of a day when God would divide Himself and send His Son, Jesus, to die on a cross as the sacrifice for all our sins. When He passed between the sacrificial pieces, He ratified the covenant with Abram. God's promise was to never leave us or forsake us.

Covenant has to do with forgiveness as well as unconditional love.

When God made His covenant with the people of Israel, He made an unconditional commitment to them. It was not a contract, it was a commitment to His people no matter how they behaved. And let's face it, they often behaved badly and sinned, but God continued to love them and accept them as His chosen people. His grace and forgiveness were constantly extended.

The Bible is clear that marriage is a covenant between two people before God. Marital covenant is an unpopular concept, because it demands forgiveness and unconditional acceptance of the other. Does that mean we ignore sin? Absolutely not. But it does mean that we have to be willing to forgive and extend grace when sin has occurred. Reconciliation is the goal.

Do we deserves His love—a love that would send His only Son to die for us? No. But God's love and covenant is not based on what we do, who we are, how much we accomplish or how well we please God. His love is freely given and a model for marriage. His love is an unbreakable promise. He says in Judges 2:1, "I will never break My covenant with you." Love is God's doing what He said He would—no matter our response.

A marital covenant is based on that same promise.

Now, I know it matters how your spouse responds. It can upset you and cause all kinds of tension, but breaking the marital covenant because you are unhappy or things are tense is not God's plan. Tracy's story is an example of a godly women who understood covenant and applied it to her marriage.

Tracy never expected to be forty-one and single. She had her life neatly planned out. Up until three years ago, there wasn't a glitch. At the age of twenty, after a courtship that was described like something out of a romance novel, Tracy married Ed and moved to Chicago. The first years of marriage were exciting as she and Ed began building their future together. She worked hard and long hours to put Ed through law school. Upon graduation, he landed the big job in international trade law. This allowed Tracy to quit her job and start a family. Three daughters later, Tracy was a content stay-at-home mom, volunteering in their community. Life was good.

The years rolled by, and Tracy had everything she wanted—money, a successful husband, leisure time, exotic vacations, daughters who excelled. She joined a "friends of the arts" group, made great friends and involved herself in hosting fundraisers. She was known as a solid and stable woman in the community. There was only one problem. Ed was losing interest in her.

Tracy didn't see the problem at first. Ed was always consumed with work. He worked late hours and rarely made it home before Tracy went to bed. Something was wrong—she felt it. When Tracy was taking Ed's shirts to the dry cleaners one day, she came across a ticket in his pocket. There were charges on a personal credit card she didn't recognize. Tracing the charges, she discovered Ed had taken a business trip with another woman.

She continued to investigate and found several similar trips—all on days she was home, and all involving another woman. Stunned, she decided it was all a mistake. After all there were several women partners and law clerks in Ed's firm. She never mentioned her findings to her husband. However, what Tracy didn't know was that her husband had been assigned to mentor a young female lawyer who was working out of the firm's Dallas office. As they traveled together and enjoyed each other's company, they eventually began to have an affair.

Spiritually things were not good. Ed stopped going to church and withdrew from the family. Attempts to talk about God were met with anger. Tracy was told to back off. If she wanted to go to church, fine, but Ed would not be bullied into going with her. According to Ed, church was full of hypocrites.

A month passed, and Tracy decided to surprise Ed for his birthday. He was out of town on a big international case. Her plan was to meet Ed secretly in his hotel room. When she called the hotel to make arrangements, she wasn't prepared for what she was told. Her husband and "his wife" were already registered at the hotel. Nervously she called the room, and a woman answered. Her heart sank. She couldn't breathe. She dropped the phone. Two hours later, she hired a private investigator. Her worst nightmare was apparently true—Ed was having an affair.

Armed with evidence she prepared to confront him. To her disbelief, he denied the affair. Now what should she do? He was so convincing about his innocence, yet she knew he was lying. She tried to bring up the subject again, and he refused to talk about it. He told her she'd seen too many soap operas and needed to believe him. Totally unprepared for his response, she did nothing. Weeks went by and things appeared quite normal, but Tracy couldn't shake the reports from the private investigator. Maybe the private eye had the wrong guy, maybe it was all a mistake or maybe Ed was lying.

Tracy became suspicious of everything Ed did. Ed became angry and more distant. She checked on his trips, called the hotels, wanted to know his whereabouts at all times. Ed withdrew and made excuses to be away from home. Tracy became depressed. She lost weight, wouldn't socialize, couldn't sleep and was highly anxious. Her family doctor prescribed tranquilizers and sleep medications. She hoped the affair was a bad dream and she would wake up in the morning relieved. Unfortunately, it was all too real.

Exhausted she called me, "I can't go on like this anymore. I know he's having an affair, but he won't admit to it. I can't sleep, eat or function. I have to get this resolved."

Tracy looked bedraggled as she followed me to the therapy room. "I can't believe this is happening to me. For twenty years, I've had a good marriage. I know you won't believe that. What in the world happened? I feel betrayed and depressed. I know he's having an affair, and I suspect it's been going on for a long time, but he won't admit it, and that is making me crazy. I love this man, yet I can't go on like this. I'm a wreck."

Tracy decided she had to confront her husband again about the affair. This time he admitted to the affair but added a twist that left her numb. He told her he didn't want a divorce but wouldn't give up his girlfriend either!

Back on my couch, she stared into space and said, "Can you believe this? He says I've never really been there for him emotionally, and this woman has. She understands his professional life. He feels a loyalty toward her and doesn't want to upset her. His girlfriend knows he is married but feels he needs her." Stunned by what she was repeating to me, she continued, "Do people really act like this? What's wrong with my husband? Has he flipped out? He's acting like having a girlfriend is a perfectly OK thing to do because he's under stress. People in my church, including my pastor, tell me to leave him. I've certainly got grounds. Am I a fool to stay with this guy? I've loved him for twenty-one years; we have three daughters. I know you won't believe this, but until now he's been a good husband."

Tracy believed in attempting reconciliation, but others thought she was crazy to try. After all the years invested in Ed and the children, she wouldn't leave just because she had a biblical out. Although no one supported Tracy, she believed in the God of the impossible.

The revelation of an affair is devastating. It's a breaking of the marital covenant. Despite all the hurt, Tracy, like many women who face this nightmare, still loved her husband. Yes, she had grounds to divorce him, but she didn't want a divorce. She wanted her husband back, restored and faithful.

Tracy's friends, many of whom were church people, told her this position was foolish. They advised divorce on biblical grounds of adultery. She had biblical grounds, but she also knew God hates divorce. With three children and twenty-one years of history, she wasn't ready to give up yet.

In Tracy's case, sin clearly occurred. Ed broke the marital covenant through having an affair. Worse, Ed was not repentant and willing to give up the affair. So where did that leave Tracy? Tracy, hurt and wounded, had to extend forgiveness to Ed even when he didn't ask for it or deserve it. Why? Because that is what Christ commanded her to do. She could not hold on to bitterness even though in the natural, she was justified. If she did, she would get stuck.

All Tracy's friends could talk about was how unfairly Ed treated her. They were right. His behavior was wrong and hurt Tracy deeply. My concern, however, was how Tracy would *respond* to Ed's behavior. She would not heal if she couldn't forgive Ed and be forthright in her emotional reactions. Bitterness could not take root in her heart. Ed never asked for forgiveness, but Tracy knew she had to extend it anyway. When she was able to forgive Ed by an act of her will, she became strong spiritually, and the depression began to lift.

Her pastor and friends continued to advise her to leave the marriage. Many called her codependent. Others told her, "You don't deserve to be treated like this. God wants you happy. You have a legal out. Don't risk your health over a man." But Tracy wasn't ready to divorce. She couldn't get past the fact that Ed was distancing himself from God, that Ed was going through bad times at work, that Ed wasn't himself. She wasn't thinking about her individual rights, immediate gratification or a quick fix to the present hurt. She was thinking long term. In all the years of marriage, his current behavior was the exception not the rule. She remembered her vows—"for better or for worse." Surely this was "worse."

God was dealing with Tracy's heart. She continued to forgive Ed as he continued to act out sexually. Because the affair was ongoing, I recommended Tracy separate and tell Ed that the affair had to end or there would be no reconciliation. Ed didn't like this accountability and chose separation.

Tracy and I then proceeded to work on her reactions to Ed—making sure she was Christ like in all the ways she dealt with him. This was not easy. It was much more natural to lash out, yell back and ruin his reputation. The anger would rise inside her, and revenge would come to mind. Well-meaning friends would encourage her to bad-mouth Ed and find someone else.

Instead Tracy stood for righteousness and did what a lot of us hope we would do under such circumstances. She confessed her hurts to God and gave them to Him. (See 1 Peter 5:7.) Then she forgave Ed. She refused to bad-mouth Ed to her friends. She stayed strong in her spiritual walk, daily fortifying herself with the Word of God, watching her tongue and praising God for His love for her even though she was being rejected by the man she loved. God heard her and had compassion on her. He helped her supernaturally to extend grace and kindness. It was powerful to witness, and people marveled at how loving she behaved under such difficult circumstances.

Tracy understood her battle—it was not against flesh and blood but principalities and powers. Her battle was not with Ed, but with the enemy of his soul. She began to intercede in prayer for Ed. Regularly we prayed, and God brought the most beautiful countenance to this woman. Her situation was not "fixed" but she was at peace. Only God could do such a thing in the middle of her suffering. Her delight was truly in the Lord.

The most frustrating thing for Tracy was knowing that biblically she was free to get on with her life. She believed in her covenant with Ed, but Ed was willfully breaking it and showed no signs of remorse. Once again, people had a lot to say to Tracy about what she should do next. My advice was to block out peoples' opinions, which ran from one extreme to the other, and to start listening to what God had to say to her.

Tracy hated living in the ambivalence of her life, and like a lot of women left by their husbands, wanted closure to the entire ordeal. The problem was, she wasn't ready for closure. Separation and divorce is like walking in an emotional minefield. The explosions may not be ongoing, but the mines are still in the ground and can be set off if you walk before they are removed. My job was to help Tracy remove all the mines before she could walk to the next place in her life.

I told Tracy to make no decisions. To sit still and work through the emotions of grief that would come and go (anger, sadness and others). Tracy was only ready to move when she was free of anger and judgment and could sincerely pray for the healing of her husband. She had to be very honest with me and God. Were all the mines gone? Was she still exploding at things Ed did? Or was she able to see the battle as spiritual?

Ed was deceived, and Tracy should pray for his eyes to be opened. She couldn't make Ed open his eyes. It wasn't her job. Whether he did or didn't wasn't even the issue. The issue was the state of her soul. Could she pray, without mines exploding, for Ed to be healed?

When Tracy came to the place where she and I believed we had cleared all the visible mines, it was time for Tracy to start thinking about the next step. Would she wait for an undetermined time for Ed miraculously to be healed? Would Ed surrender his will and be repentant? After the divorce was final, would Tracy start to date? This was between Tracy and God. My job was to help her get to a place where she could seek the Lord without the minefield.

Tracy is no longer depressed. She trusts God to take care of her now. Ed has yet to repent and change his ways, but Tracy can say, "When I lay my head on the pillow at night, I have the confidence to know that I handled the situation as a godly woman. You don't know how good that feels, and although I don't like the separation, God has helped me release Ed. I'll never stop praying for him. I know he's confused and deceived. I honestly can say I want him whole. That's all that matters, because I've learned not to look at my circumstances or at any man, but to look to God.

Tracy's story is a powerful example of a woman who honored her covenant and stayed faithful to God. Not all of us do so well when faced with divorce and an affair. Rest assured that divorce isn't an unforgivable sin, and you should not feel condemned about your past actions. If you are divorced, God knows your heart and your responses to the situation. If you need forgiveness, all you have to do is ask. If you have asked, it's done and over in God's eyes.

You need to remember that marriage is an easy target for the enemy. We aren't wrestling only with our spouses, but spiritual forces as well. The enemy's plan is to deceive you into unhappiness until your marriage is destroyed. We are in a battle and often don't have our armor on to fight back. Ephesians 6:10–18 tells us how to protect ourselves with God's armor—truth, righteousness, peace, faith, salvation and the Word. Add prayer, and you have a powerful defense against any attack.

But the enemy attacks us in slow and insidious ways. He begins by creating doubt, self-pity, envy and disillusionment. He uses temptation to test us and builds dissatisfaction. Dissatisfaction grows until we think escape is our only solution for unhappiness. We allow the larger culture to influence our thinking. We think that if our needs are unmet, we have a right to find someone better. If we give and get little back, what's the point? Contract is invoked and away we go—literally.

Perhaps you have been on the other side of marriage—the one who is unhappy and wants to leave. Jolanta was that person when she came to see me. Jolanta was mad at me. She didn't want to hear what I had to say and didn't want to be sitting in a therapist's office. She only came to see me in order to ease her conscience. Her plan was to tell people that she saw a therapist and couldn't fix her marriage. She hoped people would notice her effort and be sympathetic.

In reality, Jolanta was determined to leave her husband, and nothing I nor anyone said was going to matter. This was Jolanta's story.

Jolanta married when she was young and somewhat naïve. Her husband, an older man, had been a star professional athlete and knew his way in the world. His worldliness and self-confidence attracted her. He was the kind of man who walked into a room and made things happen. When she was with him she felt safe and protected. He was interested in Jolanta and wanted to help promote her jewelry-design business. He saw her talent and decided she was his next project.

Jolanta's dad had abandoned the family when she was five. Jolanta remembers kissing Dad good night on a warm summer evening. The next morning he was gone, without leaving a trace. She couldn't make sense of this at five. He had been there all her life and suddenly, with no warning, he was gone. She missed his hugs, his bedtime stories, his silly jokes and his big strong arms that threw her wildly around the family room in play that was somewhat scary but mostly fun.

Jolanta's mom did her best to give Jolanta and her baby brother a normal life, but the family never really recovered from the loss of Dad. They did all the typical family things—went on vacations, barbecued in the backyard, went to the beach—they just did them without Dad. His absence was always noticed. Finances were limited, but Mom found ways to supply the basic needs.

Surprisingly, no one ever mentioned Dad after he left. It was a strange and eerie silence. Mom tried to be happy but Jolanta always noticed the sadness in her mother's eyes. Mom never remarried, saying one man in a lifetime was all she could handle. Mom's strength came from God. Yet the sadness in her face was ever present.

As Jolanta grew up, her design business became a way to express her pent-up feelings of loss and grief. Although her jewelry designs were being purchased by top New York buyers, she still had little confidence. She constantly worried about whether people liked her work. She wondered if her work reflected her deep-seated feelings of insecurity. Because of this, she stayed a comfortable distance from most people. Despite her warm and friendly facade, she felt like a fake.

John was the one man she allowed to get close. She tried to keep him emotionally at bay, but couldn't resist his charm and constant gestures of affection. No man, since her father, had treated her this special. She married John, not because she was madly in love, but because John took care of her and attended to her. The two were like great friends; he the "good daddy," and she the needy daughter.

After four years of marriage, Jolanta needed John less. Her jewelry designs were selling like hot cakes in all the major stores, and her talent was in demand. She toured, lectured and spent hours consumed with her designs and success. John, believing the jewelry business was Jolanta's love, helped promote her.

Jolanta was busy every minute of the day with more orders than she could fill. But the height of her success was starting to wane. She became bored with her designs, lost her creativity and slumped into depression. She described her life like a treadmill from which she couldn't get off. And she blamed John for pushing her, saying he demanded too much.

When he tried to encourage her to take a break, she refused, afraid her success would falter if she wasn't driven.

Exhausted, she collapsed. She began to withdraw. John asked if he could cancel some of her orders so she could rest. This time she agreed. But the depression worsened.

One night, unbeknownst to John, she left him. She decided she was no longer happy in the marriage, and that she and John hadn't functioned like lovers for a number of years. Instead she felt more like his business partner and wanted out of the contract. But John was a good guy and loved by most of their friends. How could she leave and save face?

She knew her friends would pressure her to work things out with John.

Jolanta became more depressed. She started spreading untruths about her husband as a way to get those around her to feel sorry for her predicament. She blamed John for her busy schedule, for problems sexually, for her depression. As she told these untruths, her depression worsened even more.

She refused counsel from friends and was determined to leave John. Desperate, Jolanta contacted a therapist for an appointment. John tried several times to talk with her, but she refused to speak to him. In her mind, she was still determined to build her life away from John.

John was devastated. Not only did he not understand his wife's desire to leave him, but he also faced the untrue rumors she had spread about their relationship. Repeatedly he tried to make contact to work things out. Jolanta refused.

Jolanta worked with a therapist who was also divorced. He had no spiritual grounding and believed if Jolanta was unhappy in the marriage, she should leave. Her therapist reinforced the idea that she needed to be alone in order to sort out what she wanted. He questioned Jolanta's commitment to the marriage and intimated that leaving might be a healthy step because she wasn't sure she loved John, may have married too early and wasn't getting her needs met. Jolanta told the therapist she no longer felt attracted to her husband and was annoyed by his constant presence.

Jolanta was convinced that her mental health depended on leaving her marriage. She would listen to no one but the people who encouraged her to find herself and do her own thing. Her happiness was the most important thing. If that meant leaving John then so be it. God would understand. God wanted her happy and wouldn't expect her to stay in a relationship that didn't meet her needs. Besides God would forgive her, and she could start a new life.

Jolanta knew her therapist didn't share her faith and started to feel guilty about the advice he was offering. So she made an appointment to see me. I came highly recommended, and she felt she should at least talk to a Christian. Jolanta didn't get me in her corner, and she knew it. What I saw was an unhappy woman who wanted to run away from her life. Her misdirected anger at her husband allowed her to keep running from the loss of her dad. Now her husband was the source of her unhappiness, and she chose the road her mom took—single and in control of her life. Jolanta desperately wanted love and control.

Her anger became directed at me. She stood to her feet and said indignantly, "If you try to make me talk about my choices, I'll get depressed again. I don't want to hear it. Don't talk to me about commitment. God understands my unhappiness, and He'll forgive me for leaving. His grace will cover me." She looked me square in the eye, called me insensitive and walked out the door.

Two years later I would see Jolanta again. She divorced John and was remarried. She was depressed and unhappy once again. The new husband wasn't working out either. He wasn't attentive like John. He didn't promote her career and was struggling with his. Perhaps she had made a mistake.

Jolanta believed only what she wanted to believe in order to do what she wanted to do—run away. Did God know she was unhappy? Of course, but she never went to Him to find a solution to her problem. Instead she bought the cultural lie about relationships—if your needs aren't getting met, get out. If you are unhappy, find happiness elsewhere.

Happiness, the culture says, is our highest goal, found in success, money, people, self.

I also suspected there was another man paying attention to Jolanta. I was right. Another man was listening to her woes at home, giving her support and showing her the kind of affection that she had wanted in the marriage. She was encouraged by this man. Something dead in her started to awaken. Emotionally, she was looking for the next "good dad" to bring happiness.

Jolanta knew I wouldn't support her position to leave her marriage and would question her about the new man in her life. I wanted her to stop flirting with what felt good for the moment and face issues in her life. It wasn't until Jolanta divorced and came back the second time that she finally agreed to talk things over with me.

First I had Jolanta tell me what she remembered about her dad's disappearance. Jolanta had little recall since her mother refused to talk about Dad after he left. Jolanta knew nothing of the details, only that she went to bed, and the next day Dad was gone. She never saw him again. Jolanta had many unanswered questions and was left with an overall feeling of vulnerability.

Jolanta's mom's silence was associated with depression and sadness. Jolanta realized she had taken that same burden on herself. When she withdrew from people, she became depressed. She learned to be by herself as a defensive posture. Retreat felt safe.

The wish to be alone was related to fear. Getting too close to anyone may lead to separation by abandonment. If Jolanta took control and did the leaving then she couldn't be hurt by someone else. She had to face her fears of intimacy. She was unconsciously transferring the fear of loss to her husbands. The progressive marital intimacy that most couples develop over time frightened her.

Career success brought the same fearful thoughts—*things are going too well; it's all going to collapse sooner or later. Don't get lulled into thinking things will stay good; they won't.*

As she faced her depression and fears about sudden loss, she began to understand that she had transferred these fears to God as well. She didn't go to Him because He didn't stop her dad from leaving. God, in Jolanta's mind, wasn't able to protect her. Ultimately, that meant no one could protect her. How depressing. She was searching for the elusive someone who would keep bad things from happening. Of course, there was no such person.

Bad things do happen but not away from God's eye. His promise is to be with us through difficulty, not remove us from it. God was with Jolanta, her brother and mom. He provided for their needs. Happiness, for Jolanta, was a choice. Thus we began to focus on what God gave her—a praying mother, a loving brother, material provision and talent, rather than what she lost (her father). Losing her dad, although traumatic, had to be accepted as part of the fallen and diseased world in which we live. God did not tell her dad to leave.

We don't always understand why things happen the way they do. When we don't understand, our faith must go into action. We either trust God to be in control or we don't. We trust God to know the past, present and future. We trust God to walk with us through rough times. We trust God to work all things for our good. We trust God when we don't see it all working out (faith). We trust God, not man, not self. We trust a sovereign God.

Jolanta had to trust God for many things—that He would help her manage the design talent He gave her, that He would help her with intimacy and closeness, that He would renew her love for her husband, that He would be her shield and protector, that He was in control and would never leave her nor forsake her.

This didn't mean she would never experience pain or encounter difficulty. It meant Jolanta had to trust in God's promises when she faced difficulty. When she faced problems and didn't run away, she became content and, yes, happy. Contentment was learned as Jolanta allowed God to rule her life. She stopped complaining about what was missing and focused on things that were eternal.

Jolanta's happiness did not depend on circumstances, people or herself, but on God. Jolanta chose happiness. Her new joy was in the Lord, not in things going her way. Like Paul in prison, Jolanta learned to fix her eyes on things eternal—on a Savior who died for her and promised eternal life. That's what made Jolanta happy.

Jolanta learned to turn her unhappiness around through getting her eyes off another person and on God. No man can make you completely happy, because you are designed to need God. Sometimes we forget that we need God and act in our own power—taking charge of our lives. Usually our efforts end in a mess. But hopefully we learn from our mistakes, admit our wrongs and move on.

THE PARENTS I WISHED I HAD

If you could choose two parents in the world, who would they be? Tough question. As soon as I think of someone, I can also think of a reason why he or she wouldn't be best. OK, I'm still thinking, and do you know what? As brilliant as I am, I can't come up with two perfect people. Now why is that? Is it because I'm brain dead from writing this book? No, it's because everyone (outside of God) has flaws and weaknesses.

We are never quite satisfied with the parents we get. Some do a better job than others, but there is still this feeling of disappointment or of being let down. Since Adam and Eve ate the fruit, we've felt the loss of perfect parents.

Many of my women clients are stuck in depression over having imperfect parents on whom they want to blame their problems. Look, problematic parents, whether crazy, abusive, alcoholic or insensitive, do not condemn you to a life of victimization. You are not a victim; you are an overcomer. Stop complaining about what you didn't get, and start looking to God to give you what you need. He has promised to supply all your needs. He doesn't say, "I can supply your needs only if you come from a two-parent, extremely functional home." There are no qualifiers on His provision except to love God and believe His promises. End of story. OK, but not end of book. We have to talk about this more.

Many of you have had lousy parents, and many of you have been lousy kids (I'll deal with that next). I've probably come across most of the possible parent profiles in twenty years of doing therapy—parents who are critical, insensitive, controlling, verbally abusive, physically abusive, sexually abusive, alcoholic, drug addicted, promiscuous, unfaithful, into pornography, rejecting, neglectful, abandoning, narcissistic, rigid, chaotic, unloving, meddling, revengeful, depressed, anxious, mentally ill...I could go on, but have you found your parents yet? In other words, find your parents in the list and join the rest of us.

I'm not downplaying the seriousness of living with parents who have major problems. It's tough, and it does affect you. The more severe the problems, the more losses you have to work through as an adult. I certainly wouldn't compare growing up in a rather uneventful family where the biggest complaint is that the parents watched too much TV, with life in an abusive alcoholic family. Jan, for example, had many losses to work through with her family.

CUTTING

Jan was a typical teen in many ways but over the edge in others. Jan's mom insisted she come see me because she was cutting on her wrists and legs. Her mom couldn't talk to her, and the school said Jan needed counseling. The cutting had to stop.

Jan sat on my couch with little to say at first. We had to go through the usual rebellious teen routine. She told me I couldn't help her. She wouldn't talk to a "shrink," and I should leave her alone.

I told her I could only leave her alone when she stopped cutting on her body. I was there whether she liked it or not, so she could stare at me every week for an hour, or we could try to talk about her pain. Eventually Jan got bored with the "I'll wait you out" routine and started telling me about her life. The story was pretty awful.

Jan cut on herself when things at home became out of control. Cutting was a way for Jan to release feelings of depression and anxiety. "One night when things were really bad, I took a knife and started to cut. It was kind of awesome. I could focus my pain on the blood running down my arm and not think about what was happening to me in the house. I stopped cutting when it hurt too much, and I couldn't control the pain."

Jan lived with a mother who was a substance abuser. No father was present in the home, and Jan was constantly subjected to the behavior of various men who wandered in and out of her mother's life. Some of the men ignored her, others were disgustingly drunk or high and hurt her. Jan's mother didn't protect her from these men. Instead she was jealous of Jan's youthful body and projected her own promiscuity onto her daughter. Blaming Jan for the behavior of out-of-control men justified their continued presence in the house. Jan's model for coping with emotional pain was to anesthetize herself.

Alcohol and drugs took her out of the moment and numbed the present. They also placed Jan in a world in which people regularly lost control and bad things happened. Rape was only one of the many forms of aggression Jan experienced. She had been physically beaten numerous times prior to our session—all by men who got high or were sexual with Mom.

No wonder Jan didn't trust me. Her experience said she couldn't. But something inside her knew she needed help, and so she took a chance with me. After all, if I was untrustworthy, it would only confirm her belief that nobody cared or could be trusted. Jan's emotional pain was enormous, and she knew it. That's why she fought so hard to avoid it. She would inflict physical pain on herself to avoid thinking about or feeling what she experienced emotionally. She was desperate and felt trapped so acted out against her body. At fourteen, she saw no other way. She could run away. She thought of that often but figured she'd end up on the street. She could report her mom but didn't want to become a foster child. She was too young to be on her own, and her father was nowhere to be found. Her relatives were just like Mom.

Jan also told me she was scared that she was becoming her mom. She was drinking and drugging to escape her life, and she hated her mom when she did the same. Cutting made her different and allowed her to focus her pain away from reality. Cutting gave her a separate identity.

Helping Jan meant I had to get her to trust me and open up her life to me. We had so much to accomplish. She needed to work through the rape and the beatings. Her mother had to learn to protect Jan, and Jan had to stop numbing herself from emotional pain. None of this could be accomplished if Jan saw me as another unsafe person in her life.

I was encouraged by Jan's first visit. Other teenagers have refused to talk and are openly hostile. Jan was willing to risk the first time out—she told me about the rape. That was a good sign. Now she would test me to see if I would be like her mother—unresponsive to her needs.

I told Jan's mother that I thought I could help both Jan and her only if she agreed to also work with a therapist. Bringing Jan to therapy was an action that told me she wanted Jan protected, now she had to take another step and learn how to protect Jan in more ways. Mom agreed.

Next I told Jan that I would work with her and, eventually, her mom. We would all meet in family therapy to work out house rules, safety issues and how to stay sober and clean.

This structure helped Jan see I had a plan, her mother was getting the needed help, and I was committed to protecting her from more harm until her mother could fully take charge of this. She would have to agree not to cut and talk to me instead. Mom had to agree to join a substance abuse program, not allow men in the house at night when Jan was present and stay in therapy. If Mom slipped on her contract, I arranged for Jan to have a number of temporary places she could go to be safe.

The goals were to stop the substance abuse and self harm, provide a safe place to live and teach Mom to parent a teenager. Jan already experienced things that no fourteen-year-old needed to experience. Jan needed her mom to be a better parent. Mom wanted to be a better parent, but had a lot of her own "stuff" in the way. It was a long road with many bumps, but Jan and her mom made it. Through it, Jan tested me to see if I would stay consistent, protect her and love her unconditionally.

In cases like this, the therapist is really a model of Jesus to the client. People like Jan and her mother have never experienced someone who loves them and wants to help without an ulterior motive. They come broken, needy and disillusioned with life, and they don't expect the gift of God's love. When they experience it, it is overwhelming and at first hard to trust.

Jan and her mom knew that God created them, and because of that fact, they knew that He loved them. They didn't earn His love, and nothing they had done could stop God from coming after them. God died for them. God wasn't ready to give up on them, so why should I? They needed to believe that change was possible, but it would take something bigger than both of them to make it happen. It would take a personal relationship with God and then a lot of hard work.

Amazingly they chose both—God and the hard work. Sober and clean, Jan's mother is starting to believe she can be a good mother. Jan has learned new ways to cope with emotional pain and feels safe in her house for the first time. Both Jan and her mother had lousy parents, but they chose not to stay stuck with that limitation. They chose to behave differently. With help and a power greater than themselves, change was possible.

Jan's story should help you understand that when I say you are not a victim, I'm not suggesting you shouldn't talk about what happened in your growing-up years, or that you should pretend your past and circumstances didn't affect you. In Jan's case, lousy parenting had everything to do with her depression. But she didn't have to stay there—depressed and cutting on herself.

You have to come to grips with your family "yuck," whatever it is. You might be able to work with your parents like Jan did or you may have to make your own changes. *You* are still responsible for how you behave. You can't spend your life blaming other people for the adult choices you make. Well, you can, but you'll be stuck and need to reread this book.

MENTAL ILLNESS

You may struggle with not-so-perfect parents who are depressed or suffer from other mental illnesses. Growing up in a family with an ill parent creates loss. Because of family mental illness, you may not feel comfortable bringing other kids home, you may miss holidays or family get-togethers, you may have to be self-sufficient before you are ready. Overall, you may harbor anger and resentment for having parents who don't function like the Brady Bunch. This was Julie's problem. She wanted parents like the TV ones portrayed in the 1960s and her family showed no resemblance.

Julie was a single, middle-aged librarian who scheduled an appointment to see me. She felt depressed and thought her depression had something to do with her father. My best guess from Julie's description was that her father was paranoid schizophrenic—an illness characterized by bizarre delusions and hallucinations. He was convinced that the government was trying to kill him by poisoning him to death. Although Julie's dad had been hospitalized a number of times as a young man, my attempts to secure his past psychiatric records came up empty.

Julie's life was not easy because of her father's mental illness. Memories of her childhood still cause her heart to ache. Although she never knew his diagnosis, she could describe his behavior. His moods were volatile, and his thoughts paranoid. He trusted no one and would talk incoherently. He told Julie there were voices in his head. He saw things Julie never saw. All Mom said about Dad was that he was "crazy." None of Julie's days were predictable when Dad was out of the mental hospital. And Dad was in and out of the psychiatric hospital multiple times when Julie was a young girl. When he was home, he would stare at her for hours and suddenly become violent. There was no pattern, just random rage that erupted from within his troubled mind.

Julie's mother had to work outside the home because the family could not survive on Dad's disability check. Consequently, Julie and her younger brother and two sisters were left alone with Dad during afterschool hours. Julie felt protective of her younger siblings, who hid behind her back whenever Dad entered the room. Julie pretended to be brave but feared Dad, too. Mostly, Julie learned to stay out of Dad's sight.

There were moments of tenderness. For some reason, Dad seemed more "normal" in the evenings. He would tuck her into bed at night and tell wonderful stories of romance and courage. She would close her eyes and be that damsel in distress, rescued by the charming prince, and live happily ever after. But in the morning, the madness would return. And after school, she never knew what to expect. Would he be loving, angry or out of control? It was all very confusing for a little girl who didn't understand mental illness. She feared, hated and loved her dad all at the same time.

Mom was less volatile but demanded too much. Julie was expected to take care of her siblings, clean the house and get good grades. Mom was too busy taking care of Dad, running to hospitals and talking to doctors she didn't trust. She had little time to deal with Julie's emotional needs. When Julie slacked on any responsibility, Mom came down hard. Mom couldn't tolerate mistakes from Julie, because she had her hands full with Dad.

Mom's constant criticism wore on Julie's fragile sense of self. It seemed Julie could never do anything right, but she would try. She excelled in everything at school. She joined the band, math club, civic groups, whatever she could find to get out of the house and feel sane. Daily, Mom warned her not to get close to anyone. No one could be trusted. So Julie lived her childhood, fearful of her "crazy" dad, trying to please her mom, void of friends and responsible for her younger siblings.

When Julie became a teenager, a neighbor invited her to a local church. Julie's mom was uncomfortable with the invitation but allowed her to go. She instructed Julie to say nothing of her home life and treat the church with suspicion.

Even though Julie had never been to a church, she'd heard a lot about it through her father's "crazy" thoughts. Church, according to Dad, was where God yelled at you and wanted to punish you. Dad said the voices in his head screamed loudest in church. God was always mad at people for their sinful lives, and church was the place for punishment. Dad only went to church when he felt he needed to be punished.

Julie didn't feel she needed punishment but wanted to see the place that Dad so feared. She imagined church as dark and dreary. She pictured a storybook-type castle with low-lit candles and indistinguishable people crying and weeping over all the wrong things they had done. Much to Julie's surprise, the church turned out to be a place of quiet calm. People were friendly and greeted her with a smile. The music spoke to her soul and was grand and glorious. She sensed God's presence. But His presence was not scary as Dad described. Instead, it was wonderful and peaceful.

She saw the crucifix and wondered how someone so wounded could be so punishing. *Wasn't He the one punished?* she thought? Julie identified with Jesus. She didn't understand why, but she knew He suffered, too. She asked the Jesus on the crucifix to come into her life and cleanse her from her sins. The neighbor who prayed with her explained that Jesus died but rose again and could live in her heart. Julie needed someone, and Jesus was available.

The once-frightened child and teen was now a depressed, perfectionistic adult—highly successful in her librarian career, extremely responsible and well liked. She was close to no one and determined to fight the demons of her past.

When Julie left home, her parents separated. Mom could no longer deal with Dad, given his state of mind. Mom was angry at life and tightened her emotional grip on Julie. She was suspicious of men Julie dated and continued to warn Julie to trust no one. She demanded Julie's loyalty. Julie was exhausted trying to please her mother and could hardly tolerate her angry criticisms of both her and Dad.

Julie prayed, read her Bible, loved God and was involved in her church. By all accounts, she was a moral, godly woman. But Julie wasn't sure how to handle her mother and father. She worried that she hated her dad. She often felt embarrassed by him and had no desire to see him. There were times she wished he would die.

Her mother became a Christian too, but Julie saw little change in the way the family related. Mom would not divorce Dad but stayed separated. She showed little compassion towards his mental state and allowed others to bear the burden of his care. Her only interactions with Dad involved money. She burdened Julie with all the misery in her life. Julie tried to talk about Dad, but Mom preferred to avoid him and pretend everything was fine as it was. Nothing Julie said made a difference.

Julie was very organized and diligent at work. She wasn't lazy. At times, she wondered if she was driven. Her hard work led to a promotion. Julie could always be relied upon at the library. Responsibility, for Julie, was an old friend. However, away from her desk, Julie was a mess.

Reluctantly she came to my office. She never wanted to see a psychotherapist. Only crazy people like her dad did that, and look how much it helped him. Besides, she was a Christian and loved God. So why would she need a counselor? Wasn't seeing a therapist a sign of weakness, an indication of failure? Her minister's words rang loudly in her head, "Jesus is all you need."

But in the past few months, Julie was sinking deeper and deeper into depression and knew it. She flew into rages over little things—a behavior she had witnessed daily from her dad. Moody, irritable, unmotivated and insecure, she felt hopeless about the future. She lost interest in her job and couldn't pull herself out of bed in the morning. She wanted to sleep all day. She was losing weight because she had no appetite. Reading her Bible was difficult. She couldn't concentrate. She prayed, but felt distant from God. Her world was collapsing, and she didn't care. She even had thoughts of killing herself.

When Julie first walked into my office, I was struck by how together she appeared despite her depressed state. She learned the lesson well from her mother—let no one see you as you really are. But when I began the interview, all she could do was cry. It was clear—Julie was clinically depressed. She asked if the diagnosis meant she was crazy like her dad.

Of course, it didn't, but it would take me a while to convince her.

In the next few weeks, Julie was ambivalent about therapy. In her mind, it was a lack of faith to see a therapist. How could she love and serve God and still feel depressed? If she were stronger, she wouldn't be depressed. If she read her Bible more, prayed more or committed to a Bible study perhaps she would feel better. The problem was she couldn't motivate herself to do any of those things.

Asking for help meant she had to trust someone. No one in her family did such a thing. She wasn't sure God could help her feel better so why would she trust a stranger? She'd never told anyone about her childhood or her present-day depression. Like Mom, she suffered silently and was careful to hide her true thoughts and feelings.

Julie's battle with depression began when she left home as a young adult. She was relieved to be physically away from her crazy family, but the crazy family organized her in a way that was familiar. She knew how to live in unpredictability; now her life was predictable. She knew how to hide from her dad's anger, now there was no one from whom to hide. She knew how to stay distant from men, now men were showing interest in her. She knew how to please her boss, now her boss made few demands. She knew how to protect her siblings, but they were grown and managing their own families. Suddenly, it was all too calm, too sane. Her new independence was like swimming in uncharted waters, and she was drowning.

Julie spent years surviving her chaotic childhood. Now, she wasn't sure what to do with herself. She was removed from the chaos. She had no clue as to who she was away from the family system. She felt very alone. Worse, she worried she might be crazy.

Julie, like many women, spent years reacting to volatile circumstances within a troubled family. She knew nothing about the person God intended her to be. Instead, she learned to react to the anger and upsets of other people. She learned to stay out of trouble, dodge emotional bullets and blend into the wall so as not to be seen. Julie was a scared little girl in a grown-up body. Her depression was a signal—find me, or I die.

I knew she wasn't really lost. You see, God never left her. Julie knew God, at least she thought she did. But her description of God was a volatile man who was waiting to punish her for things she didn't even know she did. Julie's God was unpredictable and waiting to pounce on her at the first mistake. He was never the same. He expected her to stay on top of things, to be self-sufficient.

Julie's image of God couldn't be bothered with her needs; after all He did big things—created the universe, parted seas, sent plagues. He didn't have time for the insignificant, which in Julie's mind was her and her struggles. Like her parents, God had more important things to do than be concerned about Julie.

Julie developed her view of God like many people do, not from the Bible but from her experience with her parents. Her image of God was not as "crazy" as her parents had been, but the similarities were remarkable. She had done a masterful job of transferring the negative characteristics of her parents to God the Father.

So we began to study the person of God. Who is He? What's He like? How does He treat us? Julie discovered that the God in the Bible was hardly related to her image of God.

God was the same yesterday, today and forever—no unpredictability there. He was consistent, true to His Word. God was on call, twenty-four hours a day and knew her so well. He even knew the number of hairs on her head. He was concerned about her every need. He said to pray about everything and bring her concerns to Him.

And here was the real surprise for Julie—He was ready to give her good things. He wanted to bless her and meet her needs. When she messed up, He was full of grace and mercy. And nothing she did won His approval. He loved her unconditionally and accepted her. Wow, this was a God Julie wanted to get to know!

Amazing things began to happen. Julie dropped her idea of God and decided to get to know the God described in the Bible. She had to read the Bible and rework her image of God according to His Word rather than according to her experiences. As she did this, her life became transformed.

Here's what Julie discovered about God the Father:

- He is love (John 3:16).
- His love for her is intense (John 17:23).
- His love is everlasting (Jer. 31:3).
- She can call Him Father (Rom. 8:15).
- He cherishes her, and she is precious in His sight (Isa. 43:3–4).
- He meets all her needs (Psa. 23:1–6; Phil. 4:19).
- He bears her burdens (Psa. 55:22).
- He is trustworthy (Psa. 9:10; 33:2–22; Matt.12:17–21).
- He never changes (Mal. 3:6; Heb. 13:8).
- She is His child (Col. 2:12–14; 1 John 1:1–2).

Julie's fear of being "crazy" was based on a reality. Several of her family's generations had a mentally ill member. I assured Julie that I noticed none of the schizophrenia in her but also prayed with her to break any generational curse that may be over her family. Julie did not have to live fearing she would become "crazy" and had the power through Christ to break the "sins of the fathers."

As Julie worked on changing her image of God and claiming His promises over her life, she also worked on behaving differently. She had to learn new patterns of behavior in order to change. At times this process was uncomfortable. After all, we were fighting life-long patterns of behavior.

One of the biggest changes was to learn to live with calm and not to expect the storm to always follow. When things were calm, she began to worry. She was used to chaos and couldn't predict it. Based on her child-hood, she knew that a period of calm meant something bad was about to happen. But Julie was an adult now and not living in the home of her parents. She had more control over the circumstances of her life and could remove herself from chaos in the family.

Julie had to learn not to be afraid of men, particularly when they got upset. She was driven at work, fearing her boss would become reactive like her dad. So she tried to be perfect. She was working herself into a frenzy and needed to give herself permission to fail occasionally or say no to a project. She also avoided dating because she didn't want conflict and believed all men would be as unpredictable as her father. Women friends were kept at bay for fear they would be critical and try to control her like her mother had done.

I encouraged Julie to renew friendships with women and accept invitations to fun activities. Dating and friendships were opportunities for her to practice asserting herself and setting limits. Much of our work focused on clarifying who Julie was in the presence of others and allowing others to see that person.

She had to forgive her dad for being "crazy" and hold on to the sane moments she had with him. She had to understand his troubled mind so she could better remove herself from his assaults. She began to intercede in prayer for her father and to ask God to heal him. Rather than accept the fact that he would always be crazy, she networked with others to pray for her father's healing.

Julie was angry with her mother for ignoring her and putting her in charge of her siblings. The criticisms and hurtful comments from Mom continued in adulthood. So Julie learned to confront her mother and set limits. She would no longer be the whipping post for her mother's frustrated life. It was hard work. The goal was to separate emotionally from her parents but still have a relationship—a different relationship, one in which she could have contact but respond differently from the old patterns that led her to depression.

Most of Julie's friends encouraged her to "forget" her family and go on with her life. They advised a total break. Many of the church people agreed. They told her—when people treat you wrong, give them what they deserve and be done with them. Your parents won't get help, so why try?

We weren't listening to popular opinion. We were reading the Bible. God says to honor your father and your mother. We checked to see if He said to do so only if your parents are sane and attentive. We couldn't find that version, so we figured Julie was stuck trying to find a way to have a relationship with parents who still couldn't give her what she wanted. So,

Julie spent time with her parents but removed herself when things got crazy or critical.

As Julie methodically worked through her past, forgiving her parents and grieving for what she didn't get from them, her depression lifted. "None of us ever feels totally satisfied with our parents," I'd tell her. "Even the not-so-crazy ones are imperfect and let you down. But they do the best they can, and they are to be honored."

So Julie found a way to honor them. And I was really impressed. She accepted them for who they were and gave up on trying to change them. She stopped judging them and became a compassionate prayer intercessor for them.

In the natural, she could only control her responses to her parents, and God and I had a lot to say on that front. She had to practice being loving, kind, patient, long-suffering, gentle—not because they deserved this response but because Julie was working on being the kind of woman God wanted her to be. There were times she had to set limits, walk away or be direct about her needs. She no longer focused on their responses but on hers. As she did, she felt stronger and more self defined.

Yet, her friends did not always understand her responses. "I think you are as crazy as your dad," one friend would say. "Your parents are so weird. Why should *you* try to be with them when they don't meet your needs? You don't deserve to be treated unfairly. Forget about them, and go on with your life."

Previously, this conversation would have sent Julie into depression. She would have fed on all the injustices done to her over the years. She would have pushed the anger deep inside and never get to the hurt behind it. This time Julie just smiled and said, "Someone I know was nice to me when I didn't deserve it. I just ignored Him. Then I got to know Him, and I was blown away by the fact that I did nothing to deserve His love."

"Really?" her friend replied, "Do I know this guy?" "No," Julie smiled again, "but you could. He'll even die for you if you become His friend. I may not have the parents I wanted, but I've got another Father, one I can trust and who loves me unconditionally."

Julie found a way to make peace with her family. She didn't want a schizophrenic father, and she longed for a mom who would be accepting and tuned in to her needs. But learning to accept her losses helped her move from depression to honor.

THE KID I WISHED I WAS

I was a pretty good kid growing up, one of those kids you wished you had. Ask my mom and dad. Except for a few years of screaming and going hormonal as a teenager, I made it out of high school with no DUIs, pregnancies or criminal records. Feeling confident that I knew what I was doing, I went to college. Living on my own was not so easy. I forgot an important part of my upbringing. I forgot to keep my relationship with God strong. Who had time for Jesus? I was a student. I was studying. I was figuring out life on my own. I was dating. I was also not living a holy life. I had let down my guard, thinking my good Christian upbringing could carry me through these first years of independence. I was wrong.

Now don't get crazy on me. I didn't end up in jail or on the streets, but I allowed sin to enter my life. A little compromise here, a little there, and before I knew it I lost my grounding. Thankfully, God never lost me.

Sin isn't a fashionable topic because it implies right and wrong. Sin was really out of style when I was in college. No one sinned; we all did our own thing. And the beauty of your own thing is that you were able to define it. In the back of my mind, I knew there were standards, but no one I knew was talking about them. The point of this self-confessional is that we can be good kids and still be living our lives out of line with God's Word.

Contrary to the opinion of the day, we are not inherently good. I'd like to say we are and spread peace and love all over the world, but we tried that in the 1960s. According to my Bible, we are all sinners, born into sin and only redeemed when we accept Jesus as our Savior.

So we are sinful by nature and pass down the sins of the fathers through generations. Our nature goes against behaving the way God wants us to behave. That's why it is so important to submit to Him. We are in desperate need of Him and His Holy Spirit to empower us to overcome our nature and the attacks of the enemy.

Where does that leave us if we don't profess Jesus and walk according to His way? It leaves us messed up and messing up others, which results in more unresolved losses leading to depression. But as I mentioned, you can profess Christ and still not live the way He instructs you to live. Sometimes the acceptance of Jesus is where the spiritual walk ends. This is not good because you lose *all* that God has for you.

Some of you remember going regularly to the altar on Sunday nights as a teenager. I did. I sat in the church service and felt convicted for the way I acted all week. Many of my friends were running to the altar with me. We all knew Jesus as Savior. We hadn't committed our lives to holiness or to knowing God intimately. Many adults are still going to the altar regularly for the same reasons. Some stop going to church at all. They don't want to feel the convicting power of the Holy Spirit.

Hopefully, we don't keep God's Word only to stay out of trouble. However, if we do keep His Word we will. We live according to God's Word because we love Him. And like a great parent, He provides guidelines to help us show our love for Him. Fortunately our sin does not stop His love for us.

But when we allow sin to rule our lives, we experience more loss— loss of self-esteem, our innocence, our good word, our trust, our sense and most importantly our intimacy with God. We become anything but the kids our parents wished they had.

I don't have to list the outcomes of sin. You know what they are, but in case you need a review, they include: sexual sin, addictions, abuse, lying, cheating, gossiping, stealing, envy, jealousy, unbelief and others. When you allow sin in your life, you give the enemy a place to attack you.

Don't underestimate the impact of sin. Nothing good comes from it. So you must stay sensitive to the Holy Spirit and allow Him to work in your life, uncovering anything that may not be pleasing to the Lord.

Don't get all defensive or offended when someone, in love, tries to correct you. Hopefully that person offers feedback in a loving way. We all need help when it comes to recognizing sin.

We need to take a daily account of how our behavior lines up biblically. Did we love our neighbor, did we treat our boss with respect, were we honest on our income taxes, did we gossip about our friend? These are the kinds of questions we should ask ourselves regularly. Then pray, be sorry that we behaved badly, ask God to forgive us, make changes and go on with life.

We are not to act as if sin is no big deal because it is. But we shouldn't get stuck in self-condemnation either. Many women can't get past their mistakes. God does. So should you. When you stay stuck in self-reproach, you are really saying Jesus didn't do enough to take care of your problem. That was Courtney's thinking.

SELF-CONDEMNATION

Courtney couldn't get past the abortion she had two years ago. She was a college student and attended lots of parties. She and her girlfriends regularly drank too much and often ended the night going back to the dorm with one of the guys. Courtney got pregnant.

Courtney attended a small private college on full scholarship and couldn't drop out of school. She wasn't ready to have a baby and didn't want to give up her studies.

Confused and scared, she did what she thought was best. She had an abortion. No one found out about it, and Courtney resumed her life. She knew several girls in the dorm who had abortions as well. They assured Courtney that having an abortion was no big deal. Courtney should be thankful she lived in a time in which she had a choice.

A year later, Courtney met Jesus at a campus rally for Christ. Courtney loved God and changed her behavior. She stopped getting drunk and being sexually active with men. She told God she was sorry about the abortion but couldn't let go of it. The result was a year of depression in which she felt ashamed and sinful over aborting her baby.

Courtney asked God to forgive her. He did, and in God's mind it was over. But Courtney couldn't let go of the abortion and was stuck.

Courtney had to be convinced of God's love. The abortion was a terrible ordeal, but Jesus died to take away Courtney's sin. She had to accept His sacrifice for her sake. Anything else was telling God He didn't do enough. Courtney had to believe what God said to her—her sin was cast into the sea, never to be remembered, as far as east is from west.

Courtney represents many of us who get stuck in our sin. We don't accept God's love as He gave it—unconditionally, no strings attached and free. It's too good to be true but it is. Because of Jesus, it's possible to be the kid He wished He had.

5

Facing Situational Loss

W hen I was six years old, my family took a trip to
California. In those days we drove everywhere, and no one
had minivans. So I and my two brothers crowded in the back seat of our
pink and white Buick, and for four weeks we saw the western country-
side as we made our way from Michigan to California.

My dad was the best when it came to family vacations. He wanted us
to experience all America had to offer on a road trip, so we stopped at
every roadside attraction of interest. We visited cowboy ranches, roadside diners, souvenir shops, carnival rides, sight-seeing points of
interest—whatever looked fun and was a momentary distraction from
the long drive.

To pass the time, my oldest brother, Gary, who was totally cool as a
teenager, would practice writing the names of his girlfriends on pads of

paper. At fifteen, girls were very much on his mind. My nine-year-old brother Denny would "ooh" and "ah" at every passing tree. That was Denny, always finding the smallest thing to get excited about. I just wanted to get to where we were going—Disneyland.

Disneyland was more fun than I could imagine. As the youngest in the family, I was into fun. For two days, I had the time of my life. After exhausting myself on the rides, as we were getting ready to leave, my parents bought me a souvenir ring from one of the shops in the park. It was silver with a white pearl in the center. It was my prized possession, and I took extra care to make sure nothing happened to it.

As we headed back to Michigan, we stopped briefly in Montana to use the restroom. Carefully, I took off my ring to wash my hands. I set it by the sink as I had done at every rest stop (for some reason I didn't think it should get wet), and then I did the unthinkable—I left it in the restroom. It wasn't until hours later that I noticed my ring was not on my finger, and we were long past the place where I had left it.

I was devastated. My ring! How could I have been so careless. I began to cry. My parents tried to cheer me up. My brother Denny offered me gum, but I couldn't chew between all the tears. Gary thought maybe one of his girlfriends could give me a ring. Mom felt bad for me. Dad's solution was to buy me a new ring at the next stop. He knew how responsible I usually was with my things. But nothing could replace my Disneyland ring. It was gone forever, and I thought I'd never get over it. (The fact that I still remember it probably means I didn't!)

Fortunately, most of us do get over the loss of a five-dollar ring, but the loss of *things* can devastate us and even lead to depression. One reason is that we allow ourselves to get attached to things. Things bring us momentary happiness (a diamond ring, a love note, a night out). Sometimes we feel things make us important (a new house, car, a cell phone, new promotion). Or we may depend on things to keep us going (a second car, our health, our intellect, money).

Things have a way of taking on meaning in our lives. When we lose them, we struggle. The problem with things is that having them and keeping them are not always in our control. We can lose things through disaster—an accident, a tornado, flood, hurricane or crash in the stock market. We can lose things like our money or our home by making bad decisions. Other things are lost through no fault of our own—our health, our mind, status, power and influence for example.

Even change that is desired brings about the loss of things. When you grow up, you lose your innocence. When you move, you lose friends and security. Positive change still brings on loss that has to be dealt with well in order to keep from getting stuck.

Remember, I am not saying that loss is bad. In fact, loss can be helpful and move you to a new place. Loss has a way of reorganizing your priorities. Loss means change. Nothing is quite the same, and something new is about to grow if you let it. But facing loss and not being afraid of the new thing is where most of us get stuck.

So far we've established that things aren't as important as we make them out to be. Losing things becomes traumatic because we don't place our trust in the things of God. As long as we stay intimate and dependent on God, we won't lose His good things—His promises. His promises include salvation, healing, wisdom, blessings, increase, salvation and much more.

LOSS OF HEALTH

But what about losing things we value like our health and our mental functioning? In some cases, we don't take care of our bodies as we should. We don't eat right, exercise or live a healthy lifestyle. In those cases, we can bring on disease.

In many cases, however, we inherit disease or the predisposition towards disease, such as diabetes, high cholesterol, heart disease or cancer. Even specific mental illnesses such as bipolar disorder and schizophrenia are believed to run in families.

The environment contributes to disease as well. I remember when I was trying to get pregnant; a leading infertility specialist in town had evidence to support the fact that chemicals in the water in a specific part of the city were contributing to an increase in miscarriages. Until the water problem was corrected, pregnant women were directed by the city to drink bottled water.

When disease and dysfunction impact us, coping with loss becomes critical. You know the old saying, "If you have your health, you have everything." When you don't have your health, you face loss of functioning.

So how do we face loss that comes with disease and health problems? First we trust that God is in control of our lives and can work all things for our good. Next we petition Him for healing. As we cope with the changes associated with loss, we have to keep our eyes on Jesus so we don't allow bitterness or depression to overtake us. Read Jill's story, and you will have a better understanding of loss associated with health and disease.

BREAST CANCER

Breast cancer—two words no woman wants to hear. But the words shook Jill's body when the doctor made the diagnosis. *It can't be,* she thought, *I'm only thirty-six years old.*

Jill had been through a lot by the time she showed up in my office. Her husband had been recently transferred with his computer software company and was sent to the Silicon Valley. The move from Orlando to California was not easy. The family had adjusted well to Florida. Orlando was the closest thing to home they had experienced in years. For once, Jill lived somewhere long enough to make good friends. Her daughter, Bobbie, loved her school. But as all relocated families know, change is the one thing that's constant.

So Jill and the family moved to the Silicon Valley the summer before school started again. Jill's biggest concern was for her daughter, Bobbie. She was finally stable and doing well, but the previous year had been a nightmare. Bobbie was uncontrollable and failing school. After months of treatment, Bobbie was finally diagnosed as having a learning disability and was receiving the necessary help in school. Her behavior rapidly improved. Moving could disrupt her stability yet again. But this time Jill felt confident she could get her help right away.

Not only was Jill concerned about her daughter, but her mother was dying of colon cancer. Her mother and stepfather lived out east and rarely spoke to Jill. When Mom did call, she was verbally abusive to Jill, swearing at her and telling her cruel things. Jill could hardly take these intense conversations and would be anxious for days after she called. Her sisters, both younger, decided just to avoid Mom. Because she was dying, having no contact was not what Jill wanted.

Jill's father died when Jill was eighteen. Her mother and dad were divorced at the time. Prior to her father's death, the family lost their home due to bankruptcy. Jill, her sisters and mother were homeless. Jill became the family provider and paid her younger sisters' way through school. Her father never helped or contacted the family prior to his death.

Now that her mother was dying, Jill wanted to renew the relationship, but knew she would have to deal with her mother's verbal abuse. Her language, vulgarity and criticisms of Jill were too upsetting. Jill decided she would confront her, tell her to stop treating her this way. She did, and her mother told her she was no longer her daughter. Jill was devastated.

The stepfather, Eugene, called Jill just before they moved to the Silicon Valley. He wanted Jill to know that he was diagnosed with very advanced heart disease and would probably not live long. He told Jill that her mother, though she still refused to speak with Jill, had her good and bad days. Jill's sisters called Mom every so often, but she refused to talk much to them.

Now faced with a move, a dying mother and stepfather and a highly anxious daughter who was afraid to leave Orlando, Jill felt depressed. But she pulled the family together and, with amazing strength and resolve, got the family settled in their new home.

She was emotionally drained but determined to make California a good place for her family. She got Bobbie settled in her new school. Then Jill began to think of ways to bring in additional income. She was very resourceful. She noticed she was tired a lot and lacked the energy she needed to get everything done. She had gained weight and rarely exercised. But she figured she had been through a lot of changes and was just exhausted. Months went by, and Jill's husband was up for promotion. He had been passed over twice.

If he didn't get promoted this time, there were no more tries, and he would face possible early retirement. In addition, her husband discovered a suspicious mole. Further testing found it was cancer and needed to be removed. He was scheduled for a biopsy and surgical removal in the next week. Prior to the surgery, he learned that he had been passed over for promotion once again. Now the family faced another transition—possible unemployment, searching for a new job and perhaps even needing to change careers. Jill started to feel overwhelmed again.

It had been a while since her last physical. Because of her husband's recently discovered cancer, he urged Jill to schedule a physical exam as well. Jill figured her run-down feeling was caused from all the family changes and stress. But at her husband's insistence, she made an appointment at the nearest recommended clinic.

Her lab work came back with elevated values. Nervously, she referred herself for a second opinion. There it was—breast cancer. She was stunned, so many of her family members were seriously ill—her mother, stepfather, husband—now her. Could this really be happening? She knew she was stressed beyond her coping abilities. She called me and needed to talk.

The illnesses caused Jill to start asking about God. Where was He? Didn't He promise not to give her more than she could handle? Did He know she was over the edge emotionally? What did she do to deserve this?

By the time the breast cancer was found, Jill had already lost a number of things—her original family through divorce, her childhood home through bankruptcy, her father through divorce and death, the security of her home in Orlando, friends, her mother's love and health, the possible loss of her stepfather who was fighting heart disease, a stable daughter and her husband's promotion and health. Even I was taken aback by all Jill faced. When she entered therapy, Jill reminded me of a modern-day Job. Her circumstances could lead to depression in the strongest person.

Jill's emotional resources were depleted. Everything seemed to happen at once. She asked if there was anything she could do or take to help her through this difficult time. I suggested she consider evaluation for a low-dose antidepressant. Under normal circumstances, Jill wasn't a depressed person. In the recent past, she showed a great deal of stamina going through a number of changes. But now, as the stress piled on, her coping resources were waning. The antidepressant would give her the lift she needed to get though this stressful time. After the stress lessened and her life was on more of an even keel, it was very unlikely the antidepressant would be needed.

Although she didn't understand why all of this was happening to her, Jill was determined not to let it destroy her. She asked me about God. Jill had some religious background, but a personal relationship with God was never a part of her life. Now that she was afflicted on so many fronts, depressed and facing an uncertain future, God was someone she wanted to discuss.

Of course her first question was why would a supposedly loving God allow her to suffer so. Good question, and I wished for an easy answer. But suffering, adversity and sickness are complicated realities of the Bible.

I began our spiritual quest with this. Adversity is not God's desire for us, but He can use it to effect something good in our lives. Facing the loss of everything we hold secure can bring us to a new dependence on God.

The Bible shows us that God doesn't always remove us from circumstances but promises to take us through them. Suffering and sickness have been part of the human experience since the fall of Adam and Eve. Even though we suffer, God's sovereignty still prevails. So nothing happens to us that God doesn't know about or that cannot be used to bring about good if we love Him and are called according to His purpose.

Clearly, in Jill's case, God had her attention. Did He give her sickness—no. Would He use her circumstances to bring her to Him—yes.

And that's exactly what happened. Jill decided she needed Him in her life. Her past strengths, though admirable, could not sustain her, and she found she needed strength beyond her own.

I made it clear that surrendering her life to God would not fix all her circumstances. It wouldn't force her mom to love her. It wouldn't bring her family home or assure her husband's promotion, but it would take care of the depression and the ache in her heart.

Jill had to work through all the grief associated with the many losses of her past—the death of her father, the resentment she felt at raising her sisters, the rejection of her mother, the impending loss of her mother and stepfather, the fear and anxiety regarding her husband, the lack of family support and her own mortality. Regarding all these things, she could not let bitterness, resentment or fear take root.

Jill took comfort in the fact that Jesus suffered much while on earth. She knew He could relate to her feelings of frustration and helplessness. She was challenged by Jesus' response to suffering and His instruction to "count it all joy" (James 1:2). How does one experience joy in the midst of suffering?

Joy, I would explain, arises not in our circumstances or things, but in the fact that Jesus loved us so much that He would die for our sins so that we could have eternal life. Our joy is because we know He has already done what we needed—He saved us, healed us and promises to be with us through any difficulty. Joy comes by praising God in all things and circumstances. We praise Him for what *He* does, not for what *we* are going through. We praise Him because...

- He loves me with an everlasting love (Jer. 31:3).
- He cherishes and honors me (Isa. 43:4).
- He rejoices over me with singing (Zeph. 3:17).
- He takes pleasure in me (Psa. 149:4).
- He bears all my burdens (Psa. 55:22).
- He guards me as the apple of His eye (Deut. 32:10).
- He fights my battles for me and wins all of them (Deut. 1:3–31; 2 Tim. 4:17–18).

- He will vindicate me (Deut. 32:36; Psa. 7:8; Isa. 54:13).
- He revives me when I am weary (Psa. 68:9; 119:107; Rom. 8:11).
- He has taken away the fear of death (Heb. 2:14–15).

Though Jill had many reasons to be depressed, she now had the best reason to count it all joy. No matter the course of her life, she is God's child. We prayed for her healing. Until we see it, Jill is counting it all joy because of Jesus.

What a testimony Jill was to my life. Like Job, she stood firm once she discovered who God was and what He promised her. She stopped looking to things for her security and put her trust in God.

LOSS OF FUNCTIONING

Aging presents a series of losses. Again, I'm not saying there is no growth with aging. There certainly is. But our bodies begin to do things that require our emotional adjustment. Our eyesight and hearing are less sharp. We lose our ability to bear children. (We gain freedom from PMS!) We forget things. Everything starts to sag and fall! I know this is a poor description of the aging process, but you get the picture. At the risk of always sounding negative, please understand that I'm concentrating on the losses because women don't get depressed with the positive aspects of aging. It's the losses that depress us.

Because of the emphasis on beauty, youth and fitness, many women have difficulty adjusting to the changes of aging and get depressed. Some actually get bitter, feeling life is unfair. Our culture doesn't help much on this front either. We don't value aging or the experiences of the elderly. We engage in ridiculous arguments about the quality of life, deciding who is viable and who is not. We forget that in God's eyes all life is sacred. No one is useless. When we take charge of when we live or die, we usurp God's timing for death. We don't own our life—God does—and He values what He creates.

There is no biblical support for the idea of "quality of life." Our value does not depend on our functional ability. Even so, it is difficult for many of us to accept the physical limitations that come with aging. And we don't always understand why we walk through certain circumstances.

My grandmother was one of God's saints on earth. The wife of a pastor, she knew how to pray and go to God when things were difficult. When my grandfather died, she moved into our house and lived with us for twelve years.

After a full and productive life, Grandma began losing track of things. The doctors called it the early signs of Alzheimer's. She left the stove on when she cooked and couldn't remember where she was when she started to wander in the middle of the night.

Grandma was doing things that could endanger her and the rest of us in the house. After a long and agonizing decision, the family agreed Grandma needed twenty-four-hour nursing care. It was the hardest decision my mother and her siblings ever made. Here was their mother, a women whose life was known for dignity and holiness, now shedding her clothes and being contrary. None of it made sense.

Day after day Grandma was losing more of her self from us. Sometimes she didn't know who we were; at other times she would have lucid moments. It was hard for my mom to watch her once strong, dependable mother leaving us and going somewhere else in her mind. We wondered what she thought. Did she know what was happening? After such a life of dignity, why did God allow this to be her end here on earth? We didn't know why, but God never left her.

One of the most memorable moments I have of the nursing home was when my mom, frustrated and upset over seeing her mother in such distress, went to play the piano in the nursing home. My mom, a former pianist in our church, began to play the old hymns. An amazing thing happened, Grandma began to sing. She remembered the lyrics buried somewhere in her mind. A calm would come over her, and God would minister to her through the music. We would catch a glimpse of the grandma we used to know. When Mom stopped playing, Grandma went back to her secret place.

I'm sure God did this for us as much as for Grandma. Somehow it made us realize that despite how difficult the situation, Grandma was still with Jesus. In some way, this was a parallel to our lives. As we go through difficulty, every once in a while we get a glimpse of heaven, of God's glory, and we have the hope of a better place.

We can't afford to get stuck in the difficulty we face. Our time here is too short, and we miss the lesson when we get caught up in the circumstances. There are other losses associated with health besides aging and disease.

BIPOLAR DISORDER

Abby faced a circumstance she didn't like, so she denied the reality of her condition. When she did, she got in serious trouble. Since her early twenties, Abby was diagnosed with bipolar disorder. Bipolar disorder, which used to be known as manic-depressive disorder, is a mood disorder that tends to run in families. It is characterized by mood swings. There is a euphoric high (mania) often followed by a serious episode of depression. Sometimes depression precedes the mania. Eventually things get out of control in the mania and the depressive episode with serious consequences for both.

The major treatment for bipolar depression is lithium or a medication like lithium. Lithium is a natural salt and replaces sodium in the brain. Without getting too complicated, bipolar patients are salt-deficient and need the lithium to prevent manic episodes. The problem is that people with bipolar disorder don't want to take the medication. They don't like to think of themselves as different or needing extra help. Without the medication, they are dealing with a loss of functioning. Many women get stuck in this loss, feeling angry about having the disorder. This lack of acceptance can result in disobedience.

The most frequent comment I hear from women is, "I don't want to be different. I don't want to have to take something to function. I don't want to have this disorder." Who would, but pretending it doesn't exist causes more problems. Listen to Abby's story.

Abby was a terrific person. Bright, fun and compassionate, she made me laugh a lot in therapy. Two years prior to Abby's latest episode of mania, I met her in the hospital when she was seriously depressed and suicidal. No one had diagnosed her bipolar disorder, and her mood swings were serious.

Prior to diagnosis, Abby's episodes of mania created marital problems. Her husband separated from her, not understanding her impulsive spending and sexual behavior. It was not uncommon for Abby to spend thousands of dollars shopping and pick up men for sexual favors when she was euphoric.

She was hospitalized, diagnosed and placed on lithium, which stabilized her mood and allowed her to function normally.

Abby and Don reunited a year after Abby was diagnosed and stabilized on medication. Both were educated about bipolar disorders. They learned that Abby could function well if she would regularly take medication. They learned to watch for signs of an impending mood swing, usually precipitated by Abby's noncompliance to the medication.

Abby, like so many bipolar patients, was stable and lived a normal life when she took her medication. The problem was she didn't always take it. She didn't want to be on medication. She refused to believe she had a problem despite her severe mood swings and periods of depression and mania. Consequently, she continued to suffer in all areas of her life. Her pride was blocking her good sense.

During depressive episodes she missed work, became suicidal and couldn't function. During the mania she acted out impulsively through spending and high-risk sexual behavior. Then she would crash and become severely depressed.

Abby didn't want to have this problem. But she did. Even when I could get her to acknowledge the mood swings, she wasn't ready to give up the high and euphoria she felt during a manic episode. The euphoric feeling was exciting, creative, productive. But it came with a price—behavior she didn't control and severe depressive crashes.

Abby saw her disorder as a loss of functioning. She refused to face her condition. She knew what she had to do—take the lithium, structure her life, exercise, get regular sleep, learn better coping skills and prevent relapse. She knew all of this but didn't want to do it.

Spiritually, there were two issues we had to tackle—healing and obedience. Let's start with healing. Abby wouldn't be healed unless she admitted to a need for healing. Oh, God in His grace could heal her anyway, but God was dealing with her pride. Abby asked, "Do you believe I could be healed?" "Of course," was my answer. "If I believe nothing is impossible with God, why would I limit who and what He can heal?" God could change the salt levels in Abbey's brain, but until we saw evidence of His healing, she needed the lithium.

Using the medication was not wrong. Diabetics use insulin, people with high blood pressure regulate it with drugs. Medications control cholesterol, heart disease and countless other diseases. Because of the strong biochemical component of bipolar disorder, taking medication is appropriate. We still pray for healing because we are instructed to do so biblically. We expect and believe for God to do the miraculous because He is able. Taking medication does not stop us from asking God to heal and believing He can do it.

Abby's reluctance to use the medication was rooted in pride. She refused to do what she could to help herself and didn't want to give up the mania. Abby knew the literal meaning to, "Pride cometh before the fall." Her refusal to do what was necessary led to a big fall, one that left her devastated and ashamed.

We all struggle on some level with rebellion and obedience. We don't want to admit when something is wrong and do what's necessary to correct it. We think that if we are in charge of our life, things will go just fine. We discover, often through pain, this is not so. Pride and disobedience can be blocks to accepting loss and moving on with life.

The surrender of our will to God's will is for most of us a life-long process. While many of us are not bipolar, we can relate to the struggle to obey. Obedience begins in childhood and continues throughout our adult lives. Rebellion and pride creep into our adult lives in ways less obvious than when we were children or teens. We have to constantly examine our hearts to see if the reason we are not doing something is because it goes against God's Word or because we are rebelling and want to do it our way.

This was Abby's challenge. Down deep she knew she needed to take the medication. God was using the medication issue to deal with pride and rebellion in her life. When she finally yielded, she had a breakthrough.

It's been five years since Abby had a major mood swing. She's now obedient and continues to focus on all areas of her life that need to come into submission to God's Word. As a result, Abby is euphoric again—not from the high of the mania but from walking in obedience to God.

Changing situations and circumstances involve loss. When we don't accept change and refuse to believe that out of it will come something new and different, we get stuck feeling depressed and discouraged. We focus on what we don't have, not on where we are going. In essence, we limit God to doing things our way.

FINDING THE IMPORTANT THINGS

What does the Bible say about things? First, it says that God wants to give us good things. "If you then, being evil, know how to give good gifts to your children, how much more will your Father who is in heaven give good things to those who ask Him" (Matt. 7:11). James 1:17 says, "Every good gift and every perfect gift is from above, and comes down from the Father of lights, with whom there is no variation or shadow of turning." The Bible is full of verses that talk about the good things God wants to give us.

And while we are talking about God, let's get our theology straight. God does not give disease, disaster and harm to teach you a lesson. He may allow things to happen in your life, but He is not the author of them. God, who is perfect and good, can only give you His goodness. He can't give you what He doesn't have—evil. Furthermore, the Bible tells us that God delights in giving us good things. This means He gets a kick out of blessing us. So stop attributing the evils of your life to God. Evil is a result of our fallen state and much of the time brought on by our own stupidity.

So, knowing God wants to bless us and provide for all our needs, we need to be careful not to hold onto things that are unimportant. In fact, only things of eternal value—the things of God—have lasting significance.

How do you determine the value of something? Value is determined by how much you pay for something. Jesus bought us with a price. It cost Him His life, which is why we say we were purchased by His blood. Obviously He places great value on us.

Losing something valuable is more upsetting than losing something easily replaced. That's why losing relationships are so hard. We value people. But we also value things. Sometimes we pay a lot of money for something that isn't valuable, and that's just bad judgment. Some things have value beyond money. They represent a part of our past, a moment in time that we savor.

Women become depressed over losing things of value. What do women value besides people? Women value security, which is why divorce and death are so difficult. We value our independence and our identities. We value sentiment, compassion, empathy and kindness. Wisdom and understanding are of great value and sought after. That's why mentoring is so important.

But we can lose all these things if we focus on the wrong priorities and don't stay intimately connected to God. God is our source for all things. He gives wisdom and identity, and because of His love we can have all the good things of God. We have to stay connected to God and know how to apply His Word to our lives.

We don't have because we don't ask (James 2:4). This is not my idea—it's biblical. (See 1 John 5:14–15.) Start asking God for all the good things He has promised. He tells us to believe that He's waiting to give us good things. This is where many of us fall down. We don't really believe God's promises, at least we don't believe they are for us. We think, *God gave that woman what she needed, but He won't help me.* Where do we get such insecure thoughts? From our experiences with people who let us down, from the enemy who loves to put doubt in our mind about God's faithfulness and from our ignorance of His Word.

The formula is simple, too simple for most. Ask and believe for anything according to His will. What's His will—His Word. Whatever it says you can have. We think we have to beg God, be good enough to receive His blessing, earn His favor. But we don't. It goes back to that covenant love He has given us. He gives us good things because He has promised them. God doesn't break His promises. God's promises are like a filled buffet table with a feast waiting to be eaten, but you have to go to the table, believe there will be food and be ready to taste all the goodies.

Many things aren't as important as we make them out to be. Losing them becomes traumatic because we don't place our trust in the things of God. As long as we stay intimate and dependent on God, we won't lose His good things—His promises of salvation, healing, wisdom, blessings, increase and much more. Get your eyes off things and on God. Then you'll find what you thought you lost.

6

Facing the Loss of a Dream

W e all have dreams. Don't worry I'm not going to analyze yours. I'm talking about dreams you dream for your life. When you were a little girl, what did you want to be when you grew up? Are you close to that ideal or far away?

For a while, I wanted to be one of the Beatles. Well, actually I wanted to marry one of the Beatles—Paul McCartney to be specific. Then I found out he married someone named Linda, and that was about as close as I would get. A back-up singer was my next ambition. I could *ooh* and *ahh* behind the best of them and look out for the dancing part. Singing was a risky profession. I was good, but not that good.

OK, how about a secret agent helping Napoleon Solo and Illya Kuryakin on *The Man From U.N.C.L.E.* (I'm dating myself now.) The problem with the secret-agent thing was that you had to do things you couldn't talk about. Pass on that one. Our family needed a medical doctor, but I couldn't deal with the blood thing. The mention of varicose veins sent me flat to the floor. I guessed that could be a problem. The one serious ambition I had was to be an attorney. I was good at arguing and liked debate so it fit my personality.

My dream never materialized because I got sidetracked from my pursuit of law and justice. Oh, I had it all planned. I would begin at the University of Michigan's prelaw program and finish at Harvard Law School (you have to dream big). Then I would be hired by a high-powered firm and spend my life serving up justice and making a few bucks. I had a plan. I had a dream, but something happened on my way to college that changed the course of my life.

It was the end of the Vietnam War. My brother Denny managed to avoid the draft because of his high draft number. God knew Denny could never go to war. The terror of war alone would have killed him before he ever got there. My oldest brother, Gary, wasn't much of the soldier type either, but he was drafted. As a biologist out of college, he went into the Army as an officer—not a dream he ever envisioned for his life, but then the draft wasn't interested in his dreams.

Soon after being drafted, Gary was sent to Vietnam. I can't tell you much about his time there. He shared very little, but when he did it was horrible stuff—kids wired with bombs, soldiers freaking out and death everywhere. When he returned stateside after a year and half, he was never quite the same. But he was still my big brother who always had something to say about my future.

Promoted and given a special assignment overseas, Gary had to be gone for seven weeks. During that time, Denny was to be married. Obviously Gary couldn't attend the wedding. He was halfway around the world. We talked it over as a family and decided that despite Gary's unplanned absence, the wedding would go as planned. Gary would miss it. No one wanted it this way, but it seemed like the only recourse at the time.

At the end of the tour, flying home from India, Gary's plane blew up before it landed. I can't begin to tell you the nightmare of that experience for our family and his. He left a widow, a baby and one on the way. Denny felt guilty that he didn't insist Gary come to his wedding. Actually we all shared that guilt. Mom and Dad did what most parents would do when confronted with the death of a child—went into shock. I mostly felt lost. My big brother, who always guided my steps, was now gone at a crucial point of my launching into young adulthood. Shaken, I spent my summer not caring much about college or prelaw.

Suddenly my planned-out life seemed not so planned. I no longer cared much about my dream to become a lawyer. I no longer cared about justice. What was just about having a brother killed? Nothing, I concluded. If I couldn't personally have justice, why would I want to fight to get it for anyone else? Now, what do I do? It was painfully obvious, Gary wasn't there to help me find my way.

I was amazed that in the middle of their grief, my parents took control. They insisted I preempt my plans for the University of Michigan and attend a small private college in the Midwest. The small college would give me the sense of community and caring I so badly needed this first time away from home. At Michigan, I'd be lost in a sea of many. That fall, I left to attend Evangel College.

At first, I was mad at my parents for sending me to the small college. I was mad they were deciding my future. I was mad that my brother was dead. I was mad that my dream had died. Searching for something to help me make sense of my brother's death, I started picking up psychology courses. At least if I was going to be confused, I could study my confusion and get credit. I did well in psychology, but not much of my confusion cleared up. I was stuck, trying to find a dream I could embrace with some conviction.

As the years passed, I often thought about going back to law school. The old dream would pop up every now and then, but I couldn't seem to muster up the enthusiasm for law any more. Way down inside, I blamed God for taking away my dream. I was stuck.

Like when Adam and Eve ate the fruit, I thought that Gary's death had derailed me from the perfect plan for my life, and I resented that. It wasn't until I realized that God didn't kill my brother—and had a plan for my life (I know it's a cliché, but true)—that I started to get unstuck. I know that sounds ridiculous, especially from someone raised in the church, but I wasn't exactly rational when it came to death. It also took me a while to realize that God was able to use the tragedy to put me on His path. He intended for me to be a therapist. When I accepted His plan as a new dream, a new ambition, I started to move from that stuck place.

When we lose our dreams, it is easy to get depressed. We feel short-changed or resentful that things didn't go the way we planned. We think we know best what to do with our lives. When we love God, we submit to His plan for our life. Submission is not a word that is comfortable for me. In fact, in a feminist statement (remember I was young and confused a lot), I refused to have the word "submit" in my marriage vows. I thought that to submit to my husband meant he could do with me as he pleased. I didn't have a clue that submission was about doing God's will and working His plan for marriage. (Don't worry, by God's grace we are still together after twenty-five years of marriage.)

Submitting to the will of God may mean giving up your dreams. It's an abandoning of yourself to the Lord, an attitude of the will. It's a response to God's love for us. The good news is His plan is always better. One of my favorite songs is by Twila Paris. She writes:

> Hard as it seems, standing in dreams,
> Where is the dreamer now?
> Wonder if I, wanted to try,
> Would I remember how?
> I don't know the way to go from here,
> But I know that I have made my choice.
> This is where I stand until He moves me on,
> And I will listen to His voice.
> This is the faith. Patience to wait
> When there is nothing clear,
> Nothing to see, still we believe;
> Jesus is very near.

I cannot imagine what will come,
But I've already made my choice.
This is where I'll stand until He moves me on,
And I will listen to His voice.
Could it be that He is only waiting there to see
If I will learn to love the dreams that He has dreamed for me?
Can't imagine what the future holds,
But I've already made my choice.
This is where I stand until He moves me on,
And I will listen to His voice.[1]

Do you have a dream or ideal you are still waiting to see? If it's from God, you need to stand in that dream. If it's not, be ready to let it die without going into despair. Or did you have a dream that was crushed by some circumstance? If so, it may be that God has other plans for your life.

LOST IDENTITY

You may feel lost and confused about your life. You have an idea about how life should be, but your experience doesn't match those expectations. You have been wounded by situations or people in your past. You have lost your innocence, your virginity or even a hopeful view of the possibilities in your life.

I see a number of young women in therapy confused about their identities. As they struggle to make sense of hurtful relationships, they lose a sense of who they are—or perhaps they never knew in the first place.

When women talk about identity, we are talking about the way we view ourselves—our unique talents or characteristics. Identity formation goes through its greatest changes in adolescence and early adulthood. That's why your experiences during those years so greatly affect your sense of self.

As I mentioned before, women tend to define themselves by their relationships and their ability to connect with other people. So what happens in those relationships is of importance to developing a good sense of self. Figuring out who you are is a confusing process and often causes anxiety, periods of depression and negative feelings.

Ellen did what most forty-five-year-olds did twenty years ago. She went to college, chose a career, made some money and married a great guy. Ellen and her husband, Steve, lived well. As a dual-income family, Ellen and Steve could afford all the yuppie toys—the BMW and SUV, the Bang & Olufsen sound system, the boat docked at the nearby lake, the summer condo in the mountains and the updated European kitchen.

Ellen lived her life on cruise control. Steve became wildly successful in his advertising agency, and Ellen played with the idea of opening her own interior design studio. As the money rolled in, Ellen took more time to dabble in her interests, unsure of what she really wanted to do with her time. She had the luxury of experimenting with a number of hobbies while having no worry about her economic needs. Steve spent long hours away from home, driven by his passion to keep the agency on the leading edge of its industry.

Ellen also had her mom and community activities to busy her time. Both her preteen children were involved in every sport and extra curricular activity possible. Ellen drove her new SUV all over town, carpooling kids and attending community events. When she and Steve would finally touch base at the end of a long busy day, both were exhausted and fell into bed.

Ellen's life was very busy but not very satisfying. Something nagged at Ellen. All her dreams had come true. She had a fabulous and successful husband, lived in a five-thousand-square foot beautifully furnished home, drove great cars, attended an upstanding community church, had wonderful and talented children and a golden retriever to make the picture look perfect. This was the life that most women dream about—all that was missing was the picket fence.

But Ellen wasn't happy. She tired of the monthly bridge meetings. The pressure to keep up with the newest and best of everything was getting to her. She was tired of all the running around from place to place. The children were well-cared for, her husband came home to a stable and orderly home, but Ellen was feeling depressed.

She didn't ask for help right away because she felt guilty for having so much and feeling so bad. But as the depression worsened, Ellen decided to see me.

Ellen's depression was rooted in issues of identity. Ellen, who moved along the life cycle at a steady and well-paced schedule, missed one crucial element. She never really had a well-defined sense of who she was as a woman.

Ellen came from a family with money. Her mom, also a bridge player, spent her life catering to the needs of her husband and doing the things defined as important by others. Mom looked happy on the outside but underneath had signs of chronic unhappiness. As Ellen became a teenager, she noticed Mom's afternoon teas had changed to glasses of Long Island tea. Her numbing continued by escaping through romance novels. Ellen saw the distance grow between her father and mother. They never yelled or fought, they simply drifted apart.

Ellen was worried that her life was taking a similar turn. Steve and she rarely had any time together. When they did go out, they had little to say to each other if they didn't talk about the children. Ellen didn't have much of herself to talk about. She worried that Steve may find an interesting woman at the office and become emotionally involved.

Ellen's identity was wrapped up in her husband, her economic status and her role as mother and community volunteer. Away from these things, she had no clue what she thought, felt or desired. Worried that she was an uninteresting woman, she started to become depressed. She should be happy; she had everything and yet felt empty.

Ellen's situation may be familiar to many of us who derive our identities solely from other people and things. We dream of a great life, have it and still feel unhappy. When Ellen began to talk about the people or things in her life, I would stop her and ask her to talk about herself. I wanted to know how Ellen was wired—what did she think, feel and desire? Ellen didn't know. She really hadn't given it much thought. Like her mother, she learned what to do to be successful but never how to think about the person she was and wanted to be. Oh, Ellen dabbled with lots of career ideas, hobbies and interests, but her lack of focus was related to her unclear identity.

Under the surface, Ellen was fearful that if she lost all her things and her husband, nothing would be left. Her sense of self depended on the ongoing maintenance of things and left her adrift and unsatisfied.

The work with Ellen was to help her find her true self. She needed a voice that was clearly hers. In order to develop her voice, she had to stop listening to the voices of others. What did she want to say? She said she didn't know, but I believed she did or could figure it out.

One of the important ways to help Ellen find a sense of herself was to help her figure out who she was as the daughter of God. Since she didn't know who she was as her father's earthly daughter (he was a workaholic), I asked her to first learn who she was in God's view. The way we discovered Ellen's identity was through looking in the Bible. As Ellen became more comfortable with her view of self through Scripture, she started to develop a sense of who she was separate from relationships. She began to speak out more about her needs, set limits, develop priorities and expect a more intimate relationship with her husband.

There were also good qualities Ellen picked up from her mother. Yes, her mother had traits Ellen wanted to avoid, but Ellen overlooked her mom's strengths. It didn't take long for Ellen to identify with the strong parts of her mom and work to change the parts she didn't want to keep.

As a result of Ellen's newfound self, her husband started to get irritated. The less depressed Ellen became, the more irritated he became. He could no longer ignore his wife and put all his effort into his business without Ellen speaking up about it. The old way of doing things was shaken.

Steve eventually joined the therapy. On the one hand, he was happy that his wife was gaining a sense of herself. On the other hand, he was distressed that he had to make changes as well. My take was this was a win/win situation for both. Ellen could now be a full-fledged partner in the relationship—one with equal voice, valuable insight and opinion, and interesting. Steve could bring balance to his life by becoming less obsessed with business and get his intimacy needs met. Both stood to gain, not lose.

When women begin to develop a clear sense of self, it can be challenging and even threatening to those around them. Sometimes the response of others throws a woman's active search backwards. Women must stand firm against the backlash of change and realize that as they become better defined, others may resist the changes that come to them as a result of the process.

In the most severe cases, a woman who asserts herself can be beaten by an insecure man who doesn't want to know who she really is but prefers to treat her as an object. When you change, a ripple is felt throughout the family system. Some families handle the change well. Others are thrown into crisis.

There are many women like Ellen who struggle to find a sense of self. Others may have more self-definition but are afraid to assert themselves. Alex was that kind of woman. Alex, a short, dark-haired, nice-looking woman, was very talented in the area of theater arts. Alex married a man who was wildly successful as an entrepreneur but wanted to control his wife. He had no interest in theater arts and preferred tall statuesque blondes.

I had to wonder why Alex would choose a man who devalued central parts of who she was. Her need for security overrode her need to be accepted. Alex's past was plagued with unsettling times in which money was tight and bad things happened.

Alex did anything her husband, Jerry, wanted. He told her to drop out of theater arts and devote her time to visible community functions that improved his status among his peers. He even went so far as to suggest strongly that Alex have plastic surgery in order to physically appear more to his liking. Sadly, Alex agreed.

Alex was uncomfortable with the unreasonable demands made by her husband, but was afraid to assert herself. She felt inadequate and lacked the economic power of her husband. Jerry's status and power placed Alex in an unequal position in the marriage.

Men with money represent power and security. In Alex's case, her need for security gave way to Jerry's control. Jerry was self-centered and narcissistic. He was concerned about his wife as an adornment on his sleeve, not for her true self. He devalued her by rejecting her talent and physical body. If he unconditionally accepted who she was or even bothered to know her beyond the external, he would not make such demands.

Fortunately, Jesus doesn't care about the external; He looks at the heart. Alex had to trust her heart and decide how far she was willing to be pushed into becoming someone she wasn't. If she spoke up, she risked losing her security. If she stayed silent, she lost herself.

SEPARATE BUT ATTACHED

A girl's view of herself is related to how she feels about being female. She primarily learns about being female from her mother. Fathers validate gender identity. They influence daughters' future relationships with men and should not pull away from their teenaged daughters.

When I was studying family therapy I was influenced by writings from Betty Carter, a well-known family therapist. Her view about mothers and daughters is helpful in understanding how girls struggle with the idea of being female. She says that mothers try to raise perfect daughters. In their attempts to do so they present their daughters with ideals, how they should be, or how they want them to be, rather than their true experiences of being female. What happens then is that daughters are left trying to live up to those ideals. When they fail, they don't always know what to do because Mom, in an attempt to be a good enough mom, has kept her true self hidden.

Becoming a separate and independent woman is a process involving loss. You leave the comfort of parental dependency to discover who you are. You are trying to find your voice among the family voices. You are trying to be female while identifying with and separating from your mother. This is not an easy process for a young woman or her parents.

You struggle to be separate but attached to your parents. You may also face the loss of a romantic relationship with a boyfriend during this developmental phase of separation. This can add additional stress. Managing loss associated with change is not easy even though we all have to do it. Many young women get stuck. Liz was stuck. Liz became very confused when trying to separate and negotiate her independence.

It's 10 A.M. on Tuesday. Time for Liz's appointment. Liz, a petite, fragile-looking blonde, was one of my "regulars." I first met Liz during semester break of her junior year of college. She plopped down on my couch and refused to speak. The intake information said Liz was depressed, and her parents were worried about her. Liz wouldn't tell me a thing. I spent many of those initial sessions waiting for Liz to speak. Occasionally, she threw me a bone.

It was hard for Liz to trust anyone. She had been hurt too many times, and college life was no exception. Dating was a nightmare. Every school break, Liz reappeared on my couch to update me on the latest male who used, abused and left her. The stories were the same. She chose men who drank, had sex with her and never dated her again.

After graduation, Liz decided to live at home for a while. Family life propelled her back on my couch. Dad, a lanky-framed man with huge features, was a rather pushy, extremely successful salesman who drank every night. He was an intense man who never had much to say at home. Liz longed for an emotional relationship with her dad. She saw him as competent, and of all the members of her family, the most approachable.

She dragged Dad to my couch. He came kicking and screaming all the way. In true salesman form, he told me therapy was a waste of time and informed me that his drinking was not affecting his family. Before I could speak, he shook my hand and told me he was there if his daughter needed him. He walked out the door and paid the bill. Liz burst out crying. It was classic Dad. And this was the most approachable family member!

Next, Liz decided Mom should sit on my couch. Timidly she crept into the room. "Do people really lie down on that thing?" (pointing to the couch). "Only I do," I replied, "Sometimes people make me crazy." She didn't crack a smile and looked horrified. When I asked Liz's mom to tell me about the family, she looked at the floor and said, "I try *not* to think about the family." But I pushed. "Liz needs to accept things the way they are. Her dad is distant, and I'm depressed most of the time. I can't help her because I can't make things better. He overpowers me. I nag but it does no good. There's too much pain. We've agreed not to talk about it."

Liz stopped bringing people to the couch. It was lonely but safer for her to sit by herself. She decided to move to her own condo near the water after she landed a job at an ad agency working as a graphic artist. Things went well for a while.

One year later, back on my couch, she wasn't talking. Another series of men had come and gone, all with the familiar themes of drinking, sex and rejection. One night she went to a party with some friends from work. She met a woman named Yvonne who threw her life into turmoil.

Yvonne and Liz began to drink together. The drunker they got, the more Liz poured her heart out to Yvonne. "Men are distant, no good, can't trust them, emotionally stupid, hurtful, powerful. All they want is sex, and then they leave you broken and empty." Her anger grew in intensity and ended in heart-wrenching sobs. Yvonne listened and quietly held Liz's hand. She put her arm around Liz and tenderly kissed her. Liz was shocked but it felt good. Yvonne continued to touch her and more passionately kissed her. Liz responded. The passion intensified, and Liz and Yvonne became sexually involved.

The next day when her head was clear, Liz wondered if she had dreamed of being with Yvonne. The phone rang, and Yvonne's soothing voice was there. "I hope you are OK with what happened last night. I loved being with you. Don't be embarrassed about what happened. Can we meet and talk?" Liz's head was spinning. What was happening to her? She didn't know but agreed to meet Yvonne.

She felt guilty about what happened and yet she longed for the intimacy she felt with Yvonne. The meeting was tense, but Yvonne was masterful in calming Liz and making her feel accepted. Yvonne suggested that Liz and she go out for dinner. Liz agreed.

The two women drank wine, told stories of misguided love and compared battle scars from male relationships. Liz felt so accepted and good. Yvonne invited Liz to her apartment. Nervously, Liz agreed. Yvonne poured a glass of wine and started to stroke Liz's hair. Liz felt excited. Yvonne understood her and knew how to comfort her better than any man she had known. She yielded to Yvonne's sexual advances.

For months, she and Yvonne went to parties, drank lots of wine and regularly had sex. Liz told no one and was secretly confused by what it all meant. Was she gay? She never considered herself gay, but her feelings for Yvonne were so strong and starting to scare her.

All Liz could think about was being with Yvonne. She needed her. No one made her feel this good. Yvonne knew how to touch her, anticipate her needs.

Liz became demanding of Yvonne's time, suggested they live together. She and Yvonne began to argue.

Liz walked into a book store one day and saw Yvonne sitting with a tall attractive woman, Mary, whom Liz recognized from the gay bars she and Yvonne frequented. Liz became insanely jealous. She couldn't eat or sleep and wondered if Yvonne was having an affair behind her back. Finally, she confronted Yvonne, who admitted she and Mary were sleeping together. Yvonne assured Liz she still had feelings for her.

Devastated Liz fell into a deep depression. Again she reappeared on my couch. "I almost didn't come to see you because I know you'll be upset with me when I tell you what I've been doing this past year. But I need to talk to you because I hurt so bad and can't concentrate on work."

Liz was deeply dependent on Yvonne. Even though she was angry and hurt over the breakup, she couldn't get Yvonne off her mind. She wanted to go back with Yvonne even though Yvonne was with someone else. She told me their sexual times were like none she'd ever experienced and was sure no man could ever compare. She must be gay but didn't feel gay. She wasn't attracted to other women.

Liz was extremely confused. If she wasn't gay, why would she sleep with a woman? Her family would flip if they knew what happened. She was even embarrassed when she thought about her behavior. Yet, the tie to Yvonne was strong.

Liz also told me that Yvonne called every now and then to tell Liz she loved and cared about her but needed to be with Mary. This threw Liz into depressive bouts in which she could barely function. Just when she thought she was making progress letting go of Yvonne, Yvonne would call or show up at Liz's apartment. Liz felt like she was going crazy, was becoming suicidal and was now ready to talk and perhaps trust me.

Liz had an emotionally dependent relationship with Yvonne that was destructive and hurtful. She thought she couldn't function without the nurturing and emotional presence of Yvonne in her life. That's why even after Yvonne broke off the relationship, Liz continued to take her phone calls and see her occasionally. She knew talking or seeing Yvonne plummeted her into depression, but she was convinced she couldn't live without her.

Liz's attraction to Yvonne did not stem from deep-seated lesbian feelings. Instead Yvonne represented a strong, nurturing woman who paid attention and met Liz's needs. Nurturance, attention and emotional intimacy were missing in Liz's family. Because of the lack of family intimacy and the rejection she felt from men, Liz was susceptible to the advances of Yvonne. Yvonne, she thought, could meet all her basic needs. Liz began to idolize Yvonne as the solution to her pain. Even though Yvonne appeared to be strong, she too was needy and needed Liz to need her.

The incredible feelings of rejection from men left an open door to the sexual advances of Yvonne. Possessing little self-esteem, feeling bitter towards the men who hurt her and upset by her family's lack of interest in developing closeness, Liz was ripe for the emotional picking. Confusing sex for love, the emotional ties to Yvonne intensified a strong dependency. Even though this relationship was causing Liz pain, she stayed in it because it gave her a sense of emotional security, intimacy, self-worth, excitement and acceptance.

The emotionally dependent relationship with Yvonne was ultimately a spiritual deception. In her desperation, Liz rationalized what she believed to be intuitively wrong as right. The sexual relationship created a strong bond, making it difficult to break off the relationship even in the face of rejection once again. Furthermore, Liz's belief that a human person could fulfill all her needs left her vulnerable to hurt.

I instructed Liz to break off ties with Yvonne—stop going to places where she would be, not to take her phone calls or agree to see her. I prepared her for the fact that in doing so, she would feel pain similar to someone going through a divorce. It was necessary for her to talk with me about her pain and not keep it inside. The temptation to see Liz would remain strong, but she had to choose not to yield to it.

Liz also needed to spend time with other friends. When she began seeing Yvonne, she saw none of her other friends. She became obsessed and possessive of Yvonne. Jealousy was always present because she believed she couldn't live her life without Yvonne in it. Liz wanted to be Yvonne's exclusive interest. Anyone else was a threat.

Liz was looking for her identity and security in another person. She was vulnerable and open to attack by the enemy. The lie was that only a woman could love her and meet all of her needs. After Yvonne let her down, she fell into despair. Men hurt her and so did women. No one could give her what she needed.

In her desperation, Liz asked me if I knew anything about God. If I did, she wanted to know. Most of all she wanted to know if He was dependable. Could He be trusted? Have I ever been let down or disappointed in His love? Was Jesus someone she could really trust? Would He hurt her or abandon her like all the others?

When Liz decided to put her dependency on Jesus, things in her life began to change. The most significant change was that she had the power to overcome the temptation to get back with Yvonne. She made a mental choice not to go back to that destructive relationship, but God also helped her with her feelings. The intense emotional pull towards Yvonne lessened as she was able to look to God for strength.

Liz knew that she had to stop looking at others to define who she was and deal with the rejection she felt from her mother and father. Her view of her mother was that she was a weak woman, always depressed and dependent on her husband to take care of the family. Her mother could tolerate very little emotionally. Mostly she fell apart at the slightest hint of a conflict or problem. Consequently, Mom struggled just to get though each day rather than help Liz with her emotional needs. At a young age, Liz decided women were victims and unable to get their needs met.

Her father was a powerful man who numbed his emotional feelings through alcohol. Liz wanted his attention and approval but found him unavailable. When she began to date, she often chose men who were powerful and aggressive and allowed them to take advantage of her in exchange for attention.

Most of Liz's relationship problems manifested when alcohol was involved. The men she dated drank heavily and would push her sexually. She drank and gave in to their sexual demands. Later, the men would reject her by having no further contact, leaving her feeling used, abused and powerless like her mother.

As an adult, Liz had to recognize the shortcomings of her parents and stop waiting for them to embrace her need for intimacy. Instead, she had to find an intimate relationship with God. He could fill the empty places and keep her from developing unhealthy dependencies with others. When God was the source of her dependency, she was healthier in her other relations.

Today, Liz is totally free of her relationship from Yvonne. She knows her only dependency is on God. He does supply all her needs as His Word promises. She is also making better dating choices and has stopped drinking alcohol. She has learned to set appropriate boundaries with men and women. She has been forgiven for her sexual behavior and walks in God's unlimited grace and mercy.

She is no longer depressed because she understands that her trust is in the Lord and not people. She is not a victim of a problematic past. Instead she walks in victory, knowing she is forgiven. She serves a God who loves her unconditionally and is highly dependable.

You may not have had all the problems Liz did in trying to find yourself, but figuring out who you are is always a challenging process. It's helpful to understand your family dynamics and how they have shaped the person you are. Self discovery, as long it's focused on improving you as a person, is a good thing.

However, your identity is not determined solely by your family or experiences. Why? Because we define ourselves through relationship with Christ as well as family and friends. We have to begin our search for self-definition in our relationship with Christ. He tells us who we are as His daughter. Jesus is the corrective experience for anyone who has problematic female and male relationships.

As Christians, we are part of God's family. When we accept Christ we become new creatures; old things are passed away. We have a new parent to whom we relate. That's the best news I can give anyone because it means we get a fresh start and a perfect parent.

Who am I in Christ? I am His daughter. I am fearfully and wonderfully made. He chose me. I am clean because of the forgiveness of sin. I have special abilities (Eph. 4:7). I have strength (Psa. 29:11). I am blessed. I am healed. I have a unique identity (Matt. 10:30). The list is long. You need to read your Bible to understand how God defines you. Hold on to God's Word about you, not the opinions of others, yourself or your family.

GIVING UP THE DREAM OF MARRIAGE— SINGLE BUT NOT BY CHOICE

Marriage is still a desire most women have despite the high rate of divorce. Single women who want to be married but haven't found the right partner have to fight discouragement. As time goes by, the reality that marriage may never come is tough to face. Even the thought of staying single is a huge loss for those who don't choose to be single.

Mary was fighting despair. From the time Mary was a little girl she dreamed of being married. She played house, imagined the day she would have three children and live happily ever after. By the age of eighteen she had her wedding planned to the detail. She was missing only one thing—the groom. But she was confident that she would be married in the next year or so. When marriage didn't happen, Mary started feeling depressed. A few years went by, and Mary's college friends were marrying. Mary was a bridesmaid four times but never the bride. At twenty-seven, she was starting to panic. She had to get married soon, she thought, or it would be too late. This was not the way Mary wanted her life to go.

Mary was an attractive woman who graduated from Columbia University when she was twenty-two years old. She majored in business and was working for a large CPA firm. Her job paid well, and she found a great loft apartment in the city. Mary was popular with friends who saw her as smart and outgoing. She always had a date when she wanted one.

Mary grew up with parents who divorced when she was twelve years old. Her dad, a stand-up comic, worked most evenings. He was a likable man and met Mary's mom in a comedy club. Mary's mom had a good paying job as an executive secretary at a modeling agency.

When Mary was born, her dad's road gigs began causing tension in the family. Mom felt Dad should be home more with his daughter. She wanted her husband to consider a new lifestyle now that Mary was born. Traveling to clubs, working nights and sleeping days wasn't fitting into the new family structure.

Although Dad could see his wife's point, he wouldn't give up his love for comedy and playing the clubs. The couple agreed to separate and then divorced. Because of her dad's job, Mary rarely saw him. When she did, things went well, which made her miss him all the more.

After the divorce, Mom and Dad had a friendly relationship and kept in touch. They communicated over issues involving Mary. When they saw each other, Mary sensed their affection.

Mary's mom was a steady influence on her—hard working and always on top of things. Mary described her mom as extremely capable. She knew her mom came from a physically abusive family but rarely spoke about it. "Life is what you make it," she told Mary. "Make yours as good as you can. Find a good man, and everything will be all right." Since Mary hadn't found a man, she went to college to look for one.

College was tough on Mary emotionally. Her choices of men were questionable. Her first boyfriend was a "jerk." He criticized her every move. He used to tell her she should be thankful to have found him. He no-showed on dates and flirted with other women. He paid her no respect and played on her insecurity. After months of feeling depressed, she finally broke off the relationship.

College boyfriend number two was even more problematic. Feeling vulnerable and highly insecure with men, she hooked up with what she called "a control freak." This guy was extremely jealous and wouldn't let Mary out of his sight. He needed constant reassurance of her love and tested her with all kinds of mind games.

For example, he called her one night, pretending to be a telephone suveyor, and began asking personal questions. When she started answering the questions, he went off on her, screaming that she must be unfaithful and couldn't be trusted. Mary knew his behavior was extreme but tolerated it all the same. His control and possessiveness escalated until Mary could take no more. She broke off the relationship. He became livid and started to threaten her. Mary was scared and went to Student Services. The counselor encouraged her to be firm with the breakup and report any future threats to the campus police.

Her boyfriend apologized but continued to call her. He followed her, watched her and wouldn't leave her alone. Scared of what he might do, she took him back. It was then that Mary had her first major depressive episode. She didn't want to date this guy but was scared and afraid he may harm her or himself. She called my office. "I'm in a destructive relationship and need help getting out of it. This is not how I expected dating to go."

After making sure the proper steps were taken for Mary's safety, we rehearsed the conversation she would have with her boyfriend. Mary was to be firm and under no circumstances waiver in her resolve. She was not responsible for the way he acted and made it clear that any attempts to harm her would be met by the police and campus officials. This time he took her seriously and backed off.

Mary's depression soon lifted. She handled the situation and was ready to go back to concentrating on her studies and believing God would send her husband soon. It was after graduation that I saw Mary again. Her depression was back, this time she felt suicidal. Even I was somewhat surprised by what had transpired.

Mary had dated off and on since graduation but was careful not to become too involved with any man. She figured the break from serious relationships could only help her. She would wait for God to send the right man. She concentrated on her new job and established herself as a single woman. She was happy with her decision not to date but at times, longed for an intimate relationship with a man. She had no one to talk to when she came home from work, no one with whom to share her successes or plans for the future. She felt lonely and a little down.

One night, bored and alone, she logged onto the Internet. Searching for a singles' chat room, she quickly located several. She'd never engaged in cyberspace dialogue but figured it was harmless. Slightly hesitant, she made a connection—"normal, twenty something, tired of dating, just looking for a good listener." That's when she met Tom.

Tom was also twenty something. He too had a number of bad experiences with women and was "just looking for someone sane to talk to." At first, the talks with Tom were superficial but friendly. He was a great listener and always knew what to say to make Mary feel better. Then, the talks became more personal and intimate. A strong on-line connection between the two was growing.

Mary couldn't wait to get home from work to check her E-mail in hopes of a note from Tom. She was amazed at how well he anticipated her moods, knew her thoughts and could relate to her emotionally. She let her guard down and became more intimate. After all, she thought, wasn't this better than her past relationships? The amount of sharing and communicating was much more than any of her previous boyfriends. And Tom was patient, loving and really interested in her life.

For months the cyberspace relationship continued until one day, Tom asked if they could meet. Mary panicked but found herself excited by the idea. What was she afraid of? She felt like she knew this guy better than any guy she'd ever dated. And since there was no one else in her life, Tom must be the one. She agreed. They would meet.

Tom lived in one state and she in another. So they chose a city that was halfway in between and agreed on a date and time to meet. Mary was nervous about the first meeting. What if she hated the way he looked or laughed? What if he was introverted and couldn't carry on a conversation? What if he didn't like her? What if...? Too late, she was on her way and committed to the meeting.

She pulled into the restaurant and looked around. So far, no sign of Tom. She decided to go inside and get a table. As she entered the restaurant, the waitress asked if she was Mary. "Yes," she smiled nervously. "You were expected and should sit over here at the corner table." The waitress left. Mary sat down, still no sign of Tom.

A slender, nice-looking woman in her twenties walked towards the table and sat down in the empty chair. "Excuse me," Mary started, "I'm saving this seat for a friend." "A friend named Tom?" the woman asked. 'Yes, how did you know?" The woman smiled, "Because I'm Tom."

"What," Mary gasped. "But you're a woman." "I know," the woman proceeded. "I didn't think you'd meet me if I told you. What difference does it make? We love each other and know each other intimately. Mary, I still want you. I love you." Mary couldn't speak. She stumbled to her feet and ran to her car.

The four-hour drive back home was unbearable. She could hardly see the road through the tears. What a betrayal! Her mind was reviewing the past nine months of the E-mail relationship. How could she be so stupid? How could she fall in love with a woman? What was wrong with her, did she miss the cues? Maybe she was gay and didn't know it. Why hadn't God sent her the man she dreamed of having? She couldn't think. She went home and fell on the couch. The ache in her heart was familiar, another messed-up relationship, only this time she didn't know the *he* was a *she!* This was worse. The depression hit.

Mary was unaware of the impact of growing up with a pleasant but absent father. She had a positive image of her dad but little experience to back it up. When her parents were married, Dad was away playing in comedy clubs. When divorced, the pattern continued. Mary longed for a man to be really involved in her life—someone with whom she could talk, spend time and share her life. Her unconscious wish was to find that man who would take the place of Dad. She longed for that intimacy.

When Mary began to date, she chose men of two extremes. One man was neglectful and absent, a behavior she knew from her father. Even though Mary was repeating a familiar pattern of choosing absent men, she also knew from experience that her needs would not get met. She had the sense to break off that relationship.

The second man was controlling and too possessive—the other extreme of her father. At first she loved the attention. Here was someone who cared about her every move, how she spent her day, wanted to know her every thought. After a while, it all became too much, too suffocating. She knew the possessiveness was unhealthy, but unhealthy attention felt better than none.

Desperate to find a man who would love her, she started to panic. The panic led to risky Internet behavior. Unfortunately the outcome of her search was negative.

The work of therapy was to help Mary make better dating choices and be content with her current single status. Like many singles, Mary panicked and made bad choices. She believed that God didn't care about her dating life. If He did, she would have met the man of her dreams and married. Being single was a sign that God had forgotten her and was busy in the lives of others.

First we established that being single was not an incomplete state, a disease or a pathology. Finding a man was not a cure for an absent dad or loneliness. Mary had to stop searching for a man to make her feel complete. Instead, I had her concentrate on her relationship with God.

To be more intimate with God, she had to start being more honest. Mary was hurt that her father chose comedy over spending time with her. That loss had to be grieved and then accepted as a choice in which she had no control. She could continue to have special moments with her father, but he would probably never give her the intimacy she desired. This she had to accept.

As a single woman, Mary was in covenant with God. She had the time and energy to develop a deep relationship based on that covenant. God's promise is that if she seeks Him, she will experience the fullness of His presence. What does that mean? It means her emotional and physical needs will be met, and she will be content with her current single status. But she had to trust God and be dependent on Him to take care of her. She had to believe, like the biblical Ruth, that if a Boaz was in her future, God would bring him to her. Acting in desperation was not trusting God.

Loneliness is an issue for both married and single people. The model of Jesus, who was also single on earth, was to immerse Himself in prayer when He felt lonely. Read the account of His death, particularly the night He was betrayed. His friends fell asleep. He faced death alone. He cried out to the Father in anguish and prayed more earnestly. Mary learned to go to prayer when loneliness overwhelmed her.

Mary also learned to develop a good support network of friends. Single people need live bodies to talk to and comfort them when they feel down. She had neglected woman friends during her dating times and needed to reestablish balance in her relationships. She had to take time for her friends even when she dated.

Ultimately, Mary had to give up trying to make a relationship happen and trust God to move sovereignly in her life. I had her focus on her present circumstances and put her energy in things she could control—doing well at work, developing friends, broadening her social life to include hobbies and interests, taking time to study the Word and pray and offering help to those in need. Mary was a valuable and useful person who had mistakenly defined herself only as unmarried. Once she gave up the search for a man, she became more productive in her work, social and spiritual life.

Mary had to give up her dream of being married by twenty. She had to believe that God knew her heart and had not forgotten her. We often talked about what marriage would have been like had she married before she worked through issues from her past. Perhaps God was protecting her from a destructive relationship. Whatever the reason, God had a plan for Mary's life, and Mary was finally ready to submit to His plan.

GIVING UP THE DREAM OF CHILDREN—INFERTILITY

Like dreaming about marriage, many girls dream of being a mom. For some, the desire to mother is so strong they can't imagine doing anything else. Sandy always loved babies. When she was little, she pretended to be the mommy for her two younger sisters. She dreamed of the day she could have a family of her own—perhaps three or four children.

As a child going to bed at night, she begged Mom to tell the story of her birth. It was such a wonderful story. Mom always said, "We prayed for a sweet little angel, and God sent you." Sandy was loved and cherished.

As Sandy grew, she never lost her desire to become a mother. She decided to become a teacher. Because she loved children, teaching just seemed to make sense. At college she met Bill, fell in love and married him after graduation. Bill shared her dream for a large family. The couple decided Sandy would teach for two years and then get pregnant. They saved and planned in anticipation for the long-awaited family.

But things didn't go as Sandy and Bill planned. For twelve months they tried to get pregnant with no result. Friends reassured Sandy that a pregnancy would happen in due time. "Don't worry about it. You need to relax. Stop thinking about it, and it will happen." But it didn't happen, and Sandy and Bill grew concerned.

Sandy decided to call her gynecologist. Perhaps something was wrong.

The gynecologist thought everything looked normal but referred Sandy to an infertility specialist. The specialist could run tests and perhaps pinpoint the reason for her difficulty conceiving. Both Sandy and Bill were relieved to finally get some answers.

The infertility doctor recommended several tests. The tests were painful, but Sandy was glad the problem would be discovered. The test results showed no problems in Sandy or Bill's ability to conceive or carry a pregnancy. This was good news but puzzling. Why wasn't Sandy getting pregnant?

The doctor suggested Sandy take her temperature every day and use an ovulation kit each month to pinpoint optimum days for conception. She took her temperature, used the kit, knew the days of ovulation and made sure the opportunities for pregnancy were not missed. Still no pregnancy.

Friends and family continued to tell Sandy to relax. They would say unsympathetic things like, "You really don't want to raise children in this day and age." "Take my children for a day, and you may change your mind." "I'm so fertile, I get pregnant looking at my husband."

People at her church were even more insensitive and misguided. One lady told her she was being punished for past sins. Another said her infertility was a curse on her generation. Another wanted to pray for deliverance. None of this resonated in Sandy's spirit. She couldn't think of any unresolved generational sins, she hadn't done anything sinful that wasn't forgiven in her past, and she didn't need deliverance. The church people actually frightened her, and so she pulled away from church.

No one seemed to understand the pain Sandy and Bill experienced. Every day Sandy monitored and charted her temperature. For weeks she underwent painful physical testing, gave numerous blood samples and was vaginally examined by residents and infertility specialists. The physical demands of infertility testing were exhausting and made her irritable and tired.

The infertility specialist recommended she try a procedure called ovulation induction in which she went to the clinic for daily shots, blood work and vaginal ultrasounds. Basically, the doctor would stimulate Sandy's ovaries with drugs to produce multiple eggs, induce ovulation and then artificially inject Bill's sperm. After ten days of waiting, Sandy would know if she was pregnant. The procedure was costly and not covered by Sandy's insurance.

Sandy had to be at the clinic early every morning and afternoon for fourteen days in order to do the procedure. She had to ask her principal for someone to cover her class so she could arrive late and leave early.

The clinic had a schedule, and patients had to fit their lives around it. The drugs made her nauseous but she felt all her effort would pay off. Through all the pain, humiliation and inconvenience, she kept picturing herself holding a baby in her arms. That got her through the ordeal.

Finally, after the ovulation induction was completed, the long-awaited news came. The news was not good; the procedure didn't work. Everything looked good, the doctors said, "You should try again." And so they did—three more times and still no pregnancy.

Devastated and drained physically, emotionally and financially, Sandy and Bill cried out to God. "Why are you doing this? What's wrong with us? Don't we deserve children? Look at all the people who get pregnant and don't even want children. We don't understand, why can't we have a baby like everyone else?"

The doctors suggested the couple do something more medically aggressive. IVF (in vitro fertilization) was a procedure in which the sperm and egg are fertilized in a petri dish outside the body. After a period of time, the developing embryos are replanted in the uterus with the hope of a pregnancy. The procedure was costly—$7000–$10,000—but the doctors were hopeful.

Sandy and Bill didn't know what to do. Should they continue to use the technology or trust God to bring a baby in His time? Maybe they would never have children. Maybe God would use IVF to help them. What should they do? What was right? They called their pastor. He didn't know much about the technology and told them to pray about it. They did but didn't feel they received a clear answer. They decided to go ahead with the procedure.

Sandy hated walking into the infertility clinic. It was a depressing place. Some of the women had tried numerous procedures multiple times with no success. They were sad and depressed hoping the next time would be successful. One women was trying to conceive a second baby. She finally did after twelve attempts of IVF at a cost of $144,000.

The women in the waiting room of the clinic compared blood levels and talked about which nurses gave the best shots. It was all so depressing; nothing like the way Sandy dreamed of getting pregnant. She was humiliated by the number of vaginal exams and residents who treated her like a case number. She was in physical pain, sick from the drugs and wanted this nightmare over. But more than all that, she wanted a baby.

The day came to retrieve her eggs. Sandy produced eight viable eggs that were fertilized. Four were implanted. Everything went as planned and the doctors were again hopeful. The ten-day wait to see if the procedure worked was agonizing. Every feeling in her body was scrutinized for a sign of pregnancy. Were her breasts tender? Was her skin clear? Did she feel pregnant?

She could hardly wait for the phone call to tell her the results of the final blood test. She and Bill nervously waited by the phone and prayed. When the phone rang, Sandy hesitated to pick it up. Would the news be positive? The nurse calmly spoke, "I'm sorry to tell you but it didn't work, but the doctor thinks you are an excellent candidate to try again." Devastated again, Sandy hung up the phone. How could this be? All Sandy could do was cry. Bill tried to comfort her, but she pushed him away. "Leave me alone. I'm damaged goods. Go find a wife who can give you children. God has abandoned me. Maybe I am being punished."

Financially drained, physically exhausted and mentally tired, Sandy became depressed. All she could think about was having a baby. She knew her thoughts were obsessive. She cried for nights on end, couldn't sleep, lost her appetite and withdrew from friends. She was moody, unhappy and irritable with Bill. Her emotions were like a roller-coaster—one moment up and hopeful, the next down and depressed.

Sandy began to hate her body. She envied pregnant women and could barely look at them on the street or in the office. She couldn't concentrate at work and felt insecure. Slowly her self-esteem began to crumble.

It seemed everywhere she went, people were pregnant—young single girls who didn't want babies, women who mistreated their children. She noticed them all and thought, *How unfair. I want children and could provide a good home. Why won't God give me the desire of my heart?*

Bill didn't know how to respond to her. One minute she chided him for not talking about the infertility, the next she told him she couldn't handle the subject. Sandy didn't understand why Bill wasn't falling apart too. She figured he must secretly want to be with another woman who could give him children. Nothing Bill said could reassure Sandy that he still loved her and that she was all he needed.

The marriage became tense. Bill began to resent the sexual demand to impregnate Sandy. He felt like a machine, called upon at all the "precise moments" to service his wife and make a baby. The couple lost their sexual spontaneity and retreated from each other. The once-happy marriage was in a state of crisis.

Christmas was approaching, which meant Sandy's family would get together. Both of Sandy's younger sisters were pregnant, and Sandy couldn't bear to be with them. Even the Christmas story was painful, focusing on the birth of a baby and the happily fulfilled mother holding the tiny child.

After numerous arguments with Bill, Sandy decided not to go be with her family. Feeling devastated and alone, she spent the season in tears. Her family didn't understand what could be so difficult about coming home for Christmas. She tried to explain but they called her self-centered.

Two weeks later Sandy was invited to her best friend's baby shower. There was virtually nothing she wanted to do less. But she knew her friend would never understand. And, she was in the hopeful part of her monthly cycle (prior to ovulation), maybe, just maybe, she could make it through the baby shower.

Sitting among the circle of friends she suddenly realized she was the only one who was childless. A women spoke, "Let's go around the room and give our best advice about being a mom to the new mother." Sandy fell apart. She bolted from the house, sat in her car and screamed at God, "Why are You doing this to me? Am I not worthy enough to have a baby too?" Grief overwhelmed her. She called her infertility doctor, who then referred her to me. Sandy was stuck.

Anxiously, she came to the appointment and told me she almost canceled twice. She had never seen a therapist before and felt that prior to her infertility diagnosis, she was a mentally healthy person. She was ashamed of the way she behaved, ashamed of her feelings of envy and guilt and exhausted emotionally. She felt out of control and depressed. She didn't like the person she was becoming. It was time to seek help. I welcomed her to my office with more empathy than she could have imagined I possessed.

It was no mistake that Sandy ended up in my office. You see, I personally went through seven years of infertility. I was tested, prodded and poked more times than I care to remember. I know what it's like to endure physical pain, humiliation and feel that no one understands. You aren't rational when it comes to this problem. The desperation to have a child is intense, and thus you endure things that you would never entertain otherwise.

I found no one to help me through the emotional coping. The church was uninformed. Friends tired of hearing about the problem, family never knew what to say (except my mother who cried with me), and the psychology community had no one who understood this problem. The infertility clinic offered no emotional support. I felt very alone and at times abandoned by God. Little did I know He was working all things for my good. Little did I know that five years later I would specialize in helping infertile couples cope. Little did I know... well God knew it all.

One of the most difficult aspects of infertility is facing the unknown. You are constantly dealing with loss or the threat of loss. As you know by now, loss involves grieving. The emotions for the infertile woman are very much like going through the emotions of grief. Initial feelings of surprise and denial change to isolation, anger, guilt, unworthiness, depression and grief. Rational, stable women can become depressed and obsessed.

In Sandy and Bill's case, the cause of the infertility was unknown. This meant they didn't know what to do to fix the problem. Neither partner was to blame, but Sandy, like many women do, assumed she was the cause of the infertility.

Sandy's identity as a woman felt threatened. Intellectually, she knew being a mother was only one of the many roles women play. For her, it was a central role. She wanted to have a family ever since she was a child. Career was not a substitute for having children. Emotionally she felt failed and incomplete.

First, I reassured Sandy and Bill that their experience was similar to my own and many other couples I treated. Not everyone responds the same but many have similar thoughts and behaviors. For example, I understood the hopeful two weeks leading to ovulation and the feeling of death when the monthly cycle occurred. It helps to know that other people respond in similar ways emotionally. You don't feel so crazy.

I also acknowledged that there is real stress associated with medical interventions (hormone changes from drugs, nausea, daily trips to the infertility clinic, interruption in work, feelings of inferiority, anger, envy and irritability). Knowing the stress is real also helps couples cope. The couple had to use each other as supports and not dump all their frustrations and blame onto the other.

Sandy and Bill also had to face the possibility of never having a pregnancy. No infertile person wants to entertain this thought, but it is necessary to consider the possibility. God is the giver of all life. I truly believe He opens and closes wombs. If we love God, we must believe He knows our future.

The Bible mentions several women without any association to children—Miriam, the sisters Mary and Martha, Esther, Priscilla and Mary Magdalene. We can only guess if they were childless but we do know they were known for deeds unrelated to children.

I also raised questions about the medical procedures Sandy and Bill were so willing to embrace. Few infertility doctors talk to couples about the ethical issues involved in the medical technology they're offered. Couples are faced with enormous decisions about which procedures to use. The technology is truly amazing, but as Christians, we have to ask tough questions about these technologies.

One of the tough questions with IVF is what happens to the fertilized eggs not replanted? The hormone stimulation of the IVF procedure produces multiple eggs. Sandy produced eight. Only four embryos were implanted. Sandy and Bill placed the other four embryos in cryopreservation (froze them). What then do they do with the other four embryos—discard them, use them or donate them?

No one addressed the ethical concerns about their decision. When does life begin? Their beliefs impacted their decision. I had Sandy and Bill talk to the infertility specialist about the state of the fertilized embryos. Their conclusion was that these were viable embryos so they could not discard them. They decided to try a second implantation and use the four frozen embryos. The important point here is that no one even raised this issue PRIOR to the procedure. Every couple must think through the ethical concerns, pray for direction and not react to feelings of desperation.

Sandy needed a sounding board for her emotional reactions. She found it helpful to talk through her feelings. I provided a supportive place for her to do this. I also helped Bill realize he had to be a good listener and wasn't expected to fix anything. He needed to hold Sandy's hand, reassure her of his love and allow her to work through the stages of loss. He also needed to think more about his own emotional reaction and share them with Sandy. He was experiencing loss, too.

I had to confront Sandy on her feelings of envy and bitterness. She had to recognize these negative emotions, repent from them and not allow them to take root. Her infertility was not fair. In the natural no one could blame her for feeling the way she did, but holding onto envy and bitterness blocked her spiritual walk.

I also had to challenge her belief that God was mad at her and punishing her. This is not how God operates. He doesn't zap us with infertility. But He can use it to get our attention. The bottom line was God is sovereign and gives good things. We didn't understand why Sandy wasn't pregnant, but God knew what was going on and had it under control. This was a time to exercise faith and believe God was working all her circumstances for good. I knew how hard this was to do in the middle of emotional upheaval.

Here's what God taught me to pass on to Sandy. The Bible advises us to put on the garment of praise when we have a spirit of heaviness. I used that scripture. We tried an experiment. Even though she didn't *feel* like praising God, I told her to be obedient to the Word. Praise Him for what He's done in other aspects of her life, praise Him for His majesty and power, for dying for her sins and for promising to bless her. This was a tough assignment because everything in Sandy's body said, "I can't. I'm too miserable." But she began to praise. As she did, she began to acknowledge God's presence in her life, and she felt less depressed. Praise is a powerful thing. In all things give praise, even in infertility.

I asked Sandy to stop asking *why* she was infertile and start asking *what now* do You want me to do, God? This changed her focus. She was still a vital woman with much to give. She had forgotten the other parts of her life and had become self-absorbed. She was assigned to do two things a week to help others—send a meal to a sick person, volunteer at the crisis line, give a ride to a friend and the like. As she focused her efforts away from herself, she started to feel better.

Coping with infertility is a process. Some days are better than others, but Sandy knew what to do when she started to feel depressed. She began praising God for what He has done, reached out to others and trusted God's hand had not been removed from her life. Not surprisingly, God used her in ways she could have never seen.

A few months later Sandy called to tell me the amazing things God was doing in her life. She and Bill finally worked through the emotions related to infertility and continued to believe God would bless them with a child. They were grateful that God had used infertility to bring them back to a dependence and trust in Him. They were also ready to replant the frozen embryos.

One year later, I received a pink note in the mail. As I opened the envelope, confetti fell out along with a picture of twins. A single line was written in it—"Put on the garment of praise for the spirit of heaviness"—Sandy.

I cried when I read that note and placed it on the picture of my two gifts from God—a boy and a girl. I touched their angelic faces and smiled. Sandy and I knew the mercy of God. We can't look at our children without remembering the miracles of their births. God knew all along that we would have these children. He used our infertility to learn dependence on Him. And now He's using me and Sandy to touch others.

MISCARRIAGE AND ABORTION

The grief of infertility is immense. You grieve for the child you may never have, and the dream of children seems elusive. Women have similar grief with miscarriage. In the case of miscarriage, a conception has occurred so there is an actual baby on which to focus the grief. In addition, the hormonal changes of pregnancy have been felt in your body. After the miscarriage, the physical sensations of pregnancy are gone. You may or may not ever see the baby, depending on when the loss occurs. In either case, the loss of miscarriage has to be grieved or depression can result.

Grieving may involve naming the baby that was not yet born. It may require that you perform a ritual in order to say goodbye to the baby you never had the chance to meet. You grieve the death inside your body. It's intense and painful. The baby that never was is remembered and remains a part of your pregnancy history.

Women tend to be sympathetic to other women who have had miscarriages. I was surprised by the number of women who shared this grief with me. Although women understand and can be empathetic, the loss is still difficult because it tends to be glossed over by others. At times, unkind remarks like, "This is God's will," or "You're better off losing the baby because something probably was wrong with the baby" cut right through your heart. Nothing makes the pain less. Miscarriage is a significant loss and should not be minimized.

My first pregnancy resulted in miscarriage, and it was devastating to walk through. After almost two years of trying to conceive our first child, I finally became pregnant. Because the conception was so long anticipated, the joy was great. It was a confirmation that my body worked, that our plans were being fulfilled, that God loved me, that my dream to have a child was finally materializing. My life was back on course as planned.

I had the usual early symptoms of pregnancy—nausea, swelling breasts, thickening of the waist—and I was delighted. I would now have my own pregnancy stories and could relate to women as soon-to-be moms. As a career woman, I was finally in the club. Pregnancy, even though it can be problematic and nauseating, is something I believe most women want to experience at least once in their lives. It gives us a common bond.

The pregnancy was moving along as planned. My nausea was increasing, which I was told was a good sign. During the eighth week, I started to bleed. I was reassured that this was nothing out of the ordinary for many women. I should just watch the spotting. If the blood turned bright red and flowed harder, I should call my doctor.

Since this was my first pregnancy, I immediately became alarmed, but the community of women friends reassured me that everything would be all right. I was told dozens of stories of women who bled at times throughout their pregnancies. Every story had a good end. So I tried to stay calm, but the bleeding continued. My doctor thought it best that I stay off my feet for a few days. I should rest and see if the bleeding lessened or stopped. So, like a good and compliant patient, I took a few days off and rested.

The bleeding lessened as I had hoped, and I thought this was a good sign that everything would be OK . One night around the beginning of the eighth week, I woke up out of a deep sleep and knew the baby had died. I can't explain how I knew this, but I knew it. I felt it in my body. I woke up my husband and said, "The baby is dead. I don't feel pregnant anymore." To his credit, he believed me and prayed with me. We tried to sleep, but knew we had to go to the doctor the next day.

The doctor's exam was uncertain but the ultrasound didn't look right. We couldn't find the heart beat. My uterus was not the right size for eight weeks of pregnancy. I was told to go home and wait for a miscarriage to happen. I probably lost the baby, and it was a matter of time before the bleeding would become intense. I was also told to look for the sac when the bleeding started and try to retrieve it for the lab. I tell you this not to be so graphic but to help you understand the tremendous emotional upheaval we face when miscarriage occurs.

Go home and wait to lose your baby. I fell apart in the office and sobbed. My husband tried to be strong for both of us, but I could see the pain in his eyes. That night, the bleeding started. I never saw an empty sac, but I was losing the baby. He calmly took me to the ER, and we both sat in silence. We knew what was happening, and we tried just to get through it. As I laid in that ER, I cried to God—why? Why do I have to lose the baby I so wanted and was so difficult to conceive?

The next day I was scheduled for a D&C. That was it. The pregnancy was over, and the baby I never saw, gone. Friends tried to comfort us. My husband, Norm, went to work and saw a dear Christian friend. Norm told him he was no longer to be a father. His friend replied, "You are a father. Your baby's just not here on earth. He's with God." That spoke to Norm and made the loss very real.

He left work and on the way home, began sobbing in the car. His baby was gone. He came into the house and grabbed me and the two of us grieved together—no platitudes, no rationalizing, no justifying. We felt the loss and grieved it together. That's when we began to heal. The grief, which hit us both in different ways, was over a shared loss. We both had to come to emotional terms with it—separate and together. We had to trust God, the author of only good things.

Another loss associated with children is abortion. Let's talk about abortion—as difficult as that is to do. Abortion is a significant loss but differs from infertility and miscarriage in many ways. It is a loss that you make happen. It is not a choice out of your control. It is usually considered when pregnancy jeopardizes the plan for your life or when the pregnancy is the result of a violent act of rape. The immediate feeling associated with having an abortion is usually relief. It's not until later that most women feel the impact of their action, and relief gives way to other emotions. Many women keep feelings repressed for a long time in order to defend against the reality of what they have done.

Years ago (when I was young and confused), I didn't give a second thought to women who had abortions. I believed what my friends and professors told me. Abortion was about choice. You know the argument well. It was our bodies, so we could decide what we would do with them.

I never searched the Bible to see what it had to say about the sanctity of life. I also never heard a sermon preached on it. I held my opinion because I was a feminist, and feminists were into choice. Christians were not talking about abortion back then. No one in my Christian circle of friends ever brought up the subject.

My opinion changed when I started dealing with real women—Christian and non-Christian—who had abortions. The loss they experienced was immense, and the women I saw developed symptoms as a result of their choice. My colleagues would argue that I saw only the problem women in therapy. The ones who did fine with abortion never darkened my therapy door. I wasn't so sure. Most of my abortion clients had no prior psychiatric history.

I also found it incongruent that during one hour of my day I would see a woman who was deeply grieving over the loss of her baby because of a miscarriage at six weeks, and I would offer her comfort and mourn with her for the child that never was. Yet during the next hour I was expected to help a woman pretend that the abortion she had at six weeks was *not* a baby so she wouldn't feel so bad. I should tell her to focus on her choice and be happy that she made the right decision. Does this make sense to anyone? It didn't to me.

As you would guess, I changed my view on abortion. I find it fascinating that when you believe in the sanctity of life, somehow you become a conservative, religious fanatic. Frankly I resent being labeled in a political way over an issue of morality. Labeling is an act of intolerance and an attempt to make anyone who thinks anything but pro choice out to be a fool.

I didn't decide that ending life was wrong to do. God did. It is possible to view abortion as sin and still love the women who do it. It's the model of Jesus—hate the sin, love the sinner. But we refuse to accept love on these terms. Believing in the sanctity of life does not make you a hatemonger, against women or ready to blow up clinics. On the contrary, it makes you sad for women who felt they had to make this choice.

I know the pain of unwanted pregnancies only through listening to women talk about them for twenty years. I understand the reasons why women have abortions. The reasons generally make a lot of sense. I've often wondered what I would have done had I allowed myself to be in that position as a young woman. But nothing I've heard convinces me that the Bible is wrong when it comes to valuing life.

I'm moved with compassion towards those who have had to confront an unwanted pregnancy, especially those who are victims of violence. The decision to have an abortion can never be easy, no matter where you stand on the issue. Please understand I'm not condemning women who have had abortions. If you have had an abortion, you need to talk to God about it, ask for forgiveness and be assured of your forgiveness. Stand on this promise from the Word: "There is therefore now no condemnation to those who are in Christ Jesus, who do not walk according to the flesh, but according to the Spirit" (Rom. 8:1). According to the Bible, one sin is no greater than another. Sin is sin and forgivable.

Many women I counsel are stuck in grieving the loss of an abortion. I have been surprised at the length of time this grief can stay with women. When the loss isn't fully grieved, it can give rise to other problems such as anxiety and eating disorders.

The difficulty of grieving an abortion has to do with a number of things—when the abortion is over there is no evidence of the baby; there is no ritual to say goodbye; most times the act is done in secret, allowing for little support; and socially people may not accept your decision, which leads to judgment and rejection.

You must allow yourself to grieve and not try to reduce guilt by telling yourself it was your only choice. Grief over the loss must be felt. You have to come to terms with the reality of what you have done and ask God's forgiveness. Feel deeply about the lost child, and accept God's forgiveness.

Anytime women deal with having and wanting children, there are multiple issues of loss attached. Infertility, miscarriage and abortion are only three of the circumstances that interfere with our dream of having the perfect child. Other women contend with birth defects, genetic abnormalities, handicaps and the care of chronically ill children. These are not easy crosses to bear, but God gives us what we need to be able to cope. He also has a way of using special children to teach us many things. These children are precious and under the care of God.

Everything considered, even having healthy children involves dying to your dreams so that you can learn to dream their dreams. Mothering involves giving up what is best for you for the sake of that child. Again the similarities are strikingly parallel with what God did for us. He gave of His Son for our need. He sacrificed all because He loved us. If you haven't been able to mother, God has not forgotten you. I would also encourage you to look around. There are many in need of a mother. Perhaps we need to redefine how we can be used to mother others.

The secret to overcoming the grief over a desire to mother is really no secret at all. You have to believe you are loved by God. It is really that simple. God's love means you are forgiven. Since He forgives you, you must also forgive yourself, and allow whatever feelings you have kept inside to be expressed. His love also means He has not abandoned you; nor is He trying to punish you. He wants to give you His best. Start asking for it. Give whatever dream you have to God, and let His love set you free. Learn to love the dreams He has dreamed for you. You are the daughter of a good and generous Father.

7

Overcoming Depression

OK, I'm going to get blunt and talk to you straight now. Just for a moment, imagine I'm your mother imparting wonderful words of wisdom. If you don't like your mother, insert a positive female here, and vow to come to terms with your mother. If you feel stuck in depression, it's time to get out. If you have had trouble letting go of a relationship loss or problem, it's time to resolve it. If you have been angry or upset by some thing or situation, it's time to get over it. Or, if you have lost hope because of a dream that has never come to life, it's time to let go of it and move forward in your life. No one likes to stay stuck. You have too much to do if you are going to be all that God intended you to be.

The goal is to move out of depression and into the joy of living. In order to do this, you must face loss and cope with the feelings involved in getting unstuck. Typically those feelings are shock, denial, anger, confusion, numbness, sadness, irritability, hopelessness, fear, isolation, loneliness, emptiness, disorganization and guilt. You must work through those feelings in order to get past the loss and grow. People who get stuck, hang onto the feelings of grief.

How do you work through those feelings? What can you do to get unstuck?

Figure out what losses you face.

Use the categories I've given. Is it a loss involving a relationship, a thing, situation or a dream? When you have identified the category then identify the specific loss. For example, "I'm facing the loss of my daughter leaving for college." "I'm facing the loss of a job." "I'm facing the loss of having my dream home." "I'm facing the loss of a move."

Identify how you feel about the loss.

Don't stuff feelings inside. You get stuck when you pretend not to be upset or try to hide your feelings. Hidden feelings work on you and can cause physical problems as well as disturbed moods. You must identify your feelings—"Am I feeling sad, angry, frustrated, irritated, envious or jealous?" Whatever you feel is not right or wrong. It's just how you feel.

Acknowledge the feeling, feel it and move on from it.

It's OK to have feelings—even when they are negative. You have been made to feel things intensely. It's not OK to hang onto bad feelings. That's where we get in trouble. Through the years of counseling people, I consistently hear Christians say, "I don't get angry." This is ridiculous. Everyone gets angry; even Jesus got angry. Anger is not wrong and is part of the way God made us. What's wrong is to hold onto that anger and let it fester inside and create bitterness or separate you from God and others. You can *have* negative feelings. Just don't obsess on them.

Talk to someone, pray and release the feelings.

Women do well when they talk about their feelings. It helps us just to tell someone. Sometimes that's all we need to do. We can always do that with God. I've had many conversations with God in which I've acknowledged how unfair something is, how upset I am or how I don't want to forgive. Then I release it. At times, I release it in faith, choosing not to allow my thoughts to take me to that bad feeling again. Other times, it is more difficult, especially if there is a deep wound involved. But I still have to release the feeling and trust God to help me through the difficulty.

Forgive those who may have hurt or wronged you.

Releasing feelings often involves forgiving someone. We forgive someone not because we *feel* like it. Most of the time we feel like making the person pay. But God forgave us when we didn't deserve it, and Jesus commanded us to forgive one another. So forgiveness is often a matter of will, a choice. Choose to forgive. Then ask God to soften your heart towards the person.

This doesn't mean you accept what that person did as right. It means you choose not to let the action have any more power or influence over your life. Forgiveness is letting go. It's saying, "I was hurt, but I'm not going to let the hurt continue to control my life. I'm releasing it to God and want the hurt gone."

Only God can take away the pain and help you move to a place of compassion and empathy for those who have hurt you. In the natural, this rarely happens. It's unnatural to love your enemies, to bless those who curse you, to do good to those who hate you and to pray for those who use you, yet these are the commands of Jesus. Would He tell us to do something that is impossible? No. But to do what He has commanded in the natural is impossible. It's takes knowing the love of God to pass along that love.

Deal with any sin in your life.

Any area of your life that doesn't line up with God's directives should be dealt with and changed. It's amazing how many times depression is a result of the sin of disobedience to God's Word. When you willfully sin, you are asking for trouble.

The sins I most often see as roots of depression are sexual, lying, greed, rebellion, pride, gossiping and holding on to unforgiveness. When you allow these things to be a part of your life, you are giving the enemy a foothold. Depression can be a fallout from these things. Ask God to forgive you, and commit to living a life pleasing to God.

Change your expectations.

Don't expect life to happen without loss. Don't expect to go through difficulty without God's presence and help. You are going to have difficulty. God says that in this world there will be tribulation. But God doesn't leave you or forsake you. He promises His presence and to equip you with what you need to face loss.

Change your thoughts.

Negative thinking makes you depressed. Renew your mind with the promises of God and with the hope that only God can give. The best way to do this is to read the promises of God over and over and commit them to memory.

Stop hanging out with negative people.

When you are depressed, negative people don't help to lift you out of that dark place. Be around those who will encourage you and not give in to defeat.

Get a physical.

Depression can be caused from physical and medical conditions. You may have low thyroid, hormone imbalance, a tumor and any number of physical problems causing depression. Check this first.

Take care of your body.

Eat well, exercise and get rest. Depression can worsen with improper diet and rest. And you know the benefit of exercise on improving chemicals in the brain that lift your mood. Sometimes just making dietary and physical changes improves your mood tremendously. Alcohol is a depressant. Drinking does not improve mood in the long run. In addition, many prescription drugs have side effects related to depression. Know what you are ingesting and how it affects your body.

Don't allow yourself to feel stigmatized for using medication.

When depression is more biochemical in nature, it's appropriate to use medication. Or if you are going through an inordinate amount of stress, medication can help you through a difficult period. Don't stop believing for healing, but medication can help along the way. I don't encourage women to take medication if they don't need it, but there are times when it can be helpful and get you back on track. Medication can help get you functioning again and clear your mind enough to work on the issues involved.

Avoid blame.

Blaming people serves no purpose but to keep you stuck. It may be helpful to understand how certain people influenced you, but you are ultimately responsible for how you live your life.

Know the triggers that put you into depression.

There are certain people, circumstances, places that lead you to feel bad. Know what those things are and avoid them or change them. For example, if going to a baby shower depresses you because you are struggling with infertility, don't go. If your sister's put-downs bother you, speak up and tell her to stop. If seeing a certain type of movie depresses you, don't see it.

Become more assertive.

Another common problem is being too passive. People may hurt or upset you, and you do nothing to handle the situation. There are many times when learning to say *no* or *stop* would prevent depression. You have the right to set boundaries. When you are assertive and people don't respond, learn to walk away and control your emotions.

Manage emotions, don't let them manage you.

The goal isn't to avoid loss. The goals are to tolerate the emotions associated with loss and let something new emerge from the loss. You have to learn how to have a negative feeling but not let it run your emotional life.

Do something for someone else.

There are two dangers when you are feeling depressed—you can focus entirely on your own problems and wallow in self-pity; or you can get carried away doing so much for others that you never think about yourself. The best thing is to find a balance between these two extremes. It helps you feel better when you do something for someone else. It temporarily gets your mind off your problems. But you don't want to do so much that you overload yourself and add to the depression.

Get support.

Have people you can talk with who will listen and support you. It may be family or friends. Having good support is linked to good mental health.

Correct your image of self.

Go back to your Bible and read about how God sees you. Read it over and over. Memorize it until it becomes a part of you. Stop listening to the opinions of others, and stop being a victim. God has told you how wonderful you are. Believe Him.

Accept God's love for you.

Until you can do this, you'll never be totally healed. You must believe He loved you enough to die for you and to make a covenant with you. Once you really grasp the depths of His love, it's hard to stay hopeless.

Trust in God.

Trust in God—not your mother, husband, friend, boss. If they are trustworthy that's great, but your ultimate trust should be in God, because people will let you down. God will never let you down. Like the old hymn says,

What a Friend we have in Jesus,
All our sins and griefs to bear!
What a privilege to carry
Everything to God in prayer!

Ask God to heal you and refuse to accept anything less.

I'm saddened by the fact that many women believe they can't be healed of depression and struggle along on antidepressants for life. Now don't get me wrong, antidepressants can help, and I'm not opposed to having people take them. But they should only be an avenue to the final destination of healing. We have settled for feeling better rather than being healed. God wants you healed—not just better. If you are taking medication, that's fine, but keep praying for God to heal you so you don't need it forever. The Bible says that we don't have because we don't ask. Start asking, and expect God to touch you.

Start renewing your mind like the Bible instructs you to do.

Read Romans 12:2 and Philippians 4:8, and begin to think on positive things. Now, I'm not talking some positive thinking "mumbo jumbo" in which you stand in front of a mirror every day and say three things you like about yourself, and then chant some mantra. I'm talking about thinking about what God has done for you. He sent His son to die for you. Jesus took it all on the cross so we could be free. What more do you need to know? Would someone so loving want you to suffer so? No! He wants to give you good things—and has. Start thinking about all He has done. Remind yourself and thank God daily (that's called prayer and praise).

Make yourself act like you are not depressed.

The worse thing you can do is give in to the depression, withdraw and stay in bed. You need to get out and get active. I know what you are thinking—when you are depressed you can't get out of bed or make yourself do anything. Not true! You won't *feel* like getting out of bed but you can *make* yourself do it.

Which brings me to another soap box of mine. We are too ruled by feelings. Yes, we are wonderfully compassionate, loving—the Venus women or whatever planet we are supposed to be—but we tend to let feelings rule our actions and, at times, override our good sense. Stop it. Get up and get moving. You can't just think you are healed, you have to get up and start acting like it. In the Bible James tells us not to deceive ourselves. We need to be doers of the Word, not just hearers.

Get to know your Heavenly Father.

The best antidote for depression is knowing your Daddy—God that is. Most of you don't. I didn't know Him intimately, and I was raised in the church like many of you. Why? Sometimes we lack good and accurate teaching. Instead of reading about God in His book, we listened to the opinions of others and read books that were interesting but never helped us understand the power of God. You get to know God by reading His Word, praying and spending time listening and talking to Him. It's like developing any relationship, and remember, women are the ones who are good at relationships.

If you struggle to do the above, there are scriptures that can encourage and help you with depression. The psalms are always good reading—they often start full of despair, but they end in hope. Many of us can relate to the intensity and openness of David's struggles. It's helpful to see that even great people in the Bible had to fight depression. The good news is that when they turned to God, they always got unstuck.

SECTION
TWO

ANXIETY

8

Stuck in Anxiety

W e've all felt anxious at some point in our lives. If you haven't, check your pulse, you are probably dead. Remember sitting at the top of the roller coaster waiting to dive down a bazillion feet? The feeling of terror was mixed with excitement. Your adrenaline was flowing; you took a deep breath, closed your eyes and down you plunged. After you put your heart back in your chest, you thought, *Hey that was great!* And back you went for more. (OK, so some of us had to throw up a few times first.)

Or remember when you prepared for your first piano recital without music? I do. I was sure I would forget the notes. Of course the fear and dread that overwhelmed me didn't help my memory either. Mom was smiling confidently, and Dad was half asleep. When it was my turn to play, the piano teacher mispronounced my name, which really built my confidence. "Just sit down, back straight, hands on the keys and play," I coached myself as my sweaty hands kept slipping off the keys. "You can do it." Amazingly I did. Well, if we don't count the time I totally forgot the piece, burst into tears and left the room!

And how about those college entrance exams? The anxiety was enough to bring me to my knees and dedicate myself to a life of foreign missions or feeding the poor. Going to Africa, or anywhere for that matter, looked real good when I opened those test booklets and was given what seemed like two minutes to answer five hundred questions.

And what about walking down the aisle to say "I do" for a lifetime? For most men, that makes the top three "Most Anxious Moments of Their Lives" list. For women, the preparations and worry about all the details of the wedding turned us into raving lunatics. You have heard of road rage? It's nothing compared to "wedding rage." By the time I took my father's arm, ready for the processional, I would have bit the head off anyone who dared veer from the plan. The minister could have asked me anything, and I would have agreed just to get the wedding over and finished.

And while we are thinking about anxious moments, let's not forget (as if we could) giving birth. It feels like the baby will never come out, and you will be the first woman on earth who couldn't finish the job. Talk about anxiety. Wedding rage doesn't hold a candle to "birth rage!"

In all these cases anxiety makes us push harder (I'm not talking birth here), rouses us to action and generally helps us cope with life's threatening or difficult circumstances. Anxiety comes and then it goes, like the perfect house guest. It moves us forward in a positive way.

But what if it persists and doesn't go away? Or what if it immobilizes us or prevents us from doing even the simplest of tasks? When this happens we may experience an all too common problem called an *anxiety disorder.* These disorders grip us with inordinate fear. They persist and invade our thoughts. We worry excessively about everything. *What if . . .* is the obsession of our thoughts. And our obsessions can lead us to do irrational things that become compulsive, like constant hand washing or counting.

Here are several more types of anxiety disorders: you might have a general sense of anxiety or experience panic attacks. You might be afraid to go out of the house, fearing you couldn't easily escape should panic overwhelm you. You may fear a single object like a dog or an elevator. You may become very anxious remembering past traumas and losses.

What I am describing is more than just a case of the nerves. It's a feeling of dread that lasts for a while and begins to feed on itself instead of going away. It's overwhelming and can sometimes lead to panic and paralyzing fear. When we are anxious our bodies react physically and emotionally. We can experience a racing heart, shortness of breath, sweating, dry mouth, dizziness, nausea, diarrhea, hot flashes, the "lump in the throat," shaking, restlessness, tiredness, muscle tension, excessive worry, problems concentrating, irritability and difficulty sleeping. If you are getting anxious thinking about this, stop reading and take a deep breath! Good; keep reading when you have calmed down.

These reactions, if they persist, can interfere with daily living. Being anxious is not fun and is the reason so many people feel desperate for help.

Since we all get anxious now and then, you may wonder why some people become more so than others. Actually there are many reasons rather than one simple explanation for everybody. If you are an anxious type, you share similarities with other anxious people. When you encounter a dangerous situation, you become overly anxious. "Overly" is the operative word here. It's one thing to see danger and become anxious for the moment. It's another to worry beyond reasonable concern.

For example, you might narrowly miss hitting another car. Most people would feel anxious for a moment, be somewhat unnerved by the event and then shake it off with a determination to be more vigilant while driving. An anxious person will obsess over the near miss, carry the anxiety throughout the day or night and be fearful for days. She might even avoid getting behind the wheel of a car for days.

Another similarity you may notice with other anxious women is a strong need to be perfect. You may believe you need to have all things under control in order to be a worthwhile person. Any letdown from doing your absolute best is unacceptable and results in anxiety. Anxious people tend to see things that go wrong as catastrophes. They think, *Oh, no, something bad will happen because I didn't handle this well, perfectly or the right way,* rather than *I did my best so that will have to do.*

Because anxiety often leaves one feeling helpless, the easiest thing to do is escape or avoid whatever makes you anxious. You avoid because you don't believe you can handle the situation. Avoidance and escape work to stop anxiety immediately, but it doesn't fix the problem in the long run.

Some people may be more inclined to inherit anxiety responses. Others don't deal well with stress and pressure. For some, medical conditions like long-time asthma, heart disease and cancer can bring on anxiety. Substance abuse can bring out anxiety as can drinking too much caffeine. We live in a very stressful world with the pace of change going at record speed. Changes in technology and modern living make it stressful to stay up with all that is new and expected. We no longer have an agreed-upon set of rules to govern behavior. The lack of standards and values leaves people trying to cope with the difficulties of life without a map or framework. Without a map you feel anxious about where you are going.

STUCK ON THE DOTS

Generally, most anxiety problems can be traced back to life's losses. When loss is not properly dealt with over time, we get stuck. Remember the game Candyland? You travel along the multicolored highway to the big candy castle at the top. Along the way, you can land on these black dots and get stuck for what seems like an eternity until you draw the right color. When you draw the right color, you can finally move on. And then your six-year-old beats the pants off you. Well, anxiety is a lot like that—stuck on the black dot, unable to move!

WE AREN'T IN CONTROL ANYWAY

When people lose someone, some thing or some ideal, fear and panic can build over the idea that loss will happen again. Losing control can be frightening. It doesn't have to be if you have a strong foundation in God and believe He will see you through any difficulty. But if you are a little shaky on this trust and faith stuff, not being in control is scary. Our natural tendency is to worry and want to control bad things from happening.

But here's the neon flashing sign. *We aren't in control anyway.* We may think we are, or develop a false sense of control, but ultimately, like the bumper sticker says, "Life happens" (I'm paraphrasing again). So should we give up and get fatalistic, dye our hair black and walk around biting our nails? Absolutely not! I can't imagine myself with black hair! We should recognize that we don't always have control. That's OK because we serve a totally great God who sees everything and has it all under control. We may not be in control—but God is. We should take comfort in this. This doesn't mean we should get lax in our responsibilities. It means we have to rely on God to work it all for our good and do our part to block anxiety.

9

Facing the
Loss of Control

The number one mental health problem for women is anxiety We are an anxious group. Why? We have a lot to be anxious about. We worry about our choice of careers, if we are good mothers, if we can raise sane children, if we chose the right partner, if we can do everything we need to do in a day, if we will get to the appointment on time, if we can schedule one more thing in our day, if . . . you know this drill. We have a lot to think about and do in a day. We are multitasked and multipurposed.

Anxiety goes beyond natural worry. When you are anxious you feel restless, tired, irritable, tense and have trouble sleeping and concentrating. Fears about living interfere with living.

Anxiety is not the same as fear. Fear is usually a reaction to something happening that is real—an attack, a missed curfew, a failed test—a danger or a serious consequence that affects your life. Anxiety, on the other hand, can be present even when danger is not present. There may be no real threat of anything negative happening, but you still worry and can't seem to stop. You are sure something bad will happen or that you will lose control. You feel apprehensive and have physical sensations in your body.

Many women feel imprisoned by a constant state of worry. They spend too much time thinking about the possibilities of danger, losing control, not being able to cope, failing, being rejected or even dying. Any stressful situation can put them over the edge.

Anxiety is worry about the loss of control. Loss of control is experienced much more today in our changing culture. How so? We feel less in control of things we used to take for granted. Here are some examples. Families may not stay together. Children grow up losing parents, and siblings may choose to live with the other parent. Families move away from extended families and are more isolated from support.

There is a loss of control over jobs. No longer is loyalty to a company valued. With changing technology, skills can be quickly outdated. Job security is low with corporate buy outs and downsizing leaving people feeling vulnerable and uncertain when it comes to the future.

There is a loss of control in communities and in schools. The recent school shootings have left parents anxious about what the school day may bring. Who is at risk? Who could act out through violence? Drugs and crime continue to dominate our concerns as children are raised without moral teaching and taught to gratify themselves or numb their own pain.

We live under the threat of nuclear and biological warfare. Natural disasters make the nightly news as do random acts of murder and violence. John F. Kennedy Jr. goes down in a plane crash, a man kills his wife and kids and then nine other strangers before shooting himself. A white extremist goes on a rampage killing people at random because of their race or ethnicity. The news alone can produce anxiety, especially if you have no frame of reference from which to make sense of it all.

The list could go on and on. Nothing is certain but God and His love for us. People who live without faith in God should feel anxious. It would be a normal response to this troubled world. Without God, you can only control what you can, and the rest is up for grabs. I'm not trying to be fatalistic, but it is easy to see why people are so scared. No wonder so many of our teens and young adults approach life without hope. They have experienced so much loss of control, they figure what's the point? They respond, "Whatever."

The point is you must have something with which to fight the pervasive sense of no control. Otherwise, you'll be anxious. I choose God. He offers the most hope and the best deal. He'll never leave. His love is unconditional. He's the same yesterday, today and forever and has it all under control. He knows the future and will give us what we need to get through the present. He is a God of hope and love and a present help in times of trouble. He's the only choice that makes sense. He's got a great record for taking care of His people and providing for all they need. Without God as a reference point, we are faced with no control.

Even women who do know God have to work not to let anxiety overtake them. To help you understand how debilitating anxiety can be for so many women, here is a quick review of the types of anxiety you or someone you know could experience.

GENERALIZED ANXIETY

If you are generally anxious and worry about any number of things, you may have something called *generalized anxiety disorder.* The constant worry is hard to control. You can worry about health, finances, your marriage, your children, parents, getting things done, making an appointment and many other things. Nothing bad is happening, but the possibility for something to go wrong always exists in your mind. You spend your days feeling apprehensive. Worry stops you from doing things because it is excessive and intense.

Diane suffered from excessive and persistent worry. Right after she married Jack, anxiety became a way of life. She couldn't make it through an hour without thinking of all that could go wrong in her day. What if she was late to the hair appointment? What if her son missed the school bus? What if she couldn't get to the store today? What if she had a terrible disease and didn't know it?

Diane was in the process of coordinating a fall fundraiser for her son's school. It was the annual major event for the entire community, complete with formal dinner and celebrity auction, and the stress nearly put her over the edge. It was Diane's responsibility to bring in the necessary funds for a much-needed building program. She worried about every detail. She worried if people would show up, if the food was adequate, if the auction items were desirable and if she was spending too much money for publicity. She worried about making horrible financial mistakes. She worried over every detail and was driving the school administrators and her husband nuts!

Because of all the worry, she was having trouble concentrating on her job, so she took a leave of absence to supervise the fundraiser. She thought quitting her job would relax her, but it didn't. Instead, her anxiety intensified, and she went to bed exhausted and unable to sleep. She lost her appetite and could only think about all the problems potentially associated with the event.

She started to feel more anxious about other things. She wasn't working and finances were tight. How would the family pay all their bills? Maybe her husband resented her staying home. Maybe he would grow tired of her worried second-guessing about all her decisions, leave her and find another woman. By the time I saw Diane she was convinced she would soon be divorced, unemployed and in debt. There was nothing in Diane's current circumstances to indicate that any of these predictions would come to pass, but then, anxiety isn't rational.

When I talked more with Diane, I found out that she felt anxious most of her life. It wasn't until marriage, a child and now the added pressure of the fundraiser that she became so overly anxious. But she remembers the anxious feelings from her childhood.

Diane's parents were divorced when she was fourteen. She remembers feeling responsible for making her mom happy. Her mom was anxious and never wanted the divorce. Her mother did her best to make things work, but Diane never felt secure. Dad remarried, and she didn't like her stepsiblings much. She resented them for having her father full time.

She visited her dad on weekends, but never felt she had a place of security. Her mother complained about "the atmosphere" at Dad's house. Dad was too lenient and spent too little time with Diane. His new wife was kind, but Diane wished her parents would work things out and get back together.

A week before her wedding, Diane's mom was mugged, beaten and stabbed in the parking lot of her apartment building. The doctor told Diane that her mother could have died. Mom was fortunate that she was alive but faced a long haul with rehabilitation. Diane worried about her mom's recovery, her finances and how she would manage. She called her grandmother who agreed to stay and help nurse Mom back to health.

Diane postponed the wedding, but six months later married Jack. Mom attended in a wheelchair. Dad attended the wedding with his new wife and family. It wasn't the happy picture Diane planned. She spent the first few years of marriage with some anxiety and noticed that she obsessively cleaned. She wanted everything neat and in order in her house. This was Diane's way of taking charge of a life that felt so out of control.

When the baby arrived, things were really difficult for Diane. Babies have a way of throwing you off schedule, and Diane couldn't get organized. She worried about being a good mother and wondered how anyone ever got anything done. It bothered her to have a messy house. It bothered her to be late to appointments, and she started getting more and more anxious. She believed her new baby was the cause of her increased anxiety. She believed that if she could just get organized her anxiety would relent.

But it didn't; her anxiety mounted. That's when she came to see me.

I felt the added stress of the fundraiser is what put Diane over the edge. But looking back, the anxiety started to gain momentum at the time of her parents' divorce. Diane's response to the divorce was that she temporarily lost control of her life. She was scared and worried about how she would survive with her dad gone and money tight. Her mom was overly cautious and constantly worried about how she would support herself and Diane. Diane felt responsible to help Mom but didn't know what to do.

When her dad remarried, she worried even more about her security. The mugging incident with her mother frightened her. In an instant her mom could have been gone. Nothing felt secure. Diane lived with a pervading sense of bad things happening out of her control.

Was it the divorce that caused the anxiety disorder? Probably not by itself. But it was a major loss in Diane's life at a time she faced personal feelings of insecurity. With no father in the home, she felt insecure about basic provisions. She also felt insecure about herself as a developing woman. She felt the burden of survival and was not focused on developing a sense of who she was.

The mugging frightened her because no one came forward to help her mom during her time of desperate need. Her grandmother was suffering her own problems but was the only person available to help her mom full time. Diane's mom was the one steady person in her life, and now she was fighting to survive.

The fundraiser became her obsessive focus. She couldn't control divorce and accidents but she could guarantee a successful event. But her focus became obsessive, and nothing satisfied her. She was looking for perfection, and anything less caused her great anxiety. Arrangements for the event consumed her day, and she couldn't get anything else accomplished.

One reason anxiety disorders are so difficult to overcome is that you don't usually know what you are thinking that leads to anxious feelings. You only have a sense of feeling bad. When I ask clients like Diane what they *think* vs. what they *feel*, they don't know. Usually the response is, "I wasn't thinking anything. I just felt bad." But they were thinking something prior to getting anxious. They weren't aware of their thoughts because the feelings of anxiety overshadowed their thoughts. The trick is to figure out what your thoughts might be, because thoughts trigger feelings.

The root of Diane's problem was found in her thoughts and feelings about the losses of the past. She had to work through her feelings about the divorce and tragic incident of her mother related to losing control of her security and the people she loved.

She had Jack, but because of her father, wasn't sure he would stick around for the long haul. Jack tried to reassure her that he wasn't going anywhere, but Diane had heard this from her father. His claim to have "fallen out of love with your mother and in love with someone else" was very unsettling for Diane. Her thought was, *I can't trust what anyone says about staying. Men leave and pursue their own happiness.* It took Diane time to figure out that she even had a thought about men and divorce.

Diane never talked with her father about his leaving. She was too scared to bring it up, fearing he might get angry and cut her off like he did Mom. Now that she was on her own, it was time to talk to him. So Diane began taking control where she could—addressing her hurt, disappointment and anger over her parents' divorce. She told him how hurt she was when he rarely made time for her—that he divorced Mom, not her.

She also faced the fact that her mother almost died. Could she make it without her? She knew she was quite dependent on Mom to always be there. She wondered, *Who can I ultimately turn to who won't leave me or let me down? Who is really there for me?*

Jack had given her no reason to doubt him, but because of her father's change in heart towards her mother, she wasn't ready to put her trust in Jack. The only one she could think of was God, and she hadn't had much to do with Him since her parents' divorce.

Her family stopped going to church right before the divorce was announced. Diane did remember things about God from Sunday school as a kid. She remembered stories on a flannel board about people who got in a lot of trouble, but God always provided a way out. The woman who taught the classes would say, "So don't worry. God has it all under control." That thought stuck with Diane. She asked Jesus into her life, but never thought about how He could help her with worry.

In Matthew 6:25–26 Jesus tells Diane, "Therefore I say to you, do not worry about your life, what you will eat or what you will drink; nor about your body, what you will put on. Is not life more than food and the body more than clothing? Look at the birds of the air, for they neither sow nor reap nor gather into barns; yet your heavenly Father feeds them. Are you not of more value then they? Which of you by worrying can add one cubit to his stature?"

God takes care of His creation. Because Diane is more valuable than the birds, He will take care of her. It's a promise. Worry is not believing God's promises. Worry is unbelief. Unbelief is a lack of faith, and without faith we can't please God. Faith is what keeps us going, because we believe in the unseen things of God.

God saw Diane's life as it unfolded. He knew the uncertainty she faced when her parents divorced and when her mom was almost killed. It was in these moments of weakness and insecurity that God wanted to make her strong, not worrisome. Jesus came to transform her weakness into strength. He came to take that worry so she could be strong. To do so, she had to give the worry to Him. She had to stop trying to control her life. Her hope for getting better depended on her willingness to give her cares to Jesus. The only hope she had was Jesus, and He promised to take care of it all.

Diane began her day with this prayer. "Today I'm casting all my cares and all my burdens on You. Here they are" (She took five to ten minutes to list every worry she had). Then, she had to stop. She gave the list to God and had to read His promises to reassure herself that leaving her worry with Jesus was OK. He would take care of it. Trusting this was an act of faith.

When the worry would enter her mind, she had to stop the thought, grab it (take it captive) and recite the promise of God—any scripture related to fear and worry. Eventually as Diane practiced this renewal of her mind, she stopped feeling anxious. Her trust was no longer in what she could control but in what God promised.

As we will see there are other steps to be taken to free yourself from anxiety and worry but the first step is to cast your cares on Him. You have to make Him Lord over your life, give Him your concerns and then believe His promises.

PANIC

I'm not much of a snow skier these days. Oh, I learned to ski in my youth. Growing up in the north, skiing was something you just did like learning to ride a bike. I joined the ski club in high school and was fairly good by the time I left for college in the south—no mountains and no snow. Then to make matters worse, I married a guy who grew up in the tropics! As a concession to my past, we skied occasionally when we moved north for graduate school but my husband never really enjoyed the sport. Then we moved to the mid-Atlantic, and the only skiing there was on water!

But my brother Denny lives in Vermont where skiing is a way of life. Yearly he buys his season pass and is quite the man on the mountain. On a trip to Vermont, we, of course, planned days to ski. My husband and sister-in-law apprehensively waved goodbye on the bunny hill as my brother and I took off to conquer the mountain. Denny is an expert. I, on the other hand, relied on the athleticism of my youth to return to me.

As we sat on the lift, I started to get a small feeling of dread. We were going too high for my comfort zone. As we pushed off the lift, I took a look down, and all I saw was a cliff. "There must be some mistake," I told my brother. "This is the expert slope." "Oh, I'm sorry," he replied. "I must have taken the wrong lift. I ski these trails all the time and wasn't thinking. Well, take your time. See you at the bottom." And off he went.

The only thing I remember is total panic. How would I get down? There I was at the top of what looked like Mount Everest with no way down but one. I started to feel dizzy, my heart was pounding, I was sweating and couldn't breathe. "OK," I told myself. "This is a panic reaction. I need to calm down and figure out a way to solve this dilemma." I started deep breathing and visualized myself at the bottom of the run, safe and sound. I opened my eyes, ready to leap forward and the panic returned. "I can't do this. I'll die, but I'll die from the cold if I stay here." So I did what any sensible person would do, I panicked again.

Then I reminded myself I was a therapist. I was trained to deal with panic. I knew what to do. I had to calm down, take deep breaths and get down the mountain. I moved to the very edge of the trail where the snow wasn't packed down as much and sat down on my bottom. With my skis sideways, I was going to slide down with as much resistance as possible. It may take me all day to reach the bottom but there was no way I was skiing down standing up. The feeling of panic left. I had a plan.

Panic is like an alarm going off in your body. You get a shot of adrenalin followed by a feeling of dread. Your body reacts with dizziness, shortness of breath, sweating, heart palpitations, shaking, cold hands and feet. You feel as if you were going to die or go crazy, and you want to run. It's a helpless and frightening feeling but useful when you are faced with a dangerous situation.

Panic disorder however, is not in response to danger. The feeling of panic occurs spontaneously or out of the blue. In other words, there is no mountain looming ahead of you with no way but one to get down.

We don't know why certain people respond with panic and others do not, but prolonged stress and sudden loss can bring on the attacks. Contrary to how you feel, panic won't result in a heart attack, suffocation, fainting, loss of balance or your going crazy. You may feel as if all these things will happen, but they won't. The problem is when you start to have these symptoms, you *think* these things will happen.

Panic can start with a circumstance or can appear out of the clear blue. Symptoms develop. You begin to worry; you tell yourself, "This is dangerous, and you need to get control."

When you try to fight panic, you usually get worse. So it's best to face the symptoms. Recognize them and let them happen. Then tell yourself that it will pass if you ride it out. It will. Panic attacks are time-limited and usually only last a few minutes. There are instances when they can last for hours or even days.

When you experience the panic feelings, try telling yourself that you can manage them. "I can ride this out. I'm only anxious, and it will pass. I'm OK. Nothing bad will happen to me." The goal is to manage the anxiety, not avoid it.

Most panic attacks happen after a stressful life event like a personal loss or a life change. They may be related to drug usage. You need to think about what happened prior to the panic. These circumstances may give clues as to what brings on the anxiety.

Then come up with strategies to stop the panic. You may want to leave the situation, not run away or avoid it, but temporarily leave and come back when you have calmed yourself. This is like a time-out for grownups.

Sometimes talking your way through panic can help. Other times, physical activity helps. When panic begins, try to distract your brain to something mindless like counting or something that requires you to focus like reading or playing an instrument. Try to do something pleasurable or think on something good and lovely.

Practice stopping negative thoughts. In some cases, I would ask clients to wear a rubber band on their wrist. When they started feeling anxious, they would snap the rubber band to help remind them to relax. Then breathe deeply, slowly. This kind of breathing is incompatible with panic. Relax your body by tensing and relaxing muscles. You can't be relaxed and tense at the same time so the solution is to learn to relax your body. Anxious people are usually unaware of how tense their bodies are.

For example, when I was a child I had a few horrible experiences at the dentist. Every time I went to the dentist as an adult, the feeling of panic would return. My body would tense. I would say, "This is stupid. This dentist won't hurt me. I've checked him out too carefully." Then I would focus on something relaxing and start tensing and relaxing my muscles. Over time, I could relax my body with just the cue, "Relax now." There was nothing weird about this approach. I was simply telling my body to relax. After I practiced relaxation enough times, l could do it quickly.

AGORAPHOBIA

You might be surprised to learn that many people, mostly women, suffer degrees of this disorder. *Agoraphobia* is a fear of being somewhere and having a panic attack. It's a fear about how awful it would be to panic in public. The loss of control would lead to embarrassment and worry over what others would think. Therefore, you avoid closed-in places like stores, restaurants, airplanes and elevators. The greatest fear is usually being away from home or away from your loved one. Should you be out alone and panic, what would you do? The fear is that something terrible would happen to you (you would panic), and you would be terribly embarrassed or vulnerable. So you don't drive, walk alone or go places by yourself. Many agoraphobics don't leave the house for fear of having a panic attack. What results is a restricted, anxious and depressed life.

Frequent panic attacks can bring on agoraphobia, although you can have agoraphobia without full-blown panic attacks. Mary Beth, for example, hadn't left her house in months. She depended on a neighbor to get her groceries and spent her days inside her house too worried to venture out. She was lonely, depressed and cried about her future. She was a college graduate trapped in her own home.

Her panic became noticeable when her husband, who was in the Navy, started sea duty. Prior to his first cruise, one of the enlisted wives was attacked on the base. She was badly beaten, and the man who attacked her was caught and jailed. Mary Beth was shaken just by hearing about the experience.

Mary Beth started to panic when her husband left for short cruises. Eventually her condition worsened until she rarely left the house. She was convinced that if she went anywhere, even the bank, she would start to panic and lose control. The more she avoided going out, the more control she felt over her safety. However, she was losing control over her life. She was trapped in the house with little to do but clean and cook all day.

She tried to get out, but the fear of panic stopped her.

Working with Mary Beth required I go to her house. I first taught Mary Beth how to relax her body. Then she learned to ride out the panic feelings. When she could show me how to relax and ride out the panic, we started a treatment called *gradual exposure*. The goal was to get from her house to my office with no panic. We broke that trip down into a series of small steps, some as small as going out the front door and standing for one minute.

At each step, Mary Beth would practice calming herself until she could successfully complete that step. Then she would add another step to the journey until she finally made it to my office. This took a lot of coaching and reassuring Mary Beth that she could do it. I praised her for any effort. She came up with small rewards for each successful step. She memorized Scripture that spoke to her fear, and commanded it to leave because of God's love. Eventually Mary Beth could leave her house for short periods without fear of panic. Over time, the panic disappeared, but her fear of not feeling safe was more embedded than I first realized.

Mary Beth grew up in the home of an alcoholic mother. There were many days when Mary Beth came home from school to find her mother passed out on the couch. Several times she wondered if Mom was even alive. This weekly occurrence frightened Mary Beth and left her feeling rejected and abandoned. She and her siblings learned to put up with Mom's drunkenness, but never accepted her unavailability.

Once when Mom was passed out her brother fell and cut his head. Blood was everywhere, and Mary Beth didn't know what to do. She tried to awaken her mom, but it was no use. So she tried to stop the bleeding. By the time her father came home, the bleeding had stopped, but her brother had a permanent scar.

What Mary Beth remembers most about her childhood is being afraid something bad would happen, and she wouldn't know what to do. When bad things happened, she felt terrible and responsible for her brother's safety. Now years later, the mugging on the base brought back those feelings of panic and led to her eventual self-imposed isolation. Mary Beth was not initially aware of this connection with her current fears. Once we addressed the losses from childhood, her fear lessened even more.

PHOBIAS

A *phobia* is a fear of a specific object or situation. Any contact with the object or situation raises anxiety. With a phobia, adults know their anxiety is excessive but feel they can't control the response. Children just react. Again, the root fear is related to losing control. Many phobias develop in childhood but can develop later in life.

You are familiar with phobias like fear of snakes, dogs, heights and flying. Anytime the person has to confront the situation or object, she experiences anxiety. There are fears about animals usually brought on in childhood, fears about storms and natural disasters, fears of seeing blood or getting injections, fears of situations like flying, going through tunnels or enclosed places. The fear usually develops after a traumatic event, unexpected panic or a situation that represents a threat. For example, a child may be bitten by a dog and develop a fear of dogs. A family member may die in a plane crash and the other family members become afraid to fly. A person may witness a terrible fall and be afraid of heights.

The object of the phobia is usually avoided. Sometimes you can avoid the feared object as in the case of the fear of snakes. You could probably live your life and never have to deal with a snake. But if you are afraid of flying and need to fly because of your job, you could have real problems. Not all phobic objects can be avoided.

Sally was a client who had a long-standing fear of flying. She never sought help because she rarely had to fly. When she was promoted on the job, this changed. Once a month she had to board a plane to fly to the home office in Dallas. Sally was gripped with fear and afraid she would lose the promotion if she refused to fly. She started experiencing intense feelings of anxiety and panic. She couldn't sleep.

She was helped by a simple procedure called *desensitization*. First she tried to imagine herself sitting in the seat of an airplane. The image made her quite anxious. She had to learn to calm down her tense body through practicing relaxation methods. When she could tolerate the thought of being in an airplane, it was time to practice with the real thing.

Her treatment was conducted at the airport. We started with small steps—first going down the jet-way, then into the plane, sitting in the seat for a few minutes, sitting for a longer time and eventually taking a trip. Without going into all the details, Sally had to learn to take a step, relax herself, move to the next step until she could do the thing she feared. Eventually she could get on the plane and not panic.

Sally's fear of flying was rooted in a loss from years ago. Her phobia began during her early teen years. Sally grew up with a critical and mean alcoholic father. He constantly belittled her and made fun of her looks. Sally was athletic and played on the soccer team in middle school. During a critical shot at goal, she missed, and her team lost the game. Her father, who was drunk, embarrassed and shamed her in front of the team. She was so wounded by his words and actions that she dropped soccer, fearing his behavior would continue should she not be perfect. His pattern of belittling continued. Sally was trying hard not to hate him. Sally's dad loved to fly and owned a small plane. One evening the plane went down, and Sally's dad was killed. Feeling guilty about her relationship with Dad and about his death, the phobia gradually worsened over the years. Sally had to confront her fears and, consequently, her loss with the job promotion.

While we treated the fear of flying through helping Sally actually get on the plane, we also dealt with the loss of living with an out-of-control father who died suddenly.

Another type of phobia is one in which you fear social situations. The fear is that you will embarrass yourself and appear stupid and weak. People with social phobias often avoid eating out, public speaking or anything that is social or performance oriented. They have an intense fear that they will be humiliated. Anticipation of the social situation brings on anxiety, and panic surfaces when the situation is encountered.

Sometimes social phobia is mistaken for shyness. Shy people don't experience the intense anxiety of anticipating a social situation. They may feel uneasy but not highly anxious. Not all people with social phobias are shy. They avoid social situations because they are anxious, not shy.

I've treated several women who thought they had an eating disorder but were really phobic about eating in front of others. They did fine with eating in the privacy of their own home but became highly anxious about having to eat out with others. The anxiety prior to eating out would become so intense they would vomit from nerves. Their fear was that they would do something while eating to embarrass themselves. It made no sense but then anxiety is often irrational.

Lucy had that fear. She and her boyfriend were engaged and loved to go out to eat. As the wedding approached she started to become more anxious at restaurants. The problem became so bad she didn't want to eat out. When she tried, she panicked and ran to the bathroom to throw up. As a result, she and her fiance had to leave the restaurant.

Dan couldn't understand why this was happening. He and Lucy had eaten out for two years during their engagement. Why *now* was Lucy so anxious about eating out. When I questioned Lucy, she had no clue and could think of nothing that upset her. Nothing terrible ever happened to her in a restaurant, and she wondered why she reacted this way as well.

Puzzled, we decided to help Lucy eat in a restaurant. We worked on desensitizing Lucy to eating out. What helped Lucy was knowing she could walk out of the restaurant with no questions asked at any time. Lucy panicked less when she knew she wasn't trapped.

The same was true when Lucy attended her college classes. She would panic if she couldn't sit near the exit door. Knowing she could leave the class at any time helped her tolerate the class.

As the wedding approached, Lucy became more anxious and started having symptoms again. Again I asked about any changes or past events that might be bothering her associated with the wedding. Nothing came to mind except one thing she didn't think was related or important: She was thinking about her sister a lot.

Lucy's twin sister and her family had drowned in a sailing accident several years before. Rescuers eventually found the hull of the sailboat with the bodies trapped inside. It was an horrific experience never discussed in the family. The mere mention of the incident sent Mom into tears. Lucy became anxious and agreed to avoid the subject as well.

As the wedding approached, the loss of her sister came back again. Her absence would be noted. Yet no one in the family talked about it. Lucy felt as if she were going crazy because getting married brought up feelings of being trapped. Once married she worried that her individuality would be submerged. She would be trapped and unhappy with the potential for bad things to happen.

Sitting in an enclosed place like a restaurant or a classroom made her feel uncomfortable. She worried that she would be trapped in a social situation, lose control and panic. The anxiety rose up inside of her and caused her to vomit—the vomiting was a way to relieve some anxiety but never relieved it all. She still couldn't sit through an entire meal in a restaurant without feeling extremely anxious.

Lucy wasn't crazy. She was afraid of losing control in social places. Years ago, something bad did happen, which involved family members who were trapped and killed. It was traumatic and out of her control and related to her anxiety symptoms today. The wedding rekindled the traumatic loss of her family.

OBSESSIVE COMPULSIVE DISORDER

Bonnie can tell you about *obsessive-compulsive disorder* (OCD). Bonnie fought obsessive thoughts about cleanliness. She had to wash her hands six to ten times an hour, wipe counters repeatedly and wouldn't touch anything with dirt. If something was unclean, she put on gloves and scrubbed the area until it was totally antiseptic.

It would take Bonnie hours to fold clothes, because they had to be folded perfectly with every edge lined up exactly right. She would spend hours on her checkbook, rewriting every entry perfectly, with all the letters the same size. Any mistake, and she would start over. Each entry line had to be just perfect.

Bonnie would awaken two hours prior to leaving for work in the morning because she had to have her makeup and hair done perfectly. She spent an hour applying her eye makeup and an hour on her hair. The frustrating part was she didn't look any different than anyone else when she walked out the door.

Bonnie was obsessed with germs, had to check things repeatedly and needed everything in order before she could move on to the next thing. Obviously these rigid compulsions interfered with her day.

Some people have intrusive thoughts of violence and fear of harm or other disturbing thoughts about losing control. These thoughts are called *obsessions* and are followed by rituals that attempt to rid you of the obsessive thought. In Bonnie's case, she thought obsessively about germs and dirt. She worried that bacteria would invade her body. Her vigilant cleaning efforts were an attempt to stop the thoughts about germs.

Loss of control is a central theme in OCD. The fear is constant and acted out by behavior. When OCD is severe, medication can help bring relief from the intensity of the obsessions. Behavioral strategies can help, too. Bonnie was helped by a procedure called *exposure and response prevention*. She was exposed to a dirty surface and then prevented from cleaning it or washing her hands. I coached her to use positive self-talk and relaxation to work through her anxiety.

Bonnie knew that her compulsive behavior didn't stop her obsessive thoughts but she behaved compulsively anyway. When she was prevented from doing the compulsion, she became highly anxious and had to learn a new way to deal with the anxiety.

People with OCD suffer a great deal because it interferes with things we take for granted—writing a thank-you note can take days because each letter has to be perfect; getting dressed in the morning can take hours because there is an order of doing it that may be repeated several times; leaving the house can take hours because of the compulsion to check and recheck things. Breaking the cycle takes practice and much prayer. When severe, it may also help to use medication. Some antidepressants and antianxiety drugs actually reduce the obsessions and lessen the need to engage in compulsions.

OCD is a vicious cycle from which people seek freedom. Is OCD rooted in loss? I can't say emphatically, Yes, because the biochemical component seems strong. But it is interesting that many clients relate histories of loss and lost control.

POST-TRAUMATIC STRESS

There is yet another way women and men deal with losing control that creates excessive anxiety—*post-traumatic stress disorder* (PTSD). We first heard about this condition from war veterans who were "shell shocked" or who experienced battle fatigue. Today we know there are a number of traumatic events that can cause PTSD—accidents, kidnappings, shootings, earthquakes, rape, torture, sexual abuse, being threatened and more.

What typically happens is that you or someone close to you is threatened or experiences a traumatic event. The threat or event involves loss of life or serious harm. This terrifying event is later relived by flashbacks or nightmares. As a result of the trauma, you can feel detached from your body, numb or easily startled. Usually anything associated with the trauma is avoided because it tends to set off the trauma reaction.

Kids who witness school shootings, women who have been beaten, children who have been abused, victims of floods, witnesses to serious car accidents and other traumatic events all have one thing in common—they experienced something involving a serious loss of control. That loss of control resulted in harm or even death.

Treatment for PTSD is usually complex and takes time because of the need to go back and deal with the traumatic event. Recall of the event can be problematic and avoidance of anything associated with the event is normal.

Rape is an example of an extremely traumatic event. Unfortunately, Nancy knows the trauma of rape. After a full eight-hour nursing shift, Nancy finished up her paper work and walked to her car in the parking lot of the hospital one evening. Driving home, she was thinking of all the things that needed to be finished before she went to bed. As Nancy pulled into the garage, she thought she heard a strange noise. The garage was attached to the house so she figured something fell from the wall or maybe she ran over something. As she opened the car door, the unthinkable happened. Nancy was accosted.

All she remembers is that someone tried to choke her and threw her into her car. She vaguely recalls a man on top of her, sexually assaulting her. The pain was excruciating as he repeatedly raped her and slapped her in the face. The next thing she knew, she was alone in the car, beaten and bleeding. Somehow she opened her purse and dialed 911 on her cell phone.

Nancy's recollection of that night is vague because of the trauma. For weeks, she couldn't pull her car into the garage or be alone in her house. Any movement around her house frightened her, and she couldn't sleep. The police believed the man slipped into her garage when the automatic door went up. There was no sign of entry to her house.

Nancy was terrified that the rapist was still at large and could come back. She started having nightmares, reliving the pain of the rape. Noises made her jump. Getting into her car raised her anxiety, and she would obsessively check the seats to see if anyone was hiding. Nancy was gripped with fear. She withdrew from people, became irritable and had difficulty concentrating at work. Nancy needed help to work through the trauma.

I've treated many through the years like Nancy who have been traumatized by different events and people in their lives. It's not the purpose of this book to go into all the treatment approaches for PTSD. Just know that these women suffer intense anxiety because they have been harmed or have witnessed the death or harm of someone else. Healing from trauma takes time, patience, a competent therapist and the healing touch of God.

If you have been traumatized in any of the ways described, anxiety can be a symptom related to the trauma, whether the trauma was recent or long ago. People tend to block out the traumatic events because they are too painful to remember. They can't recall or think about what happened because it is buried deep inside. Then symptoms of anxiety develop.

Recalling the trauma can be part of the healing process, but may or may not happen. You need to work with someone who is trained in PTSD. Ask God to heal the memory and take away the fear.

By now you should have a clear sense that all of these anxiety disorders are based on a lack of control, whether perceived or real. Facing the loss of control is something none of us like to do. We all want to feel in charge of our lives and competent to handle any difficulty. But some things really throw us and create intense anxiety. I've mentioned some of the helpful things that can be done, but let's talk more about ways to help us overcome anxiety.

10

Overcoming Anxiety

Now that you have a better understanding about anxiety and can recognize the signs, you need to learn how to overcome it. Anxiety is not something you need to be resigned to having for the rest of your life. You can be healed from anxiety disorders.

Obviously you can't always stop things from getting out of control. So the first place to start is to become more comfortable with the idea that not everything will be in your control, and that's OK. The reason this is OK is because God is in control of all things. He sees the big picture. Nothing happens that He doesn't know about. That's got to be reassuring. God is always with us and knows what we are going through.

Expecting everything to go well all the time is a setup for anxiety to build. Most of living is a rough and bumpy road. It's actually more rare for things to go without a hitch. This doesn't mean you should be a pessimist and expect problems all the time. It means you should be a realist and expect glitches along the way. So having realistic expectations is important.

You also need to learn to be a problem-solver. The more confident you are in your problem-solving skills, the less anxious you'll be. When something doesn't go as planned, the problem-solver says, "OK, that didn't work, now how else could I get to the goal?" The anxious person says, "Oh no, that didn't work, now everything will fall apart, and I'll never reach the goal." A problem-solver hits a roadblock and finds a different road. The anxious person hits a roadblock and stops. Be a problem-solver—look for the new road.

There are very practical things you can do to eliminate anxiety in your life.

Sometimes they are simple changes:

Consider your diet.

It's a well-known fact that food, stress and mood are interrelated. What you eat and drink can directly affect anxiety. It's worth a try to limit salt, alcohol, preservatives and hormones from food intake. The more natural and organic foods you eat, the better you feel. There is so much research now on the relation of food to mood that it's worth making changes to see if you feel better. I'm not a registered dietitian, but a good one knows which foods can trigger anxiety. You can try making changes and see if you feel less anxious.

Eliminate or cut back on caffeine.

Caffeine can trigger anxiety. When I was in college, I studied all night in the dorm. The trick was to stay awake. Fortunately, someone owned a coffee pot. We consumed potfuls of coffee to stay awake and help us concentrate. After weeks of this habit, I started to feel shaky and anxious from drinking too much caffeine. When I stopped, the tension went away. Try eliminating caffeinated coffee, tea and sodas. Other items like chocolate and over-the-counter drugs have caffeine in them as well. If you can't stop your intake of caffeine, then at least cut back and see if you feel less tense and calmer. Keep in mind that when you do stop taking in caffeine, you may go through a period of withdrawal in which you may feel irritable and sleepy. Caffeine can be an addictive substance, and some people experience withdrawal symptoms similar to other drugs.

Stop smoking.

Smoking is also a stimulant and has similar effects to caffeine on anxiety. If you haven't already stopped smoking, here is another good reason to do so. Stop smoking, and you will feel calmer, which is a claim smokers tend to deny. Smokers say cigarettes calm them down, but they don't. If fact, smokers tend to be more anxious than nonsmokers and don't sleep as well.

Evaluate your use of any medications or drugs you take.

Other drugs contain stimulants as well. If you are an adult woman, for example, who takes Ritalin or some other stimulant for AD/HD, you may be triggering panic or anxiety. Check with your doctor to make sure your anxiety is not a side effect from a prescription drug.

Cocaine can also bring on panic. Obviously, if you are taking cocaine, you need the help of a drug and rehabilitation program. The point is that anxiety could be a side effect of certain drugs taken for legitimate or not-so-legitimate reasons. Don't assume anxiety is unrelated to something you ingest.

Talk to a doctor about antianxiety medications.

There are antianxiety drugs that are not addictive and a far cry from their earlier versions. You can treat anxiety problems without medication, but there are times when treatment proceeds better with them. The treatment of serious panic may be aided by medication.

Medication is also helpful, sometimes even necessary, in the treatment of obsessive-compulsive disorder (OCD). OCD appears to have a strong biochemical component. For reasons we don't completely understand, certain medications can decrease obsessive thoughts and compulsions.

As in the case of antidepressants, you shouldn't feel condemned for using these medications. They are designed to be helpful but should not be the only intervention you use. Work with a physician who knows these medications and can prescribe wisely. Work with a therapist who can help you develop behavioral strategies as well.

Try vitamin supplements.

You may want to add B and C vitamins to your daily intake. These anti-stress vitamins may increase your energy. Women also know the importance of taking calcium, and calcium has a calming effect on the nervous system as well. Try these simple changes to see if you feel differently.

Ask your doctor about natural herbs.

Research on the use of natural herbs for decreasing depression and anxiety shows promise. I am not an expert in this area, but some clients have had success using natural teas and herbs. For example, the herb Kava Kava has helped some clients with mild anxiety symptoms. The use of herbs continues to be evaluated by established medical associations, and you must be careful with what and how much you take, especially if you are taking perscription medications. My advice is to check with a reputable doctor who supports alternative medicine and see if there are any natural approaches that might ease your anxiety.

Exercise.

I know this sounds so simple again, but exercise affects mood positively. The problem is finding the time and motivation to do it. Maybe you are one of the fortunate ones who love to exercise and make time for it. If so, congratulate yourself and start a self-help group. If you are like the rest of us, you need help.

I hate to exercise, but I feel so much better after I do it. I gave up trying to learn to like it. I figure it's like eating brussel sprouts—you do it because it's good for you, not because you enjoy it. I used to run six days a week for months and never, I repeat never, got that runner's high or fell in love with it. Instead I had to talk myself into doing it daily.

Exercise is one of those things you just commit to doing because of the benefits. It's something you do because you are a grownup. Exercise reduces tension in your body and discharges anxiety. It has multiple health benefits and improves your mood. If you are anxious you should try to exercise. You don't have to sign up for a triathlon, just get out and walk. We'll talk again about exercise in the section on eating disorders.

Relax.

Several times, I've mentioned the need for relaxation. Anxious people have tense bodies and problems relaxing those tense bodies. When I start treatment with an anxious person, I start by teaching her relaxation skills. Usually, I make her practice in the office in front of me. The reason for this is so that I can watch how easy or difficult it is for her to relax her body. With an anxiety disorder, you are very tense and can't relax your body. So you practice until you know the bodily *feeling* of relaxation.

Some women don't know what it feels like to be relaxed. Once you feel the difference between relaxation and tension, you know what to do. You learn to recognize the sensation of tension. This sounds simple, but many women walk around with a lot of physical tension in their bodies and don't even know it.

There are several ways to do relaxation. One is to breathe deeply and slowly. When you breathe from your abdomen it's hard to stay tense. When you are anxious, your breathing becomes shallow and speeds up. Another relaxation method I like to practice is tensing and relaxing each muscle in my body. I usually give clients a tape of my voice working them through each of the muscle groups, coaching them to tense, then relax. What I are doing is training them to train their body to relax when they want it to, rather than becoming automatically tense. Remember my trauma in the dentist's chair? I used muscle relaxation to teach my body to relax on cue. I silently say, "Relax," and my body will do it. This is nothing wacky or new age. It's simply teaching your body to calm down. If you tend to carry tension in your muscles (neck and back), this is the technique for you.

Some people relax by imaging a peaceful scene in their mind. They may think of a warm beach with palm trees swaying and the waves gently lapping on the beach. Concentrating on a peaceful scene can relax you, especially if you are the type whose mind is always running a million miles an hour.

Other people like to meditate. I'm not talking mantras and Zen. For the Christian, meditation is prayer, praise and reading the Bible. The Bible tells us to think on or meditate upon things that are good, pure, noble and praiseworthy (Phil. 4:8). Thinking about your blessings and all the good things you have is a way to relax you and praise God at the same time. Being still and listening for God to speak to you is also beneficial spiritually and physically.

Pay attention to your self-talk.

Remember I said that anxious people don't usually know what they are *thinking* before they get anxious. They just *feel* anxious. But anxious people have negative self-talk. In their heads they are thinking things like, *I can't do this. I'm going crazy. This is too scary. No one will help me.*

Part of the work of overcoming anxiety is becoming aware of your thoughts that lead to anxiety. Thoughts are related. They influence mood, which influences perception, which influences thoughts. This circular process continues all through the day. When you learn to recognize your thoughts, you can change them to thoughts that are more positive, *I can do all things through Christ who strengthens me. With God, I can't fail. I'm never alone.*

Learn to identify and express feelings directly.

Lurking behind anxiety can be unexpressed anger, depression, hurt and a host of negative emotions. When women have trouble saying how they feel, they can become anxious. Some women don't even know what they feel and can't identify emotions. This is often true in the case of anorexia as well.

The work then is to learn to identify *how* and *what* you feel and find an appropriate way to express those feelings. "I" statements are best. "I feel…"

rather than "You make me feel…" No one makes you feel anything.

Learn to be assertive.

Related to this issue of expressing emotions is the need to be more assertive in your life. You don't have to go around telling everyone what to do or what you need every minute, but you do need to learn to speak up at the right time. Women get anxious and feel out of control because they let other people direct their lives. They end up doing things they are uncomfortable with or would prefer not to do at all. Well, speak up, girl. If you don't say what you need, no one can respond to you. Assertiveness can reduce anxiety.

Know what you believe.

Down deep do you really believe God loves you and cares about you? Do you really believe His promises? We may give lip service to God's promises, but when it comes to applying them to our lives, we don't do so well. Sometimes we think God's promises are good for others and not us. This relates to our self-esteem. Self-esteem is built through intimacy with God. Knowing what He says about you will make you feel great. You know how He feels about you by reading what He has to say to you.

Unfortunately, most of us listen to what *others* have to say about us. We give them way too much power over how we see ourselves. When you are a child, it's hard to correct your image of yourself if you live with people who criticize and put you down. Families and peers are powerful influencers of how we see ourselves. But when you are an adult (and even as a child), you can check out what you have been told by reading what God has to say about you. It is surprisingly good stuff. Then you have to choose who you will believe—people or God? Why do we so often choose people? Probably because they are in our face. So get in God's face, and get intimate with Him. Correct your view of yourself.

Remember God promises His presence.

The Bible says that nothing can separate us from the love of God. There will be trials. There will be times when we feel we've lost control.

But God is always with us and will walk the path with us through the difficulty. Who else do you know who can promise to never leave you and always be present in a time of trouble? You are not alone.

Be anxious about nothing (Phil. 4:6).

How is this possible? Actually the verse *tells* us how we can stop being anxious. According to the scripture, we first thank God. Then we talk to God through prayer and tell Him our requests. Verse eight instructs us to meditate on things that are noble, pure, lovely, of good report, virtuous and praiseworthy, and God will give us His peace (v. 9). The result is a peace we can't understand in the natural but one that guards our hearts and minds.

Pray away anxiety.

Try this prayer to get rid of anxiety:

> God, I thank You that You gave me a sound mind. Even if I don't
> feel sound this minute, Your Word says You have given me a sound
> mind. Thank You for the promise. Now I'm asking for You to take
> this (insert your anxious thought here) that keeps bothering me
> and remove it. I'm choosing to think about Your Resurrection,
> how You died for me so I could live in the fullness of Your glory.
> This anxiety is not from You, so I don't want it. Anytime it tries to
> come in my mind, I'm stopping it and thinking about life through
> Your risen Son. You told me to ask, so I'm asking. You told me to
> believe, so I'm believing. You told me You will give me Your peace,
> and You only give good things, so give me Your good peace now.

Meditate on the Word.

This is what the Bible calls "renewing your mind." God tells us not to fear and worry about many things. Look, He made us so He knows how fearful we can be. That's why He instructs us how to deal with it.

We are not to worry about:

—provisions (Matt. 6:25)
—enemies (Deut. 1:21)
—death (Psa. 23:4)
—wars (Psa. 27:3)
—reputation (Psa. 71:24)
—evil days (Psa. 49:5)
—children (Psa. 127:3)
—the future (Psa. 139:1–6)
—sudden terror (Prov. 3:25–26)
—safety (Matt. 10:28)
—events beyond our control (Matt. 8:26)
—health (2 Cor. 12:7–10)
—fearful thoughts (Phil. 4:6–7)
—words of others (1 Pet. 3:14)
—suffering (Rev. 2:10)

That about covers everything, doesn't it?

And there is more—He tells us *why* we are not to worry and be fearful. Here's why.

—We are His creation (Gen. 44:2).
—He fights for us (Exod. 14:13).
—He loves us (1 John 4:9).
—He is our helper (Heb.13:6).
—We are more valuable than the sparrows (Luke 12:7).
—We have God's presence (Rom. 8:15).

Still not convinced? Boy, you are a tough cookie! OK, let's keep going.

The Bible is our guide for living. We should make all our decisions based on His Word. So if He tells us not to be anxious, would He tell us to do something impossible to do? With God, all things are possible (again this is His Word, not my fantasy).

Believe you can be free of anxiety.

The Bible also says that all things are possible to them that *believe*. So you must have faith and believe you can be set free from anxiety. What gets in our way of doing this? Even the psalmist admitted, "I believed, therefore I spoke, 'I am greatly afflicted'" (Psa. 116:10). So the first step is to *believe* that we don't have to stay afflicted with anxiety. Then we need to *say* that we can rise above it. Too many people resign themselves to living an anxious life. Again, why would God direct you to do something and then not give you a way to do it?

Don't give in to fear and anxiety.

Know the Word so you can fight back when you feel anxious. Look at the great men and women in the Bible for example. Joseph was thrown in the pit by his lovely brothers. Pretty lousy circumstances; enough to make most of us anxious. Did Joseph sit in the pit and say, "Oh no. My life is over?" No. When he met up with the brothers later in Egypt, he said to them, "Now don't get fearful. Everything is cool. What you meant for evil, God meant for good" (Gen 50:19, author's paraphrase). Joseph knew in his heart that God would take care of him despite his desperate circumstances.

People may harm you, do bad things to you, die on you, treat you poorly but God can turn it around. Why? Because God is working in our favor.

If we start believing the promises of God, fear will leave us. When fear leaves, the provision comes. What's the provision? His promise to supply all our needs. If He says I can have perfect peace, then I can. What a great way out of fear and anxiety!

Think about the many losses you have experienced.

One of the most common losses relates to people. We have been let down or disillusioned by others. This can cause deep wounds if we let it. We have to put our trust in God and not people.

God will not let you down. I'm not saying that life is a piece of cake or that this is easy to do. In the natural, it's really hard. With God it's possible though. Even though losses like a physical death, a divorce, an abusive parent or a tragedy occur, God is still in control. We can trust that nothing gets past His watchful eye. He sees it all and can identify with our pain and suffering. He wants us free from worry and anxiety over the present and potential losses we face.

Let's go back to the example of when my brother was killed. It was a horrific time. He was married, had a pregnant wife and nearly three-year-old son. My brother loved God and always was a model for me in taking a stand for Christ even during the rebellious days of the 1960s. When he died, it was scary. Suddenly in a moment, someone I loved was gone.

Unaware that I carried around a fear of losing an intimate other, I married. I was highly anxious whenever my husband had to travel, thinking he would be killed like my brother, and I would be a widow like my sister-in-law. For a period of time, I allowed this fear to grip me. I'd pray and think all kinds of nutty stuff like, *God wouldn't take two important men out of my life, would He?*

One night, I had an "ah ha" experience from the Holy Spirit. I finally realized I didn't really believe God was sovereign, and that I didn't trust God to be faithful. I had to repent and confess that I was too busy making up stuff in my head rather than reading God's promises and believing them. I was too busy being upset with God to focus on the good things He had done for me. I was not living in the truth of Philippians 4:6–7. When I started applying the scripture to my life and took authority over the fear through the power of the Holy Spirit in me, the fear left. The fear would try to pop up again and again but I knew the source was the loss I experienced, and I knew what to do to overcome it.

You have the same ability to deal with fear and anxiety. Recognize the source—usually loss of control. Give God thanks for what He has done. Ask Him to stop the thoughts and body responses. Think on the good things of God, and believe His promise for healing.

Don't get depressed if you aren't better instantly. Some of this takes time and persistence. Changing your thoughts from negative to positive is usually not an overnight accomplishment. It took you a while to develop a negative thought pattern; it may take you a while to learn a positive one.

Give thanks in spite of your circumstances.

Women also ask me how it is possible to give thanks in the middle of yucky circumstances. Let's revisit Joseph. Remember his lousy circumstances? His thanks wasn't for His circumstances. He didn't sit in the pit and say, "I'm so glad to be in this dirty, dark, smelly old pit. Isn't it great that I can suffer for God here in a hole?" No. His thanks was because God promised to take care of him. He didn't know how or when he would be delivered, but he believed God would deliver him. Even more than what Joseph had, we have the Comforter. Thank God for sending Jesus, giving us the Holy Spirit and always providing the way out of the pit!

SECTION
THREE

EATING
DISORDERS

11

Stuck in
Eating Disorders

The Duchess of Windsor has said: "You can never be too rich or too thin." Doesn't this quote make you want to go to a buffet and dive into the fried chicken with everything you have? Come on, Duchess. A more realistic axiom would be, "You can never be the Duchess of Windsor!" If this is the thinking of a duchess, leave me out (like I'm in line for the job anyway!). Now don't go getting all upset with me for picking on good 'ole Wallis Simpson (the Duchess of Windsor). All I'm saying is that this type of thinking has to stop. We *can* be too thin. It's called *anorexia!*

Ladies, as Joan Rivers says, "Can we talk?" This dieting, "thin is in" stuff is way out of control and causing too many women major problems. Unless you were born with the perfect body (please send photos so I can verify this, and plastic surgery doesn't count!), you probably don't like your body very well. With thirty-four million of us overweight and half of us dieting, this is a safe guess.

In today's society, it's hard to be comfortable with our bodies. At five feet four inches tall, one hundred forty-four pounds and a size twelve, the average American woman doesn't measure up to the five feet eight inches tall, one hundred ten pound, size two model. We look at ourselves in the mirror, then look at a magazine and get depressed. We have to face reality. We don't look model perfect. Is it OK with you, or do you feel anxious about it? (See Section I if you get depressed, Section 2 if you are anxious.)

The cultural pressure to look fit, thin and healthy is immense. So much so that our daughters, at the age of nine, are already dieting and talking about losing weight. Plastic surgery among teens is at an all-time high, and we are all secretly waiting for the new pill that will make all that cellulite melt like hot wax.

With all our attention and focus on losing weight and looking like Cindy Crawford, "we have trouble in River City." According to the National Association of Anorexia and Associated Disorders, eating disorders impact more than eleven million of us, and that's reason enough to be concerned.

IT'S NOT JUST ABOUT FOOD

For the past fifteen years, I've specialized in the treatment of women with eating disorders and have seen hundreds of bright, attractive women damage their bodies to the point of near death. I've watched family members and loved ones shake their heads in disbelief asking, "Why would someone with so much potential harm her body this way?"

First of all, we must recognize that food really isn't the problem. I know it's an *eating* disorder but it's not just about food. Food is the thing we outwardly wrestle with, but emotional and spiritual emptiness are the real culprits. Now don't get me wrong, I treat the food symptoms (starving, bingeing and purging) but unless we deal with deeper issues, the food problems return.

So what are those deeper issues? One is the cultural pressure mentioned above. But if that were the only cause, then we would all have an eating disorder. So there must be more to it.

If you have developed an eating disorder, your family plays a part. I'm not blaming families, I'm just saying they have an influence. All of us live in not-so-perfect families. But for those of you with an eating problem, the not-so-perfect family creates big problems.

Families can actually be places of emptiness and loneliness. If your family emphasized looking good but paid little attention to your inward struggles of growing up, you become vulnerable to eating disorders. Furthermore, if achievement was overemphasized and love had to be earned through perfection and compliance, food can be used to soothe the anxiety. Or you may have grown up in a family that was chaotic and out of control. There was little structure, and you didn't feel safe. Someone in the family may have been depressed and unable to handle conflict. Someone may have been alcoholic or out of control in other ways. Whether you grew up in a family that neglected your emotions or one that was chaotic, food can be used to fill the empty places and calm you down.

Individually, you may fear the loss of childhood. Adolescence may look turbulent or adulthood, demanding. Staying small and childlike protects you. You may be frightened by the prospect of leaving home to become an independent adult. You don't feel confident pushing for independence and handling the normal challenges that go with that effort. You would rather starve, binge and purge than face the growing pains of becoming a young woman with an identity to solidify.

Or you may feel that you just can't measure up—that you have to be perfect. You also experience intense emotions that feel out of control and scare you—emotions like hurt, anger, disappointment and frustration. So you pretend emotions don't exist, or you numb those emotions with food.

Instead of facing loss, growing and moving on, you hide behind the "perfect body" or give up trying to have the perfect body and lose control. Loss, in your mind, is best fed or starved, rather than experienced.

179

Having an eating disorder is about living life in the extremes. You starve or binge emotionally and spiritually. There is no in between. No moderation. No working through the tough issues. It's avoidance or indulgence, whether you are talking food or functioning with people.

There is incredible deception. Deception over the truth about one's body: The body is too fat or too thin. The true self is hidden. You are convinced that if anyone really knew how you thought, felt and wanted to act, they would hate you and never want to be with you. So you maintain an outward appearance of having it all together.

Eating disorders become all-consuming. It's a "twenty-four/seven" problem. The obsession with eating takes over and interferes with everyday living. The thought of food is constant. The urge to starve or purge is always present. You are desperate to be free but often don't know how.

Freedom is found with a lot of hard work and a willingness to embrace loss. Once again, loss is a significant factor in the development of eating problems. Loss is related to control and giving up the quest for the ideal body. The obsession with how you look is really a distraction from more important issues of the soul. Who you are is the central question. You are not your weight. You are so much more, but you are stuck thinking about your weight.

So we have to free ourselves from weight obsessions in order to discover the other parts of our being. Weight is superficial. How you love God, others and yourself is what gives you depth and meaning. Find your freedom from the thin ideal. Let God love you so you can love others without being weighted down. He wants to lift you up and out of that stuck place.

12

Facing the Loss of Childhood—
Anorexia

Y ou have seen pictures of emaciated women who think they are fat. You have watched news magazine shows about girls who slowly starve themselves to near death. Those of us who grew up hearing the smooth pop voice of Karen Carpenter remember when she died from complications related to anorexia. Models, actresses and ballet dancers are well known for having high numbers of anorexic women in their professions—professions in which the body and appearance are of great importance. Famous people like model Kate Dillon and actress Lucy Lawless admit to having an eating disorder. Others, like Kalista Flockheart (Ally McBeal), deny being anorexic and say they are naturally skinny.

The point is that today we all talk about this subject. Anorexia is no longer just buzz talk among mental health professionals. It's common jargon in the culture. You probably know someone who is or has been anorexic. If you live in a college dorm, you don't have to look too far to see evidence of this disorder. For one thing, it's a visible disorder. It's rampant among college women.

It's not my intention here to do an exhaustive study of anorexia or any eating disorder. Instead I want to give you a taste, so to speak, of the complexity of these disorders and help you understand some of the struggles as they relate to loss. There is so much more I could say since this is a specialty practice of mine, but I'll focus my efforts on a basic understanding of major issues.

These disorders usually require treatment by a mental health professional trained in eating disorders as well as good medical follow-up by a physician, because they can lead to serious medical complications and lifelong problems.

The medical complications of anorexia can include loss of menstrual cycles, osteoporosis, constipation, stunting of growth, abdominal pain, stomach bloating, electrolyte imbalance, decrease in muscle mass, heart problems, anemia, EEG abnormalities, low blood pressure, hypoglycemia, kidney abnormalities and more. Obviously the condition is life threatening, and you can die from the disorder.

You know that anorexia is about people intentionally starving themselves. Usually anorexia begins around puberty. There are cases of anorexia that begin in childhood and some that start after the age of forty. These are special cases with unique issues. In this book, I am mostly going to talk about anorexia among adolescent and young adult girls.

When you are anorexic and have lost at least 15 percent of your ideal body weight, you still aren't convinced that you are too thin. Your family and friends have a hard time understanding how you can be so deceived. That's because anorexia involves a physical, emotional, relational and spiritual battle. Anorexia involves much more than food, even though food is the object of struggle. Anorexia is about facing loss—the loss of childhood.

One way to think about anorexia is that it is a wish to stay childlike. The turmoil and sexuality of adolescence can be a frightening time.

Some girls shrink from that fear and regress to a time when they felt safe—a time when their bodies weren't changing and relationships weren't so confusing. That time was childhood. As children, we are dependent. We've yet to face the challenge of firming up our identities. We don't have to think about leaving home. Think about Wendy and her brothers in *Peter Pan.* When their father tells them to stop pretending because they are too old for such nonsense, and then abruptly announces this will be the last night for Wendy in the nursery, Wendy feels sad (leave it to the girl to have the emotion) because she's not ready to grow up. But Wendy resigns herself to the fact: "Tomorrow I have to grow up." Then, Peter Pan shows up and provides a temporary way to escape such sadness. The modern-day story would be for Wendy to develop anorexia and go into psychological Never-Never Land!

When you starve, your body appears more like a child than an emerging adolescent or young women. Your hips stop getting round, your breasts don't develop and you often lose your periods or don't start them at all.

Anorexia keeps you childlike in appearance and interrupts budding sexuality. You may wonder what the big deal is about becoming a teen and growing up. We all have to do it and don't necessarily become anorexic. We all do face specific challenges, however, in making the transition from girl to woman. Why some develop eating disorders is still somewhat of a mystery, but we have many clues.

Most American teen girls have an obsession with dieting and calories and want to look a certain way based on a cultural standard. Girls who develop eating disorders, however, take the normal fixation about their bodies during adolescence to an extreme. Eating disorders are about doing too much or too little around food, calories and dieting. There is a preoccupation with weight loss and fear of getting fat way beyond normal concerns.

Here are signs of anorexia you can look for if you are concerned about yourself or someone you love:

- You are at least 15 percent below your ideal body weight and refuse to gain or stay at a normal weight for your height and body frame.

- You fear gaining weight and getting fat.

- Your image of your body is distorted. You think you look fat when you don't.

- You have missed at least three menstrual cycles.

- You compulsively exercise.

Not every person fits perfectly into this description. You can have some of the characteristics listed above and not be a full-blown anorexic but still struggle over eating. For example, I've seen girls who are very thin, obsessed with feeling fat, who haven't lost their periods. They still have a serious problem with food, but don't technically meet the definition of anorexia. Or you may have all the symptoms but be only 10 percent below your ideal body weight. I've also seen others who go on starvation kicks when stress gets high. The anorexic behavior comes and goes. All of this is to say that there is a continuum of eating problems that many of us face.

The question from most families is, "Why is this happening?" The answer is, "For a lot of reasons." Let's start with the culture in which we raise teenage girls. Ask yourself, What do you think of when you think of *thin?* Competent, successful, controlled, attractive? What do you think of when you think of *fat?* Laziness, unattractive, lack of control, undesirable? Your view of thinness is, in part, shaped by the culture. You would have to be living in a cave not to notice how much focus there is on beauty and weight in our society. Pick up any magazine, turn on a television show, go to a movie, get on the Internet, go to a clothing store, listen to teen conversation and you will see and hear continuous themes of beauty and weight.

I can still remember seeing my mother push her body into a girdle when I was a child. I'd watch, thinking, *That must hurt, but it must be part of what we do to look good.* Since the nineteenth century, women have pushed their bodies into all sorts of undergarments in an effort to have the right look. Don't kid yourself. We still have the nineteenth century mentality. Just go to a Victoria's Secret and check out the body-slimming gear.

In an ironic twist, we tell girls they are so much more than their outward appearance and then inundate them with images of body beauty. It's at the very least a confusing message. We live in a society obsessed with youth, beauty, fitness and attaining the perfect look. Thanks to plastic surgery, you can even pay for near perfection.

I saw a woman on a talk show who had undergone something like twelve plastic surgery operations to correct what she thought were flaws in her appearance. Her *before* pictures showed a pleasant-looking women who was a housewife and mother of two. She was convinced if she were beautiful, voluptuous and perfectly sculpted, her life would be happy and satisfying. She told the talk show host that after her twelve surgeries, she was now happy with her life and had no regrets. Her two young daughters knew that Mommy had surgery to make her happy. What a sad and misguided message for her daughters as well as to herself. Someone needed to get that woman off TV and into therapy.

Happiness does not come from having a perfect body even though the culture tries to instill this message. Sadly, our girls buy into the lie. We are told there is a "right look," and we'll do most anything to get it.

I remember the angst of adolescence and trying to attain the right look. The top half of my body was great. The bottom half needed work to fit into those low-hipped, tight pants. At five feet six inches tall and one hundred twenty pounds, I was not fat. But the thighs bothered me because they didn't look like the ones in the magazines or on TV. I was physically fit; I just didn't get the genes to look "right" in the jeans. You all know what I am talking about. Pick a part of your body you didn't like and tell me your story.

What happens with all this cultural emphasis on thinness, which I believe has worsened in the past twenty years and not improved despite the efforts of feminists, is that we experience loss. We lose the acceptance of God's unique design for us. The "right" look is how God designed us. For many of us, this takes a lifetime to accept.

Anorexia involves a dissatisfaction with appearance that usually precedes dieting. Dieting is often an entrée into the disorder. Many girls talk about being teased about their bodies prior to dieting. Dieting is an attempt to take control of that teasing.

The culture is only one layer of the problem. Eating disorders tend to run in families. Families play a role because of the developmental issues involved in the disorder. When I do an evaluation of a girl with an eating disorder, I ask the entire family to be present. One of the reasons for this is because I'm taking family history. I typically ask about other members of the family—including aunts, grandmothers and others. I almost always find that other family members have struggled with eating problems, and the family knows all about them.

It's not uncommon to find a depressed mother, an alcoholic father or a traumatized sibling. There is "stuff" going on other than the eating disorder. While the anorexic girl has to be responsible to stop the symptoms of her disorder, the family is my "patient." I tell them, "You are all a part of this. I'm not saying this to blame anyone, but to help you to realize that your daughter isn't the only one that will be asked to make changes."

The family then stares at me with this "What in the world is she talking about?" look, but soon they understand. Anorexia doesn't take place in a vacuum, and it's not just about the daughter. It's about a daughter whose family is enveloped by one or more of the following:

- Silent fighting
- A sense of inadequacy hiding behind a facade of excessive togetherness and respectability
- Rigid protection of the status quo
- Overprotective nurturing

- Chronic unhappiness
- Depression and anxiety
- Poor regulation of emotions and mood
- Pressure on the daughter to deny her own identity for the sake of the family
- Favoring rules over feelings
- Avoiding problems and conflict resolution
- Indirect communication, which is characterized by family members speaking for each other
- Fear of the daughter's emerging sexuality
- Preoccupation of family members with their own dieting and looks

There is no one profile of an "anorexic" family, but family relationships are the key. Developmentally, anorexia can begin when daughters start to separate from mothers and seek their own identities. Girls must fight to be separate, and mothers must let them go. Anorexia can be a sign of problematic separation.

The challenge for the daughter is to find her own identity while still having a relationship with her mother. The challenge for the mother is to allow the daughter to find herself and still mother. Moms spend a lifetime trying to give daughters what they need. As daughters grow, they pull away—not because they don't need their mothers anymore, but because they are trying to firm up their individual identity. During puberty, many mothers grieve the loss of closeness and not being as intimately connected to all the details of their daughters' lives.

When this separation process becomes problematic, anorexia can develop. Anorexia is seen by girls as a solution—a solution to get unstuck in the separation process. Anorexia allows them to stay dependent and undefined but still have a unique identity—anorexic. Anorexia allows them to develop a false sense of self and independence. They develop a sense of competence and self-control with food, not people. Obviously, the problem is that their solution gets them stuck in another way (they develop symptoms).

Fathers also play a role in this separation process. Fathers help girls develop their identities and successfully leave home (psychologically). Fathers show girls how a husband nurtures his wife. Fathers show unconditional acceptance of daughters and bring out their sexuality. Fathers help girls feel beautiful, loved and cherished, and they show interest in their age-related development—dating, school, self-reflection and ambitions. When fathers fail to do these things, girls experience a loss of Dad, which leads to insecurity in their abilities to compete with other women and develop sexual maturity.

Many girls with anorexia talk about how, when they were little, their fathers played with them. They felt close to their daddies. As they approached adolescence and their bodies began to develop, Dad pulled away. They experienced a loss of dad.

Dads have told me they are uncomfortable with their daughters' emerging sexuality and don't know how to relate to this change. This only confirms the suspicion of girls—dads do pull away. Dads experience a loss of their little girls as well.

Girls then are facing a time in their lives when their identities are firming up in the context of separating and becoming independent. The root of an eating disorder is usually found in this issue of identity formation. We are expected to leave the dependency of childhood and forge ahead into the unknown world of independence. If we are encouraged in healthy ways along this journey, we somehow manage to push our way along. But if we get scared or can't grieve the loss of childhood, we can get stuck.

Anorexia is a way of developing a new identity. At first, dieting and losing weight are attempts to take control of feelings that feel out of control. It is a way to mask feeling scared and insecure. It is a way to hide. As the anorexia takes hold, feelings are lost, sexuality wanes and self-development gets stuck. Anorexia is an idealistic false return to the dependency of childhood, while at the same time hating it. The girl's dilemma is, "I'm sick; you'll have to take care of me, but I hate being taken care of because that means I can't take care of myself as I'm supposed to be doing."

Girls with anorexia don't know how they feel. You ask, and they stare. There are no words for feelings, just body experiences. For example, an anorexic daughter may be angry at her mother for demanding she eat. Instead of recognizing the anger as such, she feels tightness in her stomach. She "can't" eat. Most have to be taught to identify their feelings and give names to them. Then they must be encouraged to express feelings, not indirectly through eating or not eating, but directly to the person. The tricky emotions to navigate are the negative ones—anger, hurt, disappointment, emptiness. Those emotions get starved and stuffed inward. Good girls don't get upset. If they do allow a negative feeling to surface, they don't know how to handle it.

When you are anorexic, you are usually compliant, the girl who never causes problems. You tend to be perfectionistic and an achiever. Accomplishments mean a great deal because you are defined by what you achieve. Even though you strive for perfection and look good on the outside, you struggle with feelings of inadequacy on the inside. You feel inept socially and avoid social activities. You prefer to stay in the arena of task accomplishment where expectations are clear-cut and can be met. Social situations feel too out of control and you can't control how other people behave.

You think, *Thin is happy. Self-denial is virtue. Self-control must be maintained at all times. Growing up is overwhelming. Perfection can be achieved, and I must please everyone all the time.*

You spend a lot of energy pleasing others and looking for the approval of others. Even in therapy, you try to please me rather than show me your authentic self. The fear is, "If you knew me, Dr. Mintle, you wouldn't like me," which of course is not true. But you believe you must hide the true self because it wouldn't please others. In some cases, this is true—anger and upsets don't please everyone. Anger may be your true emotion, but not pleasing. Pleasing others isn't the goal. Being true to self is. But you feel you can't risk the rejection. Better to hide, do what others want and fight with your body vs. others.

You feel incompetent, powerless and helpless to deal with relationships and developmental tasks. The discipline of anorexia gives you a feeling of power and control. You are often physically hungry but determined to deny yourself food as a way to feel empowered.

You get depressed, obsessed and anxious. You are a smart girl who knows this eating thing has gotten way out of your control. Now you can't eat even when you try.

Tara's story will help you understand some of the dynamics of all of this.

Tara grew up in a small coastal town along the shores of the Atlantic in North Carolina. She loved to sit by the ocean and listen to the tide gently lap against the sand. She'd laugh at the young fiddler crabs as they burrowed in the sand, narrowly escaping for their lives each time the wash of the waves rhythmically smoothed the surface. The ocean was teaming with life and wonderfully soothing. It was the one place Tara felt calm and free from worry.

Tara's family moved to North Carolina when she was a baby. Dad was tired of the pressures of city living and uprooted the family from their upscale Manhattan brownstone. Dad believed New York City would make them all crazy sooner or later. The stress of his job was taking a toll on his physical body. His cardiologist told him to make changes or he'd be a dead man.

Mom, who grew up in Brooklyn, loved the city. Her husband, a successful business investor, made it possible for the family to enjoy all the city had to offer—plays, museums and a social life of interesting and prominent people. The idea of moving to the ocean, not to mention the South, was hardly appealing. But she, as the dutiful wife, worried about her husband's near heart attack, agreed to make the move.

The South suited Dad. The slower, quieter way of living helped him to reduce stress, and his physical condition improved. The community was safe, a good place to raise a family.

The family's house on the beach was a delight for the children.

Tara was too young to notice the change in Mom, but her oldest sister, Sue, was acutely aware that Mom was not the same person she was in New

York City. In New York City, Mom was energized and ready to take on the challenges of a new day. She bundled up the three sisters and dragged them all over town, taking full advantage of all the city had to offer. There were parties, lots of parties in the well-appointed brownstone. Ellen remembers Mom always laughing and pleased with life.

When Dad moved the family to the South, Mom never recovered her zest for life. Instead, she became sullen and withdrew from socializing, feeling she didn't fit in with the community and couldn't relate to the women in her social circle. Her eyes, tired from crying behind the door of her bedroom, looked depressed. Mom never complained, but she wasn't her former happy self. Her bedstand was strewn with bottles. Sue said she took antidepressants and tranquilizers.

Tara's two sisters were quite a bit older and left for college when Tara was in junior high. Both went to schools in the North and rarely came home on break. Mom went to see them as often as possible, using them as an excuse to see her friends in the city.

Tara missed her sisters terribly. She missed their walks on the beach. It was lonely without her sisters to cheer her up, and Mom's depression was worsening.

Tara was a good student and liked school. She was a bit of a loner, but she felt accomplished in her school work. Her father was proud of her grades and told her she was probably the smartest of all the girls.

At home, life was tense. Tara's mom and dad rarely spoke to one another. Tara knew her mother was chronically unhappy and secretly blamed her dad for taking away her life in the city. She missed her two daughters and envied them for being back North. Mom was too depressed to notice Tara was losing weight.

Mealtime was unbearable. Too depressed to cook, Mom opened canned goods and placed them on the table. Although disgusted, Tara wouldn't dream of making a fuss. Dad rarely ate with Tara and her mom. In the evenings, both parents retreated to the den and quietly sipped cocktails most of the night. They never spoke; finally they drifted off to bed.

Tara felt guilty and sad about Mom's unhappiness. She too was lonely and missed her sisters. She rarely saw her dad, and she had a mother who was barely functioning. She had no one to talk to but the fiddler crabs in the sand. They were good listeners but could do little to help her figure out how to make the family happy again.

Tara threw herself into school work and rarely socialized. She quickly learned that good grades got her attention, so she studied day and night and graduated from high school with top honors. She wanted to go to college in the North, but she wouldn't think of leaving her mother in such a depressed state. Instead, she took classes at the local community college and tried to cheer up her mother. There were moments when Tara saw the old spark return to her mother's eyes, but it quickly faded, and life would go back to its tense and unhappy state.

Tara dated only twice and felt too inadequate and anxious to go out with men. She hated her body and felt she was too fat to be of interest to anyone. Not recognizing her social anxiety, she decided to diet. The more she lost weight, the more in control of life she felt. No one in her family noticed her weight loss. In fact, her mother was terribly thin, taking pills all day and drinking cocktails at night. Tara hardly ever saw her eat, and the canned goods she opened were unappealing anyway.

At the end of her sophomore year, Tara transferred to a four-year college. She chose a college close to home so she could regularly check on her mother. When Tara left for college, her mother's depression worsened. The marital relationship became more distant, and Tara wondered if her parents would separate. Tara often felt guilty for leaving her mom. She worried about her mother's state of mind.

Her dad's drinking increased. He became more and more distant from anyone in the family and was now spending weekends away. Tara tried not to think about what he might be doing, but she suspected there might be another woman in his life.

Tara focused more on her studies, but she was increasingly uncomfortable with college life. She compared her body to the women in the dorm and was determined to become the thinnest. She avoided men, feeling too afraid to date. Privately, she felt inadequate to handle the demands of the social life on campus. She retreated and became obsessed with thinness. Every day she exercised compulsively and studied hours on end. She took pride in her ability to resist food and not gain weight like the other women. Self-denial became her friend.

Tara met Tim at a medical conference on nutrition. He was taken by her beauty and intelligence. They talked for hours about their studies and discovered both loved the ocean. Tim, whose mother was also depressed, wanted to take care of Tara, and Tara welcomed the attention. They married after only a few dates.

Tara was terrified about sex. She felt too fat to be seen by Tim and hid her body by wearing baggy clothing. She made excuses to avoid sex. Tim was too tired from the demands of running his health food stores. Rarely did he see Tara. When Tim was home, he wanted to spend time with Tara, but she was going to aerobic classes. Too exhausted and too preoccupied with his new business, Tim didn't push for intimacy in the marriage.

Tara continued to lose weight. Periodically Tim would notice and tell her to get help. She complied, gained a few pounds and then went back to food restricting. Tara felt best when she was losing weight, even though she noticed her energy was depleting.

One morning as Tara was showering, Tim opened the door to say good-bye and was shocked by what he saw. Naked, Tara looked skeletal. He couldn't believe how emaciated she appeared. He waited. When Tara came out of the shower, he told her to get on the scale—eighty-four pounds! *How could I have not seen this?* he thought. "You have to get help," he pleaded.

Tim was upset. He didn't know what to do to help Tara. For the past year, he had denied the seriousness of Tara's problem and focused his attentions on his new business. When he did mention Tara's weight, she always promised she would eat and gain weight, but nothing changed. This time, she pleaded with Tim to give her one more chance: "Please, I can do this on my own." So Tim gave in, and Tara continued to lose weight.

Tim didn't know that Tara had struggled with anorexia for years. Now married, her anorexia worsened. She thought marrying Tim would make things better. After all, she found someone to love and take care of her. Unconsciously, she hoped Tim would be her "good mom."

Now aware of Tara's eating disorder, Tim watched her every move at mealtime and encouraged her to eat. He would sit with her for hours until she was able to swallow a few bites of food. Away from Tim, Tara ate nothing.

Tim was building a chain of health food stores. His hours were long, and the demands intense. When he was gone for days at a time, he could not monitor Tara's eating. He felt guilty and responsible, but he had to attend to the demands of his new business.

Tara's physical condition was worsening, and her day job as a hostess in a restaurant was affected—because she was too tired to make it through the day. She felt guilty because Tim needed her income. Tara's only thought was not to be a burden to Tim. She couldn't let him down. He needed her to be strong during this tough time of business start up.

Again Tim pleaded with her to get help. She promised but didn't follow through. Tim became angry and told her to see someone immediately. Because she didn't want to upset him, she called me.

I was very concerned when I first met Tara. Her physical condition was so severe, I referred her to an internist. The internist confirmed the need for hospitalization. She had to gain to at least ninety pounds, and neither of us believed she could do it alone. Tara refused to go to a hospital. We made an agreement. She had one week to show me she could gain a pound, or she would have to be hospitalized.

The next week, Tara dropped a pound, not gained. According to our agreement, she admitted herself to the psychiatric hospital. Her physical condition had to be stabilized. Tara was not thinking clearly due to her state of starvation, and she still wanted to lose more weight.

Tara was dying, and we both knew it. The anorexia had ravaged her five-foot-four-inch frame. She sat quietly in my office, looking more like a ten-year-old girl than a twenty-year-old woman. At eighty-four pounds, she was facing a fight for her life.

Tara felt hopeless and abandoned by God. Her sunken eyes stared desperately at me, "I don't want to eat because I am already so fat. I wish I could just disappear into the sand like the fiddler crab. Then I wouldn't upset anyone."

Seeing and hearing her intense pain, I asked Tara about her relationship with God. "God doesn't have time for me," she insisted. "There are too many people with bigger problems. I haven't been abused. I come from a good home. I went to good schools. I shouldn't bother God. Think of all the people who really need Him, like my mom."

Tara was wrong. She needed God. She needed Him desperately. She fought the staff whenever mealtime approached. She was terrified of becoming fat and highly anxious when food was placed in front of her. Her refeeding program was carefully monitored so she would gain weight slowly and safely. Still she trusted no one and refused to eat. The dietitian prescribed a liquid supplement to boost her calorie intake, but Tara fought drinking it.

In our initial therapy sessions, Tara had little to say. She felt empty, depleted and unwilling to comply with the eating disorders protocol of the unit. Instead, she wanted her husband to take her home. Like a sad little girl, she waited by the window for her husband's daily visits.

Her husband, relieved she was in the hospital, felt powerless to help her and knew she could die if nothing changed. At least he could go to work and know she was being monitored. Knowing Tara was in the care of people who wanted to help her, he tried to catch up on work and put in extra hours. Although she didn't say so, Tara was mad that he was not taking care of her. How dare he leave her in the hands of others? Repeatedly she told him she needed him and not the staff.

I confronted Tara on her attempts to get her husband to discharge her and not work the eating disorders program. It was time for her to learn to feed herself. It was time to face her emptiness and stand on her own. She responded with silence. Tara was mad at me. Like most anorexics, Tara would not admit to anger, but it came out through her refusal to eat.

Timidly she confronted, "I'm a little irritated with you. You keep acting as if I can make myself eat. Do you have any idea how hard it is to put that horrible food in my mouth at every meal?"

"Yes," I replied softly. "Do you know how hard it is for me to watch you slowly die? You have to trust me and eat. I'll help you any way I can, but you have to gain weight. You don't have to like it; it won't feel good, but you just have to do it." Since there was no way around it, Tara slowly gained one to two pounds a week.

As her weight increased and her thinking became clearer, Tara began to talk. She started telling me how inadequate she felt, how fearful she was of being alone. How worried she was about her mother and how disappointed she was in her dad. The more ill she had become, the more Tim tried to help her. When she was sick, he paid attention to her, and she felt special. She really never saw Tim as a person to know, but more as someone who could support her and be there for her.

She recounted times in her childhood in which she felt utterly alone and a burden to her parents. Despite all her efforts, she couldn't make her mom happy nor bring her dad back to pay attention to her. She talked to no one about her pain. Only the tiny fiddler crabs on the beach knew how she felt.

Tara, now a twenty-year-old women, curled up in my chair. Anxious about her weight gain, she whispered, "What will change? I'm scared and frightened. Truthfully, I want to lose weight. I know that upsets you and my husband. It would be easier if I could just disappear under the sand like the fiddler crab."

First and foremost, it was necessary for Tara to gain weight. Her weight was dangerously low, affecting her ability to function and think. If nothing changed, she could die. From the many past failed attempts to gain weight, I knew Tara didn't *want* to gain weight, and despite her good intentions, she would not be able to gain on her own. Being hospitalized forced her to eat and took the control of food out of her hands.

As she slowly gained weight, she could think more clearly and was less irritable. Her recovery involved much more than weight gain, however. Tara had to deal with underlying family and spiritual issues that contributed to her starved state.

The most important issue in Tara's healing was letting go of the tremendous responsibility she felt to fix her parents' unhappy lives. Sensing the tension throughout childhood and having no solution to the ongoing conflict between her mother and father, Tara set out to do what her parents would not—fix the marriage.

Finding herself powerless to make Mom happy and bring Dad back into the emotional involvement of the family, Tara felt inadequate and guilty. Not knowing what to do with those feelings, she turned them inward toward her body. She felt empty and lonely from having parents who neglected her emotional development and who unconsciously put her in the role of parenting them. Tara took care of her mother, and her dad let her do it.

Dad, ignoring his wife's unhappiness and distancing himself from his daughter, turned emotionally away from the family. It was easier to put his efforts in his work where he was consistently rewarded. Under mounting family stress, he reverted to an old familiar pattern—workaholism. Forgetting his near-death experience, he once again allowed work to consume him and numbed himself through alcohol when he had to be present in the home. He ignored his daughter who asked for nothing but was quietly wasting away.

Mom, feeling powerless and angry about the changes in her life, did nothing to resolve the situation. Instead, she became depressed and emotionally unavailable to her daughters. Her inability to take care of her own unhappiness left Tara scared and not wanting to burden her mother with the normal questions of adolescent angst.

Tara used to sit on the beach and ponder, "If I could be like the fiddler crab and burrow my body in the sand, I would be safe when life's waves rush over me." Down deep, she wished she could leave home like her sisters. She was mad at them for abandoning her and leaving her with a depressed mom.

Tara was in a terrible dilemma. Eventually she had to leave home but couldn't because of guilt and worry over her parents' instability. If she left, her mom would fall apart. If she stayed, she would fall apart. Better she than her mom, she thought. Her mom seemed so unable to cope with life. What if Dad left? Then Mom would really fall apart.

In order to reduce tension in the home, Tara tried to be the perfect daughter and give her parents no extra cause for worry. She would not burden them about her changing body, dating boys or problems at school. She didn't want to think about her problems. She was too worried about her family.

Tara felt lost and confused about many things, but so did her mom. However, the two never spoke about their unhappiness, but the underlying current was felt by both. Unconsciously she hoped Tim would be her new caretaker. She soon learned that Tim, like her father, was too busy taking care of himself.

Even though Tara only came to the hospital to avoid an upset with her husband, it was a start. On the one hand, she longed for someone to talk with her about her life On the other hand, she was afraid to tell anyone what she felt. It may be too much of a burden.

Anorexia was a way for Tara to hide her true feelings of anger toward her parents' neglect. Convinced that her parents couldn't handle her problems along with theirs, she didn't express any needs. She led others to believe she was self-sufficient, even though she was starving both physically and emotionally.

Anorexia gave Tara a false sense of control. She had to deny hunger and took pride in this. At first, Tara couldn't see her starvation as self-destructive. Tara was deceived. Since the enemy's purpose is to deceive and destroy, he was clearly at work in Tara's life.

Tara had to confront the deception of anorexia. She was killing herself. She prayed for God to open her eyes to clearly see what she was doing. In order to let God help her, she had to trust He wouldn't abandon her, too. Erroneously she believed that when things got tough in North Carolina, God, like her father, took off. She had to read her Bible to correct her understanding of God. God promised never to leave her or forsake her. He didn't take off when she moved. Her family stopped including God in their lives. He was there, patiently waiting, but was ignored. Tara and her parents tried to work out their difficulties without God's help.

Tara was afraid to call on God. She believed she was too far gone for Him to help. God would probably be overwhelmed by her neediness. I assured her He could handle the job and was a loving parent she could trust. He wanted to be there for her and to fill the void she felt. She had to depend on Him—not Tim or me. God was the only one who wouldn't let her down.

Like gaining weight, Tara had to trust that God would slowly and steadily help her. In many ways, Tara was still a little girl who never matured because of her concerns for her parents and their neglect of her emotional needs.

There is a verse in Luke that says, "The child grew and became strong in spirit..." (1:80). This scripture is speaking about Jesus' life on earth, but it also applies to Tara. She had to grow psychologically and physically and become strong in spirit. She had to believe that although it would be hard work, she could become a competent adult and give up trying to fix her parents. Better to put her effort in prayer where real change was possible.

We had to work on healthy boundaries with her husband. Tim was not the "food" police. She had to assume responsibility for eating and stay accountable to God, me and the doctor. Instead, her interactions with Tim were directed at developing a meaningful intimacy. Tim was not her "good parent." He was her partner.

Tara was changing. Through prayer and trusting God's Word, she was able to see the anorexia as self-deception rather than self-identity. She knew, through Christ, she could be an overcomer. It was time to put 1 Corinthians 13:11 into action: "When I was a child, I spoke as a child, I understood as a child, I thought as a child; but when I became a [woman], I put away childish things." With God's help, Tara grew up.

Giving up anorexia is a loss in and of itself. If you think of the disorder as a wish to stay a child and a way to have an identity, then giving it up means loss. The words of Jesus are so meaningful here. Jesus said in order to find life, you have to lose it. This is so true for the anorexic. In order to find life both literally and psychologically, she has to lose the anorexia. Grieving the loss begins the transformation to living, not dying. That's the hope of getting better. You are losing childhood, but you are giving birth to new life.

13

Facing the Loss of Structure—
Bulimia

In recent years, more people have talked openly about bulimia. You
may have heard Tracey Gold (*Growing Pains*), gymnast Cathy
Rigby, Ginger Spice, Jane Fonda or possibly the most famous self-
disclosed bulimic, Princess Diana, speak out about their secret
obsession. Why don't more women speak up? It's embarrassing to tell
people you eat out of control and then throw up. Shame is a big silencer.

When you are bulimic, you often suffer from depression, anxiety, substance abuse and other psychological problems as well. You might be an
episodic drinker—not drinking for periods of time and then going on
drinking binges. Psychologically, drinking binges are similar to food
binges. Alcohol and drug binges are more ways to numb the body from
feeling loss or pain.

Dieting can start the course of bulimia. If you are a girl who is overweight or has overweight family members, you can be teased by friends and family. Losing weight, you think, is a way to stop this teasing. Or you may have been anorexic and can't control your eating once you decide to gain the needed weight.

But issues around dieting are not the single cause of bulimia. Like anorexia, food is the abused substance, but there is much more of an internal struggle with yourself and an external struggle with others.

Bulimia usually begins later in the teen years than anorexia. It's also not uncommon to see women in their twenties and thirties struggle with the disorder. The reason for this seems to be related developmentally to the task of becoming independent and firming up your self-identity.

It's not easy for young women to figure out who they are and what they want to do with their lives, especially given the mixed cultural messages about the feminine role. In addition, family problems complicate the emotional side of leaving home. And certain personality characteristics like perfectionism, low self-esteem and mood swings complicate self-development.

Jessica was a young women who had a lot of confusion and started to binge. Jessica anxiously waited for her parents to leave the house to run an errand. She would have the house to herself for an hour—a prospect most teenagers enjoy. She waved good-bye, closed the door and then it started.

She popped a pizza in the oven and ate half of it; then she drank a liter of soda. She reached for the bag of chips and began to munch until the entire bag was empty. She wanted sweets. A gallon of ice cream was in the freezer. She finished half the gallon. Cookies go with ice cream, so she ate a half dozen. The rest of the pizza was sitting on the counter so she finished it off. She stopped, having eaten all of this in just twenty minutes. Jessica felt sick.

She made her way to the bathroom. Leaning over the toilet, Jessica knew the routine. She stuck her finger down her throat and began to vomit. Feeling dizzy and unsteady, she cleaned up the mess, turned on the fan and retreated to her room. Her hour of freedom was spent bingeing and purging. Such is the life of a bulimic.

Perhaps you read the story of Cherry Boone O'Neil in her book, *Starving for Attention,* in which she described a binge that included eating scraps from the dog's dish. Does that sound sick? It is, and that's part of the shame bulimics face. Binges feel totally out of control, so out of control that many women describe them as "taking over the body."

A binge followed by a purge is one of the symptoms of bulimia. A binge is the rapid consumption of large amounts of food in a short time period. Many women binge on sweets; some prefer carbohydrates; while others will eat anything they can find. I've seen women in therapy who have binged on uncooked macaroni, dried oatmeal or whatever was in the cupboard. One client binged on canned pumpkin. Pizza is a favorite, and ice cream is loved because it's easy to throw up.

Binges are usually followed by some form of purging behavior. Purging is doing something to get rid of the food eaten. There are lots of ways to purge, although vomiting is the most popular. You can also purge by taking laxatives, compulsively exercising, taking diuretics (water pills) or diet pills, giving yourself an enema, fasting and in some cases, using ipecac syrup to induce vomiting.

Purging follows a binge in order to prevent weight gain. When you are bulimic, purging helps maintain normal weight. Like anorexics, you fear gaining weight because you think your worth is determined by your body shape and weight. Purging also serves to relax you while "purifying" your body.

When bingeing and purging becomes a habit and causes physical damage, hospitalization may be needed. I've worked in a number of inpatient units that housed eating disorder programs. Most programs lock the bathroom doors of your room so you can't go in and purge. You have to eat meals and snacks prescribed by the registered dietitian. You are prevented from bingeing and purging, which really makes you anxious.

This structure of an inpatient unit leads to a lot of anxiety, because you are forced to eat and then have no way to purge. I've been amazed, though, at how creative some of my patients become trying to find a way to purge. Some try to compulsively exercise, vomit in trash cans or in the plants in the unit. One woman I saw was so desperate to purge that she vomited in the magazines in the day room. The urge to purge is so strong that women can become sneaky and sabotage their own treatment.

Reading this you are probably thinking, *Oh come on, do women really do this? It's disgusting.* The urge to binge and purge is hard to understand when you are an outsider. Men really think it's odd behavior and look at their daughters and wives with utter amazement. How can someone do such disgusting things? The answer is complex. (You expected simple?)

When you are anorexic, most people can tell just by looking at you because your physical body gives away the secret. When you are bulimic, people can't always tell because your weight may be normal.

There may be telltale signs of purging, such as swollen parotid (salivary) glands, dizziness, fainting, fatigue, burns on the knuckles or fingers from vomiting and dental enamel erosion. But the other medical complications are not as visible and include dehydration, electrolyte abnormalities, perforations in the esophagus, gastric rupture, constipation, EKG and EEG abnormalities, dry skin, pulmonary symptoms associated with vomiting, menstrual abnormalities and pancreatitis.

As you can see, the medical problems can be serious and should be taken as such.

There is no one "bulimic" personality. But if you have bulimia, you tend to feel inadequate, lonely, helpless, impulsive and moody. Low self-esteem is then coupled with very high self-expectations that you or others place on yourself. You may have trouble saying no to requests and demands, wanting to please others. You don't set good boundaries and are afraid if you do, someone won't like you. The ultimate goal is to be loved by and please everyone. Saying no to a request, assignment, job or anything means you might lose love or acceptance.

You lack a sense of balance. You do too much or don't try at all. You think in "all or nothing" terms. There are no in-betweens. For example, you wouldn't be satisfied with three As and two Bs on your report card.

You have to have all As, or you feel like a failure.

You are either all good or all bad, and you fluctuate between feeling these two extremes regularly. Consequently, you often feel burdened and overloaded (like a binge). Then exhausted, you try to do everything (like a purge).

You are overly compliant, and the drive for succeed is intense. You have to be the best, the top, the outstanding one, or you are a nobody. Since you are so outwardly compliant and in control, you rebel through the food by losing control. Then you feel bad that you have lost control (binged), worry about getting fat, try to get back the control (purge) and the cycle repeats itself.

You care deeply about what other people think of you. You live your life to please them. So instead of saying no or setting limits, you take on everything and then have to find a way to release the tension and stress that goes along with doing too much. But the way of release has to be secretive so no one will know you can't do everything you take on. Vomiting can be done alone, in private and doesn't affect anyone but you. It can release your stress, relax you and solve the problem of potential weight gain from bingeing.

You may have problems with impulse control. You have difficulty tolerating frustration. When something doesn't go the way planned, there is panic or terrible upset. You have little patience to sit with negative feelings and work through a problem. This was Barb's struggle.

IMPULSIVE

Barb was a twenty-three-year-old energetic women who was in college and working various jobs to finish paying for school. Like so many women with eating disorders, Barb got a job waiting tables in a restaurant. Her food binges occurred late at night when the restaurant closed and she helped clean up. Barb didn't like going home to an empty apartment. Feelings of loneliness bothered her and often led to a binge.

Barb binged and purged other times during the week and desperately wanted to stop. She was in a destructive relationship with a man who occasionally lost his temper and hit her. She tolerated his behavior because of her own low self-esteem, and she held the fantasy that her love would change his temper. I suspected that she also related to his feelings of inadequacy and impulse problems.

Barb's parents were horrified that their daughter was dating an abusive man. The family was well to do and embarrassed by Barb's bruises. If their friends knew that Barb dated a guy who beat her, they would be the talk of the town. People would know that Barb's family had problems.

Barb admitted that dating a man who was physically out of control was a way to get back at her parents. Dating a guy who was disturbed really upset them. She wanted them to be disturbed because she was mad at them. According to Barb, her childhood was lonely. She felt lost and out of control during her early teen years. She felt unprepared to deal with boys and felt she got no help from either parent in this area. Her choices of men reflected this.

Her parents, busy making money, never asked about boyfriends. When Barb was in high school, her parents handed her the keys to the car, gave her credit cards and told her to navigate the life of dating on her own. They were confident she could handle dating. They were preoccupied with other legitimate concerns about the family. One of those concerns was Dad's dying mother.

While Barb was the envy of all the other girls in high school, she hated the total freedom; she wanted her parents to guide her or talk to her about her feelings of inadequacy. She didn't feel competent or ready to take charge of her life. Dating a loser was an indirect way for Barb to get back at her parents. It was a high price for Barb to pay to make a point, but Barb didn't feel worthy of dating "healthy" men.

Barb was doing other things to get her parents' attention. Barb went through periods of fasting as well as bingeing and purging. She also drank periodically. When she drank, it wasn't one or two drinks. She got drunk. There was no moderation. Like the food, drinking was impulsive and an act of bingeing. As a result, she received several driving-under-the-influence (DUI) charges. Because she didn't drink daily or every weekend, friends and family denied the seriousness of this problem.

Barb also told me she used speed every now and then. When her bingeing was going full speed, the drug speed would take away her appetite and help her lose weight. She had a history of experimenting with street drugs; she admitted she liked using cocaine in the past. Barb had a lot of problems. Bulimia was only one of many in her journey to become an adult.

Barb represents one subtype of bulimics who have multiple addiction and impulse-control problems. She binged on alcohol, food and relationships. She numbed her pain rather than do the slow and difficult work of figuring out who she was and practice self-control. She had problems regulating her anger and being direct in her communication.

LOOKING FOR LOVE IN ALL THE WRONG PLACES

Like food, alcohol and drugs, sexual behavior can be impulsive and out of control. You can binge on sex, believing the more you have, the more accepted or loved you will become. Kelly was a young women who looked for sex to calm her anxiety about marriage and loneliness.

Kelly married an international trader and lived out of the country due to his job. The winter months were long, and Kelly's husband, Ben, was gone on assignment a lot. Kelly was lonely.

She described a father who was never affectionate to her while she was growing up. According to Kelly, Dad controlled the family with an iron fist. Mom had little to say about family decisions. Kelly saw her mother as a coward who was only courageous when she divorced Dad after he admitted to an extensive extramarital affair.

Kelly's mother was depressed and couldn't give much emotionally to Kelly or her siblings. The divorce occurred when Kelly was six years old. Her brother and one sister went to live with Dad. Kelly and another sister stayed with Mom. Her sister was thin, popular and a cheerleader. Kelly felt like the ugly duckling of the family and believed, from an early age, that if she were thin like her sister, she would be loved.

Eventually both parents remarried, and Kelly saw more of her dad after the remarriage. She soon discovered he had a gambling problem and bet on the horses. Kelly's mom married an alcoholic when Kelly was fourteen. Kelly was often caught in the middle of her parents' conflicts. To make matters worse, the stepfather teased Kelly about her weight, and Kelly became moderately obese.

When Kelly was twenty, she had surgery and lost twenty pounds. She vowed she would never be overweight again. Men started to notice her, and she loved the attention.

When Kelly was twenty-one, she tried to commit suicide by cutting her wrist. She didn't want to live alone and was deeply upset that losing weight didn't snag her a stable man. Kelly moved back home with her depressed mother and alcoholic stepfather.

Kelly finally married Ben because he was stable, though not affectionate. Ben didn't drink often, but when he did, he did to an excess. Ben's folks divorced when he was nine years old. His mother remarried a man who later died in a fire. Ben believed his stepfather committed suicide. Ben rarely talked about anything related to his past. He preferred the subject closed.

Ben was a good man who was kind to Kelly and tried to give her things to make her happy. Kelly was not happy. Her bingeing and purging became more serious, and she used alcohol and drugs at night to fall asleep. When she attended social events, she drank too much. She couldn't stand Ben's long trips away from home. His absence left her lonely, but his job gave her the financial stability she longed to have.

The bulimia worsened whenever she felt out of control with her life. Now married and unhappy, she felt bulimia was a very special private part of her life. It gave her an identity. It was her secret, and no one could stop her. Purging relaxed her from the stress of the day. It distracted her from feeling alone.

Kelly was lonely, and she went out for dinner quite often. She met men at the restaurants and became quite flirtatious. At first her flirting was harmless fun, but men started responding. She longed for passion, excitement and felt out of control with her sexual feelings. She was tempted to have sex with one of the men. She yielded to temptation and gradually started having one-night stands with different men. After having sex, the men would leave Kelly's house, and Kelly would binge and purge. She convinced herself that her sexual exploits were OK because she didn't love any of the men. She just wanted the excitement of sex and a man who, for an hour or two, would be consumed by her.

She started having an affair with a local executive. He was divorced and married for a second time. Kelly described him as very attentive to her needs. He was extremely affectionate and wanted to "binge" on her. She adored his attention. The affair grew more intimate, and Kelly's eating disorder worsened. She found herself thinking about this man all the time. She started making excuses to be out of the house. She couldn't get enough of his attention and sex.

Ben continued to be clueless and sweet. Kelly had pangs of guilt but learned to put the guilt out of her mind. She couldn't stand the double life or the thought of hurting Ben, so she didn't think about it. Instead, she thought about her need for passion and sexual gratification. Without it, she felt dead.

Kelly was stuck and reacting to her impulsive need for gratification because of an emptiness she felt inside. She was bored with a good man and loved the excitement of the affair. But she felt guilty about her behavior because Ben did nothing for her to treat him like this.

Kelly had multiple impulse problems, one of which was bulimia. Kelly chose to mess up the one stable relationship she had because she was more comfortable living in chaos and conflict. She also thought her behavior would satisfy a deep craving for acceptance and love. Guilt bothered her, but it didn't stop her. Kelly longed for someone to love her unconditionally and be passionate about her. Kelly needed an intimate relationship with God to fill the void she felt. Then she could work on finding true intimacy with Ben.

Bulimic episodes are most often brought on by stress, anxiety, boredom or an intense feeling of emotional emptiness. Hunger is rarely the motivation for a binge. Kelly didn't want to binge and throw up, but she found herself unable to control the urge when tension built up. Her tension was related to poor management of negative emotions. She didn't know how to deal with boredom, loneliness, feelings of emptiness or feeling unloved. Her way to handle these intense negative feelings was to feed herself with food, sex, alcohol or drugs—anything that might fill the empty hole inside. She learned from her family to numb pain.

Food thoughts are always on your mind when you are bulimic. You think about and plan binges. When will I be able to do it, what will I eat, what do I need to buy? Food distracts from the tough issues of living. Food gratifies, is always available and doesn't give you a hard time. Food is pleasure.

THE PERFECT TEEN

You develop high expectations of yourself thinking that perfection will solve your problems. But when you aren't perfect, you get really frustrated. If you are perfect, maybe you won't have to experience loss. Perfect people have no problems. Ask Amy. She tried to be the perfect teen.

Amy was the all-American girl who had a great future ahead of her. Bright and attractive, she accomplished everything she set out to do. She was president of the senior class, had the lead in the high school musical, was chair of the yearbook committee, a member of the band and orchestra, a national honors scholar, voted most likely to succeed, popular with most groups in school and president of the youth group at church.

As you can see, Amy's yearbook summary will read like a who's who among high school students. You probably guessed that Amy binged on activities. What people didn't know about Amy was the pain behind her so-called perfect life.

Amy never gave her parents any cause for worry. She was responsible and sensible. She achieved so often that achievement was the norm and expected.

One afternoon during the first semester of Amy's senior year, she came home from school and announced to her parents that she was now a vegetarian. According to Amy, the popular girls in her class refused to eat red meat. They skipped meals in the cafeteria and prided themselves on eating only low-fat yogurt or power bars for lunch. Junk food was definitely *déclassé*.

Amy, not wanting to be left out or less than the perfect senior, joined the vegetarian crusade. Like most of the girls, she didn't understand how to be a vegetarian. She just stopped eating meat and any food with fat.

When her diet drastically changed, Mom's cooking began to cause problems. Amy couldn't possibly eat what the family ate. It was too unhealthy. She asked if she could make her own meals. Her parents felt this was a harmless request and agreed. Mom and Dad were impressed with Amy's interest in healthy eating.

When salad became Amy's main dinner course, Amy's mom became concerned. Mom encouraged Amy to add other foods to her meals, but Amy refused, stating she had to stick with her vegetarian plan. In Amy's mind the list of healthy and "legal" foods was diminishing to only a few items.

For a while Mom tolerated Amy's vegetarian flight, figuring it was a fad and would soon pass. But it didn't pass, and Amy became more and more consumed with dieting and losing weight. Amy's mom noticed she was losing weight and once again asked her to eat more. Before long, Amy and her mom were locked in a power struggle over eating. Amy ate less, and Mom pushed more. Amy's weight dropped ten pounds. Mom knew the vegetarian diet was getting out of control.

The tension between Mom and Amy was heating up. The perfect teen was now asserting her independence over food. Her quiet rebellion caused an uncomfortable and unfamiliar friction between mother and daughter.

Feeling guilty about upsetting her mother, Amy finally promised she would eat more if Mom would leave her alone. Mom gladly agreed, hoping her daughter would go back to eating with the family again.

In true Amy form, she held up her part of the bargain. At each meal, she took a portion of what was served. She even added a little meat to her plate and occasionally asked for dessert. Mom was pleased and believed the problem was resolved.

The second semester of Amy's senior year became more stressful than the first. Amy was involved in her usual overload of school activities and still highly praised for her accomplishments, but Amy struggled to stay on top of it all. By the time she arrived home each night, it was late, and she was tired. But she needed to study. So late at night, she pulled out her books and worked until the wee hours of the morning. Then, she would catch a few hours of sleep and start her day early that morning. The sleep deprivation was taking a toll, but she couldn't let up.

Her dating life was another source of stress. Josh was a nice enough guy, but demanding more of her time than she was willing to give. He was too possessive, and she felt suffocated in the relationship. She wanted more freedom but was afraid to hurt his feelings. So she quietly swallowed her growing resentment and gave in to his demands. Josh was, after all, one of the most popular guys in the senior class. Every girl wanted to date him, and everyone said they were the perfect couple.

Despite all of Amy's academic success, she worried intensely about failing and letting others down. She found herself obsessing over her grades. Her new fear was that she wouldn't be accepted to the college of her choice. She had applied to Dad's alma mater and didn't want to let him down by not getting accepted. So she pushed herself harder. The more she achieved, the better she would feel, or so she thought. But she didn't feel better; she felt worse. She was tired, hypersensitive to criticism, depressed and moody.

Amy could tell she was more irritable and isolated from the family. After dinner she retreated to the upstairs and spent long hours in her room. Mom noticed Amy's isolation and mentioned it to her husband. Dad was oblivious to Amy's life. He reassured his wife that Amy was a great teen. She was no cause for worry. Amy was probably just going through a stage. Whatever it was, Amy would come out of it. She always did.

Dad wasn't the best observer of Amy's behavior. He was consumed with the intense demands of his work schedule. He was rarely home for meals, feeling the pressure of a new boss who was bringing in younger people for management positions. When he finally arrived home for the evening, he was exhausted and Amy was studying. He was grateful that Amy added no stress to his life. Amy had always been a great kid. Why would anything change now?

Dad was never good at talking much to Amy about her emotional or dating life once she became a teenager. When Amy was a little girl, he felt close to her and spent more time with her. They used to take long walks in the park and sit under the shade tree and play cards.

Dad was fun and enjoyed his time with Amy, but as she grew older, he felt awkward and unsure of his role as the father of a teenage girl. Uncertain as to how to be with her as she developed into a young woman, he unconsciously pulled away. He had no sisters growing up and was now living in a house with two women he didn't pretend to understand. So he did what his father did—he threw himself into work. Work, unlike relationships, was easy. If you followed the rules, you could be successful. He also felt the pressure of providing well for his family. He loved them dearly.

Mom, on the other hand, grew up in a family with little structure or organization. Her parents were successful people but routinely entertained, neglecting the care of their children. Mom was a lonely child who always felt responsible for the subtle but constant tension between her parents. Perhaps if she were perfect, the tension would lessen. When she tried to be perfect as a child, her efforts went unnoticed. Something about Amy's current behavior felt familiar to Mom.

Mom begged her husband to slow down and not be so obsessed about losing his job. He was a talented man and could always find another job if the boss pushed too hard. But Dad didn't want to lose his job to a younger man who could put in the long and extra hours. Powerless to make him change, Mom started building up resentment. She worried that Amy might sense the marital tension. She never directly asked Amy about it. Confrontation was not easy for Mom. She preferred to believe her husband and reassure herself that everything would work itself out over time.

One afternoon, Mom was cleaning up the bathroom. She found a towel that smelled sour stashed in the back of the laundry. She noticed the bottle of air freshener was almost empty. Didn't she just buy it last week? Something didn't feel right.

Mom mentioned the towel to Amy. Amy made an excuse about an upset stomach, but Mom wasn't satisfied with that answer. The air freshener was used up, and she noticed how quickly Amy left the table after every meal. Even more suspicious was the constant running of the bathroom fan. Amy was hiding something, and Mom wanted to know what it was. Things were not adding up. Mom pushed.

Too tired to fight and being the compliant teen, Amy decided to confess. What Mom didn't know was that for months after dinner, Amy sneaked upstairs and vomited in the bathroom. Amy cleaned up the mess masterfully, wiping down the toilet, spraying room freshener and turning on the fan so no one could hear her purge. There was no evidence of Amy's vomiting. It was Amy's secret. Amy found a way to relieve her stress and anxiety.

Amy was also bingeing. Thoughts of food ruled her day. All she could think about was her next binge. She hated herself and felt disgusted with her body. She hated feeling out of control but couldn't stop the binge/purge cycle. Nothing she did seemed to work, and she was tired. Thoughts of food coupled with all her responsibilities were overwhelming her.

Whenever Amy felt stressed, which was most of the time, she binged. Worried that she couldn't get everything accomplished, she binged. Unable to set limits with her boyfriend, she binged. Fears about grades and college acceptance led her to binge. She felt competitive with other girls and wanted to be the thinnest.

She binged anytime she felt out of control. Then, feeling fat and uncomfortable, she purged. It was a never-ending cycle that led her to depression. She wanted to isolate, feeling certain that if people found out what she was really doing, they would be disgusted with her. However, she could no longer hide. It took too much energy to maintain her perfect appearance. Amy wanted help.

The confession helped Amy's mom make sense of a nagging suspicion she had carried for the past month. Amy stopped fighting over food because she ate and then threw it all up. That's why Amy always left the table in such a hurry after mealtime. It wasn't because she had to study. It was because she had to make herself throw up.

Purging after a binge allowed Amy to remain the perfect daughter and not gain weight. Bingeing and purging allowed Amy to please everyone most of the time. However, the cost to Amy was great. Maintaining the perfect image while secretly struggling with an eating disorder took a toll on Amy's body. Amy was weary, having trouble concentrating and was food obsessed. She was ready to make a change, but she didn't know how to do it. She told Mom that she tried to stop the bingeing and purging for months and always failed. Perhaps it was time to get more help from one of those eating disorder specialists. That's when Mom telephoned me.

It was good that Amy realized she needed help. Her bingeing and purging were seriously out of control. She had to stop harming her body, which meant she had to stop trying to be perfect.

Amy wouldn't allow negative feelings to surface. She had them—hurt, anger, disappointment, fear, anxiety. But admitting to negative feelings was admitting weakness. No one could see that side of her. Consequently, Amy didn't know what to do when she felt bad. It was improper to rebel outright. Good girls do what they are told, don't complain and never question what is being asked of them. The most important thing was to look good regardless of how she felt.

Amy incorrectly assumed she had to be perfect or that no one would love her. No one could know that down deep she really didn't have it all together. At all costs, she had to appear strong and in control.

What Amy failed to see was that anything taken to an extreme is a problem. Perfection is an extreme and, in the natural, is impossible to accomplish. Adolescence is a time of defining the self, of taking steps of autonomy that sometimes lead to failure. Failure is part of the learning process. When Amy avoided failure, she didn't grow. She didn't learn how to deal with life's difficulties.

Amy also believed that if she was perfect there would be less tension in the house. Dad was already stressed by his job, and Mom was upset with him for allowing work to overwhelm him. Amy's eating disorder took the focus off the family stress. Amy could obsess over her body, which she believed she could control.

Amy, being the dutiful daughter, never wanted to rock the family boat by going against the rules. There were many unspoken rules that Amy figured out early in life. The most important one was succeed, and don't fail; be perfect, and nothing bad will happen; appear strong, and you will be strong; put on a good appearance no matter what goes on inside; weakness is bad, so never let it show.

Showing weakness was not acceptable for anyone in Amy's family. Dad appeared strong and in control. In reality, he was afraid to set limits on the job, fearing he might be replaced and wouldn't be able to provide for his family. He took pride in the fact that he was successful. Nothing would get in the way of his continued success.

Mom was not much help in showing Amy how to cope with weakness either. The lesson from her family was, "You are on your own." As a child, Mom found that prospect frightening. She received little guidance from her parents and always felt insecure and uncertain of her actions. Because of this, she depended on Amy's dad to make decisions.

Amy never allowed herself to fail. She learned from Dad that nothing was too difficult that hard work couldn't fix. When she realized she was upsetting her mother with the vegetarian diet, she didn't know what to do. She wanted to fit in with her peers and be the perfect vegetarian, but didn't want to upset her parents. Besides, it was hard to stay on the vegetarian diet. She had to deny herself foods she really enjoyed. The more she dieted, however, the easier it became, and she found a weird satisfaction in denying herself the pleasure of eating.

It was tough being perfect in high school. Amy couldn't imagine and didn't want to think about college. The idea of leaving home caused Amy to feel anxious. How would she do her school work, make decisions by herself, cope with other girls, date and compete with more talented young people at a big university? She felt overwhelmed just thinking about it. She preferred staying in high school where she could be dependent on her parents.

The perfect teen was beginning to fall apart. When it became too much pressure to please her parents, friends, school, church and others, the bingeing and purging began. She could eat what her parents wanted, not upset them and get rid of the food by vomiting.

When she began to eat foods off her vegetarian regime, they tasted so good. She felt guilty. She couldn't love the food, enjoy it and give in to the pleasure. But having deprived herself from the food, she binged. Worried she would become fat and feeling guilty for enjoying herself, she vomited.

The problem was that the bingeing and purging became more frequent as the stress mounted to always appear perfect. The binge/purge behavior got out of her control and took on a life of its own. She tried to stop and couldn't.

In order to stop the cycle, Amy had to give up the idea that perfection was possible. She was insecure, believing that the young woman God made her to be was somehow not good enough. As a Christian, she intellectually knew that perfection was not possible. (See Hebrews 13:20–21.) Only through Christ could she be made perfect. Sadly, Amy wasn't looking to Christ for help. She was trying to be perfect in her own power.

Philippians 3:12 says, "Not that I have already attained, or am already perfected; but I press on, that I may lay hold of that for which Christ Jesus has also laid hold of me." Amy had to give herself permission to fail, permission not to be perfect. She had to let God help her press on. She was not a finished work. No one expected her to have arrived at eighteen years of age—no one except Amy!

Amy had to allow people to see her true self, not the perfect facade she so impeccably maintained for years. For example, if Amy was more honest with her boyfriend about his demands, she risked not being the perfect girlfriend. If she told her parents about her problems, they would see her flaws and have to deal with her. Perhaps people wouldn't like the new, imperfect Amy.

She needed to know that it didn't matter if she was liked all the time. It was more important for her to be real and authentic in relationships. The only one she needed to please was Jesus. He knew her heart and wasn't impressed by her strong appearance.

When Amy was willing to embrace weakness as a part of her growth, she became free of the pressure to be perfect. She had to trust God and others to love her no matter how she behaved. She had to be willing to let others see her struggles and not hide behind the food. She had to stop pleasing everyone and be honest with her feelings and needs. As she became more comfortable with letting down her perfect facade, she took control of the bingeing and purging.

It was OK to relax, to enjoy herself and let down from the pressure of achievement occasionally. I even had to assign her to have fun, to not study for hours on end and to bring balance to all parts of her life.

Amy didn't need to be perfect before she could approach God for help. As we talked, she realized that she didn't call on God because of pride. Pride said she had to be self-reliant. Asking for help was weak and dependent.

When she realized that God was waiting to help her, to empower her to overcome her fears and weaknesses, she asked God to forgive her for pushing Him away. She didn't have to be successful for God to love her. He just did. Her unwillingness to receive His love was wrong. She was rejecting the sacrifice Jesus made for her on the cross. To not call on Him in the time of trouble was to say that His sacrifice was not enough and that she didn't need Him.

Today, Amy is striving for perfection, but not in a way that is unhealthy and prideful. She knows she can only be perfected through her relationship with Jesus Christ. It is not up to her to make everything perfect, but to let Christ use her weakness to make her strong.

In many ways, Amy's struggle with perfectionism was self-imposed.

Sometimes the issues are more clearly related to lack of family structure. Relationships are a source of much tension and strife. Families with a bulimic member are often chaotic places with little structure and con-flicted relationships. Conflict is not resolved and tension stays high, though not directly discussed.

Anger is an emotion not well controlled. Just like the bulimic, other members of the family don't regulate their emotions well and tend to operate on an all-or-nothing basis. Anger is often hidden away.

Shared meals are a rarity. Everyone is so busy doing their own thing that family time is not valued or can't be organized.

One of the first changes I ask families to make is to schedule one meal they can all share. You would think I was asking them to find a way to discover a cure for cancer!

Impulsive and addictive behavior is not reserved only for the bulimic member. For example, you might have an alcoholic father or a highly reactionary mother who can't cope and is taking prescriptive drugs for anxiety. Family structure is lacking, and no one has good management skills to bring needed balance.

MY LIFE IS A SOAP OPERA

Hope was another teenager whose family life was making her life crazy. Hope's parents had been married eighteen years and now were divorcing. The divorce was a nightmare. Dad was having an affair with the neighbor. The neighbor had a husband and family as well, but she was content to be Dad's mistress. Hope's mother discovered the affair by accident and was enraged with her husband. Her anger spilled everywhere, including to Hope. Hope began to worry about her mother.

Dad left the house, and Hope's younger brother, Adam, sided with Dad. He didn't care that much for the mistress, but Mom was impossible to be around once the affair came to light. Dad at least was calm and let Adam do what he wanted to do. Adam spent his spare time at Dad's new apartment, and Mom was livid.

Hope felt caught in the middle and sided with her mom. She felt guilty about her brother's lost loyalty and was equally mad at Dad. She hated what the divorce was doing to her mother and to the family. Her mother was stuck in anger, and Hope felt responsible to make her mother better. Since Dad and her brother deserted Mom, she felt she couldn't. Mom looked as if she were falling apart.

This all happened the summer of Hope's senior year of high school, and Hope was a mess. Her mom and dad were still having ugly conversations, and Dad was now bringing his mistress to family functions. Hope could hardly take it. Here was her mother, dad and his mistress. *This is a scene out of a soap opera,* she thought. *Only this is my real life.*

Hope tried to talk to her father, but he was angry that she couldn't get past the divorce and accept his now soon-to-be new wife. He saw no problem including her in family functions. She would soon be a legitimate part of the family. No one in the extended family was angry like Hope, so she should get over it and start making plans for college.

Hope was so confused. The bingeing and purging that started just prior to the divorce was in high gear. By the time she came to see me, she was one stressed teen. Her mother was angry and distant. Her brother moved to Dad's home. Her dad was mad at her for not accepting his girlfriend, and the girlfriend wanted to be her friend. It was enough to make anyone throw up.

Hope had to face the fact that as much as she hated her parents' behavior, she couldn't control it. She couldn't make her mom and dad reconcile. She couldn't stop her father from having an affair. She couldn't stop her brother from moving to Dad's house. She couldn't control her father's absurd views of God's grace. And she couldn't stop her mother from being so angry. It all felt so awful, and Hope responded by losing control.

The loss she had to grieve was the divorce. She lost her intact family, and nothing was the same. When she was supposed to be enjoying dating, her father was doing the same. Her father taught her to abstain from premarital sex, and now he was having it! She wanted her father home, talking with her about her dates, not talking about his.

She wanted her mother happy again and not feeling rejected. She wanted her brother home so they could talk and be friends, not split over where to live.

Deep down, Hope was mad. Under her anger was sadness. She wanted her dad back. She wanted him sensible again. She wanted him controlled and concerned about her needs, not his. Hope had to grieve, forgive and move on with her life. She was disillusioned but not defeated. With my help, she went on to beat the bulimia. Her healing came from accepting the losses involved with divorce, knowing God never left her and learning how to make her own decisions based on the beliefs she held dear. Her spiritual foundation had been laid even though her family was cracking.

CONFRONTING SEXUAL ABUSE

Sexual abuse may also be related to bulimic symptoms. While not all women who are bulimic have been sexually abused, sexual abuse and bulimia do coexist. Sexual abuse, as you know, can take many forms—fondling, rape, date rape, penetration, lewd gestures, pornographic acts, incest and so forth. Over the years, I have been disheartened by the large number of women who have been scarred by sexual abuse. This is one of the most horrendous forms of loss of control. It involves the loss of innocence, safety, protection, boundaries and the self.

Mandy's conversation with me is typical of how sexual abuse and bulimia coexist. Listen to Mandy talk about making peace with incest. She could not control her dad's sinful behavior as a child. Now as an adult, she was ready to confront the past.

"Mandy, how did you do this week? Did you food restrict or binge and purge? According to my scale, your weight is about the same."

"I restricted. I went two days without eating. Then I became so anxious, I binged and took laxatives. A lot of laxatives."

"How many is a lot?"

"About forty."

"Are you still taking laxatives?"

"No, I stopped."

"Good, I'm glad you were able to stop. Have you been eating regularly as well?"

"No, I've skipped a few meals."

"A few? How many?"

"Three, but I knew I would be seeing you today and that you could help."

"What triggered the binge? What was so upsetting?"

"I had to see my father this week. It was Father's Day, you know. We all went to church together, and then Mom cooked dinner. I just couldn't take it. Seeing him really upset me."

"So what made you decide to spend the day with him, especially knowing how upset you get every time you see him?"

"Guilt, I guess. You know, Father's Day. He is alive, and he is my father. As a Christian, I'm supposed to have forgiven him. But nothing has changed. He hasn't admitted to anything, and Mom still pretends nothing ever happened as well. How can they sit there so calmly, knowing what they did to me? All I could think about was bingeing. I felt totally out of control."

"What is it you want from your parents? You don't want to see them, but then you do. You want them to admit to what they did, but you never bring it up. I'm confused."

"Me, too, that's why I'm still having trouble, I guess. OK. I've thought about it. Here it is. I want them to admit to what they did so I don't feel so crazy."

"You'll be crazy if they don't admit to the incest?"

"No, you know what I mean. I want them to admit to what they did."

"But they may not, even if you bring it up."

"OK then, I just need to bring it up. I would feel better and more in control. At least then we wouldn't be pretending nothing happened. I've been trying to forgive, but it's hard when the incest has never even been talked about."

"That's really clear. Do you suspect they will bring up the incest on their own?"

"Well, they haven't yet, and it's been almost fifteen years now. Look, you and I have worked on this incest thing for months. I've dealt with my anger. I've tried to forgive them. I've been grieving the losses involved. I just can't let it go without saying something to them. But they never bring it up."

"So let's guess they will continue to avoid and act as if nothing ever happened. Here are your options as I see it. Bring up the incest and see what happens; join them in pretending it never happened; stop seeing them; or try to see them and deal with it alone. Can you think of any other options?"

"No. I've tried doing the last one you mentioned—not bring it up and deal with it in here and with friends, but that doesn't seem to help. I end up bingeing and purging after I talk about it. I don't want to stop seeing them. I tried that for a while and didn't like it. They are my parents. They are so old and pitiful now. I don't understand how they can go to church and act like they never did anything to hurt me. Wouldn't they feel convicted or something?"

"I don't know. You would have to ask them. But what your father did was wrong."

"I want to bring this out in the open, but what do I say? 'Hi, Dad. Did you know I hated you for years because you sexually molested me between the ages of five to eight? You had no right to touch my genitals and then rub your penis on me. And by the way, the time you tried to penetrate me hurt more than you could imagine. And Mom, where were you when this was going on, pretending not to notice—in la-la land? Didn't you wonder why I didn't eat for days? Didn't you think it was strange that I started losing weight and the doctor couldn't find a reason for it? Didn't you think it was odd that Dad insisted on putting me to bed every night and didn't want you in the room? What did you think he was doing in there? Certainly not praying like Dad said.'"

"Sounds like a good start."

"Are you serious? I couldn't say that to my parents. Not now. Not when they gave me money for college and are trying to be nice."

"You'd rather continue to have an eating disorder? It's easier to hurt your body than confront them, I suppose."

"Yes, no, sort of. I'm tired of this food stuff. First my parents hurt me; now I'm hurting myself. Great, who needs them!"

"So let's go back to how you can stop hurting yourself."

"I need to confront the sexual abuse. I can't ignore it, and I can't make peace with it without confronting it. I want to do it, but I'm afraid."

"I can understand that. The scary part is that you can't control how they'll respond. But you sound like you know what it is you want to do. Now let's think through what might happen if you do, and how you might handle it. For example, they may say you made the whole thing up. Or that it was in the past. Or they may get mad and not speak to you, cut you out of the will. It's also possible that they could be sorry and ask for forgiveness."

"What do you think they'll do?"

"I don't know. I'm not very good at mind reading! But I will help you prepare for any of those responses if you want to do this. I think you are right—your food problems are related to this issue."

Incest between a child and adult is never right. It is now recognized as the most prevalent form of child abuse. Even though the incest may not be committed in a violent or abusive way, it is still wrong; it is a violation of the child, and it damages the child in unseen ways.

Incest, in its essence, is a narcissistic gratification of the adult self and an abuse of power. There is no thought as to how this misuse of power and aggression harms the child. Children are not capable of giving consent despite recent trends suggesting they can. They submit to incest because of fear, powerlessness and naïveté.

In Mandy's case the incest was committed by her dad. He fondled her, rubbed his penis on her and tried penetration when she was five to eight years old. From the information I had, it was unclear why he stopped when she turned eight. Mandy did have a younger sister, and perhaps he turned his attentions to her and molested her as well. Mandy's sister wouldn't talk about it.

Family is supposed to be the protected place for children. All the while the abuse was happening, Mandy was told she was loved. For years, she held the secrecy of the incest, feeling powerless to do anything about it and accommodating her parents' unwillingness to address it.

It was a big step for Mandy to talk with me about the incest. Initially, she believed, as many do, that she somehow provoked the behavior and was a bad little girl. Of course, the incest was not her fault, and she was not bad. Her father, as the adult, was solely responsible for his out-of-control behavior.

The undercurrent of rage she felt was directed inward toward her body. It is not uncommon for sexual abuse to manifest in an eating disorder. In Mandy's case, she wouldn't eat, and then she would binge and purge. Mandy would get control (not eat), lose control (binge) and then punish herself (purge).

Mandy needed much reassurance that she was not to blame for her dad's wrong behavior. He was the offender, and she was not in control of the situation. She had a right to feel angry and yet still love her dad. This confused her, but it is often the case with children who are sexually abused. Hating what her father did to her didn't mean she had to hate her father. Her father wasn't abusive twenty-four hours a day, which doesn't minimize the impact of the abuse. It simply explains why she still loved him.

Mandy was determined to break the silence about the incest. She was stuck and was convinced she had to confront her father to get unstuck. She knew if she did this, her eating symptoms would improve.

So I began to prepare her for the confrontation. First, I asked her to write a letter to both parents. The letter to her father was to focus on how she felt about the abuse. Her mother's letter was to address feelings of not being protected. Mandy was not to edit these letters, but she was to write from her heart with no concern for their reactions. The letter writing was a way to help her identify her feelings and articulate them.

She was not to send the letters, but she could use them later in the confrontation if she so chose.

Second, I had her role-play the confrontation. I played her mother and father. We practiced every possible way her parents could react. She had to think through what she would say. This built her confidence. If she could anticipate a response, she could rehearse her reaction and be ready for anything.

Third, I had her pray about the confrontation. She had to exercise forgiveness over her parents many times and make sure she was doing this to improve her condition rather than blast them with anger. The confrontation would certainly disrupt family relationships, and Mandy had to be ready for this.

Mandy had to consider the possibility that her mother may not have even known about the incest. If so, this revelation would shatter her mother's view of her husband and shake the marriage. Mandy was not responsible if this resulted.

Her father stood to lose his wife and stellar reputation. He may deny or try to discredit Mandy. Mandy could not control any of this.

Although Mandy sensed a softening in her father with age, and intuitively felt he might be relieved to get the secret in the open, she wasn't sure what her mother would do. She decided to go forward with the confrontation. She was ready and clear about what she needed to do, knowing she couldn't control their reactions.

We spent the week in prayer about the confrontation—searching motives, expecting God to move in the situation and preparing for whatever may come. On a sunny Sunday afternoon Mandy went for dinner at her parents' house after church once again. She asked if she could pray before she began to talk with her folks about the incest. They agreed.

Firmly, but gently she addressed the secret hidden for so many years. Silence. Her mother started to cry. Her father looked away, and then the best thing happened. Her father rose to his feet and asked for forgiveness. Mandy could hardly believe what she was hearing. She prepared herself for his denial or his discrediting of her, but he admitted his wrong.

The three wept together for a long time and asked God to forgive. Emotions were intense.

After that Sunday, they all agreed to come for family therapy. The confrontation was just the beginning of the healing process. Her father was racked with guilt. He had given his life to Christ in his later years and knew he had to deal with his past sin. He lacked the courage to raise the issue himself. Weeks earlier, he had confessed what he had done to his wife. She was waiting for him to talk to Mandy. She was quietly interceding behind the scenes. Up until his confession, she was unaware that the incest occurred in Mandy's childhood. She apologized to Mandy for not protecting her, for not knowing and not confronting her father on many things.

Mandy called her sister to tell her what had transpired. She admitted to Mandy that Dad had also sexually abused her. She arranged to meet us in the next family therapy session.

As you would guess, Mandy's eating symptoms improved. She no longer binges and purges or goes through periods of not eating. Not all cases of incest end on such a positive note. This one did because of the courage of one woman and the life-changing power of Jesus Christ. Mandy's family found God and in the process found His forgiveness. The secret was out in the open, and the truth indeed set them free.

Mandy's family responded in a way I always hope families will respond when confronted with the horrible sin of incest, but many do not. Some become incensed at the accusation and do everything they can to hurt the person confronting the abuse. Others become distant and refuse to see or speak to the abused. Confrontation of sexual abuse is something to plan carefully with a therapist or knowledgeable helping person. You need to earnestly pray about your decision and ask God to help you. Your confrontation may not have the outcome you desire because we cannot control other people. And God does not force people to confront sin.

Also remember that sexual abuse can be perpetrated by people outside the family. I have dealt with cases of date rape and molestation by friends, stepparents, babysitters and other significant people. Sexual abuse is a violation. You are left feeling very out of control and invaded. Bulimic symptoms can reflect those out of control and shameful feelings.

FILLING THE LOSS WITH FOOD

Whether it's stress from trying to be the perfect teen or young adult, obsession with dieting that has gotten out of control, individual personality traits such as impulsivity or inability to manage negative feelings, family problems, sexual abuse or a list of other problems, know that bulimia involves loss. The loss is temporarily filled by food.

Loss cannot be successfully grieved when food is used to numb the self. You have to face the loss of control over food as symbolic of the loss of control in other areas of your life, or you will stay stuck. Food symptoms provide a distraction from the important issues related to emotional emptiness and grief. You can't be perfect and have everyone love you. You can't do what feels good and expect no serious consequences. You can't hide away feelings of anger or hurt and not expect them to come back in other ways. You can't avoid family problems and not expect them to be reflected in your other intimate relationships. And you can't go through the loss inflicted by abuse and not deal with the feelings of vulnerability and personal invasion.

Loss will be expressed in good or not so good ways. The key is to learn how to do express it without hurting yourself—to work through all the emotions to a point of acceptance. The power to do this comes from God's Holy Spirit abiding in you. He is the Comforter. He is the One sent to empower you and heal all your hurts and wounds. Jesus came to take our wounds. By His stripes we are healed.

14

Facing the Loss of the Thin Ideal— Compulsive Overeating and Obesity

Weight matters to women. No matter how emotionally healthy you think you are, you still obsess a little about your weight. Admit it. When you try on bathing suits in the spring, isn't it a little depressing? I could swear department stores install special mirrors designed to make us look like we all need liposuction. I've often thought I could have a thriving therapy practice if I just put two chairs in the swimsuit dressing room of any department store.

And what about those yearly physicals when the nurse weighs us? She always acts as if it's no big deal, which of course it is. We make certain that our shoes are off (that's another two pounds), our watch (gotta be worth a few ounces), our earrings (a few more ounces) and our jacket (easily a pound). Stripped to the lowest common denominator—a flimsy lightweight dress over underwear—we pray the scale will be kind.

After all, we fasted for a week prior to the appointment. That number better be low, because it stays in our chart for a year! It defines our success or failure.

Have you lied about your weight on your driver's license? Pull it out and take a look. Does it list your weight from high school or your actual weight now? Think about it. What if you get in a car accident, they take you to the hospital and mistakenly treat the one-hundred-twenty-pound woman instead of you, who weighs one hundred sixty pounds?

Or are you dieting because of a wedding, class reunion or special event? If we are going to see someone once in ten years, it doesn't matter how fat we've been during those ten years. We'll go to extraordinary measures to be thin for one day. Let's face it; we're all a little nuts when it comes to our weight.

Who can we thank for our corporate neurosis? Lots of people, actually—our culture, our race and ethnicity, our socioeconomic status, ourselves, our families and our biology. Our weight is influenced by all these things.

Weight loss is big business in America. We are desperate to find a magical way to shed pounds. We hate being fat because we've come to believe that fat is not where it's at. And yet a third to a half of us are overweight. We spend billions of dollars trying new products, pills, programs and anything else that promises to melt away pounds and give us the body of Cindy Crawford.

But the reality for most of us is we don't look like the *Sports Illustrated* models in a bathing suit, and we probably never will. For all the money spent on weight loss, we have epidemic rates of obesity. Why in a society so health-and-fitness conscious are we still so fat?

As you know by now, I never have a simple answer to any of these tough questions. But let's think for a moment about how our daily life impacts our weight. We eat tons of processed food, much of it high-fat, fast food, loaded with empty calories. We exercise very little and spend much of our leisure time in front of screens—movies, TV and computers. We are too busy to structure mealtimes and end up doing what dietitians call "grazing" on food all day long. We eat not because we are hungry but because of emotional emptiness and stress.

And food is everywhere. If you are a churchgoer, food is the accepted addiction. Every function has food attached—spaghetti dinners, pot lucks, coffee and donuts and so forth. My friend Diane, who hosts my Bible study, makes the best breakfast goodies! All the women look forward to sampling her gourmet delights!

How do we celebrate holidays and special events? We eat. What do we see every few minutes on TV? Food, glorious food. We can't live our lives without seeing, smelling and being tempted by food daily. Food is almost sensual. Some of you will argue, It is! I've had women tell me they would give up sex before giving up eating certain foods!

It's not easy to maintain a healthy weight. If it is for you, consider yourself blessed and hated by most women. Ask any woman; she will say she has at least five pounds to lose to feel better about herself. So how do we deal with this weight thing? How do we resolve our love-hate relationship with food?

BIOLOGY MATTERS

First we need to understand a few things in order to keep our expectations realistic. Let's start with our biology. Biology influences our body size and weight. There is a strong association between the weight of biological parents and children. If you have obese parents, you have a greater chance of being obese than if you don't.

Metabolism and growth patterns also influence weight and are genetically influenced. Fat cells multiply at three important times in our development—before birth, infancy and adolescence. Related to this, there are three periods of development that are conducive to obesity— late infancy, early childhood (about age six) and mid-to-late adolescence. Also, children who mature quickly may be more at risk for obesity.

There are many other biological factors that complicate our understanding of obesity. We discover more about obesity every day, but we still don't know everything. While biology is important to consider, you are not doomed to be obese because of it. Just remember that genetics play a role. You got what you got and have to work from there. If you inherited a high metabolism, be grateful. If you didn't, join the rest of us grieving this loss!

Once fat cells increase, we don't lose them. We simply shrink or expand them. If you have more and bigger fat cells than someone with smaller and fewer fat cells, you'll be fatter. This is an important and often depressing thought, because it means the fat cells don't just melt away. Go ahead and throw away all those products that make this claim.

When you gain weight, you gain fat cells that only shrink with weight loss. You are not shedding a bunch of fat cells when you lose weight (unless you have liposuction or surgery). Even though you keep your fat cells, the size is still influenced by the way you live and eat.

Have you ever been to a doctor who handed you a twelve-hundred-calorie diet and said, "You need to lose a lot of weight. Instead of two hundred ten pounds, you should weigh one hundred ten pounds according to the insurance chart"? I bet you felt real encouraged to meet the challenge. Handing you a diet doesn't help and is a setup for failure. You know how to diet. You could probably write books on the topic; you have dieted a number of times in your life. The problem is keeping the weight off.

Furthermore, you need to set realistic weight loss goals. For example, if you weigh two hundred ten pounds and have been obese all your adult life, you may want to begin by aiming for a twenty-to-thirty pound weight loss instead of one hundred pounds. This is more realistic than setting your sights on the one-hundred-ten-pound number. Any weight loss improves health. Be reasonable and don't set yourself up for failure.

Many of you gained weight after pregnancy. Pregnancy is one of those times we add fat cells. Sometimes it's hard to shed those extra pounds after the baby is born. I've known many women who never had a weight problem until after a pregnancy or two. And then there is mid-life and menopause to think about. The point is, people gain weight for a number of reasons. Losing weight is not simple and not just a matter of will power.

Most of us, particularly medical doctors, have little compassion for those who are significantly overweight. Discriminatory remarks and fat jokes are evidence of this. It starts young. I pounce on my kids if they make unkind jokes about an overweight person. You should do the same. My kids know that the person they tease could be Mom's client—someone hurting and trying to deal with her size. We don't make fun of people's struggles.

Just the other day my six-year-old came home from school and told me about a girl we'll call Alicia. "The girls in my class say that Alicia is fat. So Alicia doesn't get to be played with as much. Alicia must eat a lot of food." Six-year-olds already know how to discriminate based on body size.

They also make judgments about weight.

DON'T JUDGE

People choose to believe that all weight problems are a result of poor self-control and large consumption of food. This is true in some cases and not in others. To judge people by their weight is something we all have to guard against.

I was a member of the eating disorders team for an outpatient practice and ran several compulsive overeating groups. One of my secretaries, I'll call Ann, was responsible for checking in the patients prior to group. Group met just prior to lunch, which Ann ate at her desk. Ann was a skinny thing, who ate constantly and drove me crazy by eating at her desk. Obviously she was blessed with a high metabolism and thin genes.

Ann had her food strewn all over the counter—French fries, milk shakes, double bacon burgers, bags of cookies—basic junk. The women for my compulsive overeating group would come to the window to check in and be dumbfounded as to how this thin woman could eat so much junk and stay thin. We discussed Ann many times in group—how unfair it was not to be Ann. Ann was eating a high-fat, junk diet and was still as skinny as a rail. It was unfair, but there was nothing we could do about it except realize that Ann had a high metabolism and that when we ate like Ann, we put on weight. We could also hate Ann, which, of course, as good people we didn't.

I first learned the Ann lesson in college. I was a cheerleader and consequently very physically active. After our first away basketball game, the cheerleading squad rode the bus back to the college with the team. We stopped at McDonald's. Everyone piled out of the bus and placed their orders for the usual high-caloried items. My fellow cheerleaders ate like wild animals, so I joined in, thinking we've all been so active, we can eat this stuff. Well, *unlike* my fellow cheerleaders, I gained weight. It took me a while (and fifteen pounds later) to realize I couldn't eat like the rest of the squad and keep my weight stable. It was unfair, but it was my body! Thanks, God!

We have to stop comparing our bodies, trying to fit into a particular look. We've done this already—it was called adolescence. We have to learn to accept the body we have, grieve the loss of the perfect body, eat healthy and be sensible about exercise. If this sounds boring and trite, it is. That's the problem with this weight loss thing; there are no short cuts, no magical cures, no happy wands to wave over the fat.

We should also keep in mind that there are cultural factors, racial differences, ethnic influences, medical conditions and more that contribute to obesity. It's not my intent to go through all the research, but to simply let you know that many variables are involved in weight gain.

TYPES OF OVEREATING PROBLEMS

I do want to talk about what happens emotionally when we are overweight or obese. Before I do though, let me clarify the different types of overeating problems. First there is something called *binge-eating disorder*. This is similar to bulimia in that eating feels out of control and bingeing occurs. The difference from bulimia is that there is no purging. You binge until you are uncomfortably full, but you don't throw up, take laxatives, diet pills or do anything to get rid of the extra weight put on by the extra eating.

Binge-eating is distressing because of the lack of control felt over eating. It becomes a habit, taking place at least two days a week, for a period of six months or more. If you regularly binge and don't purge, you gain weight. This adds to the upset associated with feeling out of control.

Another type of eating problem is compulsive overeating. This too is uncontrolled eating that is followed by guilt and shame. Compulsive overeaters can be bingers. They can also be "grazers," which means they eat constantly throughout the day. They don't eat because they are hungry but because they are emotionally empty. Food is used to cope with stress, emotional conflicts, daily problems. It is used to soothe and block feelings, and it usually begins in childhood.

Obesity is not a psychological problem. It's a medical condition defined by an excess of fat tissue resulting in impaired health. Most medical doctors consider weight that is 20 percent over your ideal body weight as mild obesity. Obesity is categorized by mild, moderate, severe, morbid and super-morbid depending on the percent overweight you are from an ideal (usually based on insurance charts or something called body mass index—BMI).

Obesity is cause for concern because of potential medical complications—high cholesterol, high blood pressure, diabetes, increased risk for gallbladder disease, heart disease and some forms of cancer, stroke, respiratory disease, arthritis and gout to name a few. Not everyone who is obese is ill, and some diseases like high cholesterol can be inherited apart from obesity.

When you think about your own issues with food, you should keep in mind a few things if you are considering trying to lose weight or gain control over eating. These questions are important because they influence how easy or hard it will be to reach your goal:

1. Have you been overweight since childhood?

If so, it may be harder to lose weight than someone who put on weight as an adult.

2. Are other people in your family overweight?

You already know that if they are, you may have inherited a biological predisposition to weight gain.

3. Do you have any underlying disease state like hypothyroidism or Cushing's syndrome?

See a physician first to make sure disease is not the cause of weight gain.

4. How overweight are you?

The more you have to lose, the more discouraging it can be to stay with a plan. You may need extra support.

5. Are you realistic about how much and how long it may take you to safely lose weight?

Don't go by the insurance chart or some ridiculous number a medical person has handed you. Start by setting the goal to lose 10 percent of your current body weight. Consider weight loss of one to two pounds a week as successful. Also, don't engage in betting contests with men. Generally speaking, men lose weight faster than women.

6. Do you binge, deny how much you eat or tend to make excuses for overeating?

If you do any of these, don't start a weight loss program until you are honest about your behavior. You'll just fail, and you don't need that.

7. Do you use food to comfort yourself?

You may want help from a therapist in order to connect eating with feelings. Losing weight without addressing the emotional component won't be successful in the long run.

8. Do you have people who will support your efforts?

When we have social support, we do better and keep the weight off.

9. Are you willing to make lifelong changes and give up dieting?

Weight loss isn't a time-limited deal. You are committing to a lifelong change in the way you eat and think about food.

10. If you never dropped a pound, would you still be a worthwhile person?

Your feeling of self-worth should not be tied to your weight. I know we feel better when we lose weight (although some women actually feel more vulnerable), but we need to love ourselves regardless of our weight. Jesus doesn't love you because of how you look or your size. He loves you because of you. He loves unconditionally.

SOCIAL AND INDIVIDUAL PAIN

Whether you binge, graze, overeat, have a low metabolism, are predisposed to obesity or whatever, you share similar social and psychological challenges. No matter the reason for your overweight, you are stereotyped. It's unfair and wrong, but true.

There is a social bias against overweight people. If you are an overweight woman, you are less likely to marry, get into college and be promoted on the job compared to thinner women. I already mentioned that doctors and other health professionals can be insensitive to you. Watch the face of the person you sit next to on an airplane, particularly if you are assigned a middle seat. Any one of you could give plenty of stories about the social prejudices and the discrimination you have felt being overweight.

In addition to the social stigma, there is personal pain involved in obesity. You typically hate your body and feel it is "gross." You rarely look at your full body in the mirror. You loathe yourself because of the fat.

A few groups and some famous people have spoken out against the self-hatred obese women feel. They have encouraged self-acceptance at any weight. Obese women are so much more than their weight, and we need to look beyond the external to see the person.

Thin people ask, "If it is so difficult to be fat in today's world, why don't people do something about it?" Thank you for that informed and sensitive question! The answer is complicated, as we've already stated, but let's try to understand more of the psychological side of overeating.

Other than self-hatred, which can lead to depression and anxiety, there is isolation and social alienation with which to contend. Girls who are overweight live in a world where their bodies are a focal point of conversation, fashion, dating and socializing. When they don't meet the standard "look" of their peers, teasing results. This cruelty reinforces a poor sense of self and a wish to drop out from the social scene. Dating can be nonexistent. They become the brunt of cruel jokes, and food becomes the one thing that is kind and comforting.

Overeating can also begin when loss piles up. Food is used to fill the emptiness or neglect that results from having no one in your life to properly nurture you. Food becomes your friend.

UNNOTICED

In my experience, most of my binge and compulsive overeaters faced numerous losses in their lives. The social histories typically include divorce, neglect, abuse, alcoholic parents, rejection and loneliness. They have experienced loss after loss and feel stuck—stuck using food to soothe and protect from pain. Jan's life was full of loss.

Jan was a very creative woman who aspired to be in film production. However, her day job was spent training people in computer skills. She was a valuable asset to the training company, yet she felt unappreciated in many ways. Her boss was a jealous man who often took credit for Jan's ideas. He demeaned Jan in front of other staff and excluded her from important meetings. Jan saw her boss as an insecure, married man who wanted to climb the administrative ladder. He used anyone or anything to boost his career. Jan, who was passive when it came to asserting herself, said nothing and quietly built resentment inside.

Jan's job stress was not the reason she came to therapy, although it was often the topic of therapy sessions. Her main concern was her growing weight and inability to control her eating. The closer to two hundred seventy pounds she became at five feet two inches, the more she was depressed and worried about her health.

She hated her body and wouldn't look in a mirror below her neck. Daily events, however, reminded her that her size was becoming a problem. There were times of humiliation when she couldn't fit into the class chairs, squeeze past a line of people, walk the stairs or put on her panty hose. When she tried to exercise, her legs rubbed together and her joints hurt. Buying clothes was a nightmare. She hated walking in those big lady stores and buying dresses that looked more like tents than anything to wear.

Even though she hated her size, the bingeing was out of control. Candy was her biggest enemy. She craved it, thought about it all day and had secret stashes hidden in her desk. The more she tried to resist, the more she wanted it. The more she tried to lose weight, the more she seemed to gain. Nothing seemed to detour her mind away from thinking about bingeing. She was scared—two hundred sixty-four pounds and gaining.

Jan had not been overweight as a child. Her weight gain was a slow and progressive process that began in junior high school. Jan's father was killed by a drunk driver when she was in grade school, and her mother couldn't support nor care for Jan and her three siblings. Consequently Jan and her siblings were sent to live with an aunt. Jan's memories of her aunt's home were not pleasant. Her life consisted of school and chores. Pleasures were few and far in between.

Jan's teachers were harsh and tolerated none of her creativity. Her aunt made her clean and take care of the younger children. Food was doled out and she was always hungry. Often, she would hide a snack or two in her room, but she paid a high price if she was caught. Whenever she could get candy, it was a special prize to be cherished.

Jan's time at her aunt's house was a blur in her memory. All she could remember was that no one noticed her or paid her any special attention. She always abided by the rules and stayed out of trouble. Attention meant she did something wrong. Food became her friend. Food gave her pleasure and helped her forget the loneliness she felt.

When Jan entered junior high, her mother had a good job and enough money to bring the children back to her home. So Jan moved back home and suddenly had access to food. This newfound freedom was hard to control, and she started bingeing. She could open a cupboard, get a snack day or night and no one stopped her.

Not much changed in Jan's life other than the freedom to eat. Her mother worked long hours to support the family, and Jan had to work constantly in the home preparing meals and doing chores.

Jan's intelligence helped her get through school. She was able to breeze through school and graduate with honors. Finally free to be on her own, she set her sights on college. Ready to pursue her own interests, Jan began to lose weight. She studied film production in college but got her first job in computer training. Excited by her independence and success, she rented an apartment and started to make contacts in the film industry. For a while, she was content. Computer training paid her bills while she explored entry into the film industry.

Slowly the bingeing returned. Upset with the weight gain the binging brought, she would not eat for a day or two. Then hungry, she would binge again. Finally she would get her bingeing under control and try to eat sensibly. The result of bingeing, then fasting for days was a slow, steady weight gain of a few pounds each month.

Desperate to find a way to lose weight, she tried every diet imaginable— Cambridge, *Weight Watchers,* protein only, high carbohydrate—whatever was the fad and promised to change her life. Then she discovered liquid dieting. It worked. All she had to do was make a liquid shake, drink it and be done with food. She lost weight and didn't have to make any food choices. If she didn't eat, she didn't binge. This all-or-nothing approach to eating suited her. She simply chose not to eat.

When Jan met her husband, Randy, she was quite thin because she had been on a liquid diet for months. Even on her wedding day she fasted. Fasting was the only way she stayed thin and in control. But fasting for months was taking a toll on Jan's body. Feeling faint, light-headed and looking very thin, she was advised to go off the shakes and start eating solid food again. When she did eat, the bingeing returned.

Jan's weight crept up to one hundred fifty pounds, but she wasn't alarmed. To her delight she was pregnant with her first child. The forty-five pound weight gain didn't bother her—she was eating for two. When

Elizabeth entered the world at nine pounds, Jan was overjoyed. She had a daughter to love and cherish. Elizabeth was a good baby and the delight of her parents, but Jan couldn't shed the extra pounds from the pregnancy. The bingeing returned, and she steadily gained even more weight.

Years later, when Jan made the appointment to see me, she was at her highest weight ever—two hundred sixty-four pounds. She was scared and felt totally out of control. Her comment was, "If I don't do something, I'll soon be three hundred pounds!"

What seemed to be significant in the initial interview was that despite all Jan's success, she still felt unnoticed. Her boss treated her poorly, her husband had little to say to her and was busy with his new entertainment law practice and her child, now eleven years old, was pulling away and spending more time with friends. All Jan seemed to do was go to work and then work at home, taking care of a husband and daughter. The familiar feelings of childhood returned. The felt emptiness of her life led to bingeing again.

Jan's level of insecurity was staggering despite how competently she functioned. When it came to work, she was organized, on time and masterful at what she did. Everyone expected Jan to be responsible, and she was. But she wanted more and was growing inwardly resentful that everyone in her life wanted her to give to them. The only thing that gave her pleasure was food. It was always available to her.

The more Jan was successful at her job, the more people expected of her. Her passive stance allowed her boss to continue to take advantage of her and not promote Jan. The more responsibility she took on in the home, the more her husband let her do things. Her plate was full, too full, and she started to feel depressed. Who would take care of her? Who would notice she was crumbling like the cookies she binged upon every day?

Apparently no one. So Jan grew bigger and bigger until finally someone noticed—her husband. Her weight was beginning to turn him off sexually. He complained that he was losing interest because of her weight.

Jan had to get control of her bingeing behavior. She felt so out of control, and it bothered her terribly. The extra weight was physically uncomfortable and was disturbing her sense of self. Even though she was two hundred sixty-four pounds, she thought of herself as one hundred fifty pounds. She was in denial about how big she had become.

I assigned her to regularly look in a full-length mirror undressed. I did this because Jan was in denial about her size and developing health concerns. Not looking at her full body helped her deny the extra one hundred pounds on her frame. As a result, she lost motivation to address her weight concerns.

The bingeing was based on a number of emotional and interpersonal factors. First, Jan was unhappy in her job and had stored up anger. She resented her boss but wouldn't confront him. Her first task was to figure out if she wanted to stay in her job, change positions, leave or do something else. Since she was unsure of what she wanted to do until a position in film came available, we listed pros and cons for each of the options. Looking at the list helped her make a decision to leave her current position. She didn't believe asserting herself would create change at the training facility. There were too many political issues involving her boss.

So Jan began exploring other positions and worked on her film production interests. Instead of agreeing to extra projects that were dumped on her without compensation, she learned to say no and spend her extra time away from the office contacting friends in the entertainment industry. Eventually Jan changed jobs and planned to work her way into a film production company.

Second, Jan had to learn to be assertive and speak up when she was overloaded with work. This wasn't easy, because she learned to comply with whatever people told her to do with little thought of how she felt about it. She did have feelings, but they were buried. Instead of dealing with people directly and setting limits, she ate her anger.

Jan's thinking was also challenged. Her approach to problem-solving was to act in an all-or-nothing fashion. Either she took on too much or was passive. There was no moderation, no middle ground, no negotiation. The same was true of food. She fasted or did liquid. Eating in moderate amounts was very hard because she would lose control. Regulation of both responsibility and food were linked together. As she balanced her load, she felt less burdened and less stressful, which helped her balance her eating.

Losing control was related to feeling out of control. Since childhood she felt small and insignificant. As a child, she had no power to make changes and felt resigned to do what others told her to do. She carried this notion into adulthood, feeling powerless and resigned to do whatever others told her. Consequently she felt out of control and binged.

She had to learn to distinguish situations in which she was truly powerless from those in which she wasn't. When appropriate, she had to take control by asserting herself. This was no easy task, considering she didn't know what she wanted or needed.

Much of the work was spent helping Jan determine who was hiding under the layers of fat. Her fat served a purpose. It hid her from confronting life. She could always blame being overweight for all her problems and not look at her inability to identify her needs, make decisions and assert herself. Her weight was not the problem (although it was causing health problems). Her lack of self-definition, assertiveness and balance were problems.

We also talked about how her big size made others notice her and take her seriously. She often mentioned how small and insignificant she felt as a child and how this feeling stayed with her throughout adulthood. Her size made people notice, but she was ambivalent about being noticed this way. She drew attention to herself, but for the wrong reasons.

Her size finally got her husband's attention as well. His preoccupation with his law practice bothered Jan, but she never mentioned it. She figured he was working to provide security for the family, a major issue for her given her history. Thus, she had no right to ask him for time or attention. Again, this was totally out of balance. He could provide security, but not at the expense of ignoring his wife and daughter.

Jan's discomfort with her size also helped her hide from growing intimacy problems with her husband. He used work as an excuse, and she used weight. The distance between the two seemed to "just happen" as they developed their careers and raised their daughter. Her husband was ready for changes. The marriage lacked passion. Jan was also ready for change. She longed for true intimacy and unconditional love.

Jan's case illustrates many issues important to the compulsive overeater. Jan experienced major losses in her childhood. She had no sense of security, lost both primary parents in her life and lost dreams of who she was and could become. She learned to be compliant because any disobedience was met with rigid criticism. Jan was dependent on others to take care of her. She was passive when it came to her own needs. Rarely did she *think* about or *identify* her own needs, because most of her life was spent taking care of others.

Jan felt deprived both physically and emotionally. Food filled her up and was used to pacify the empty feelings and anger she often felt. She binged when she was anxious and unable to confront her anger directly. Jan needed to be more assertive and set boundaries.

Jan was uncomfortable with her body and out of touch with her sexual self. Her fat was a way to keep her husband distant and keep her own sexual impulses hidden. If any man paid attention to her, she worried she might feel attracted and unable to control herself. She was secretly angry with her husband for neglecting her needs and always demanding she do for him and their daughter. She told me she was too angry to feel sexual toward him. Her need for love was great. Food, love and sex were all confused in her thinking.

Food is an available object that gives pleasure and is often used to calm anxiety, cover anger, protect from sexual issues and much more. We have to eat, so food cannot be avoided. Food doesn't give you a chemical high like alcohol and drugs, but food can be psychologically addicting. Food is often equated with love. If you experience a lack of love, you can fill yourself with food. Food fills the empty places.

We eat when we are anxious. Even as I write this book to make the deadline, my intake of cookies and chocolate has increased. Food is calming and soothing. We eat out of anger, too. Remember, we go internal with anger. It's safer to go to food than assert yourself in a situation that could get ugly.

We eat to protect ourselves sexually. In Jan's case, she was afraid of her own dormant sexual feelings. She knew if a man started coming on to her, her self-control was questionable. In her case, the fat kept men at a distance and kept her from feeling sexy.

ABUSED

Other women keep a protective layer of fat because they have been physically or sexually abused and mistakenly feel that they did something to incur the abuse. Gail's story is one of those cases.

Gail lived on the west side of the city of Chicago. Her husband, Dave, was a respected mechanic down at the local garage. He was a steady man who had held the same job for the past fifteen years of marriage. The couple lived in a well-kept multicultural neighborhood where people were friendly and concerned about the safety of their children.

Gail and Dave faced the same problems most middle class families do, nothing earth shattering, just everyday "normal" stress. They worked hard, paid too many taxes, budgeted their money and went to church on Sundays. Gail's two children had their basic needs met, and Gail couldn't complain.

As Gail drove her children to school each day, she passed by the house she grew up in as a child. Still standing on the original lot, still the ugly green that her father painted it, the house was a sobering reminder of unpleasant times. Most days, she looked away and wouldn't think about her past. Occasionally one of the kids would yell, "Isn't that the house that Grandpa lived in before he died?" Gail nodded and reached for a candy bar. Some days she couldn't get those memories out of her head.

One cool October evening, the family was driving to a nearby suburb for the obligatory family get-together. Tonight it was at the home of Gail's youngest brother, Sam. Gail had two brothers, one older and one younger than she. When her mother died two years ago, Gail promised to stay close to her brothers.

Her oldest brother, Jack, lived on the north side of the city. Gail liked Jack but was uncomfortable around his family. Jack was the only one of the three who went to college and landed a high-paying job. He married and moved his family to an affluent suburb. Gail always felt out of place whenever she visited. Jack welcomed her visits but her sister-in-law had little to do with her. On the few occasions her sister-in-law spoke to her, she talked incessantly about things she bought and suggested Gail try dieting. Gail, at two hundred fifty pounds, knew her sister-in-law was embarrassed by Gail's weight. The sister-in-law wasn't more than one hundred pounds dripping wet. Gail suspected she was probably anorexic.

Tonight, it was Sam's turn to host the family dinner. Gail didn't like going to Sam's anymore than Jack's for very different reasons. Sam's drinking was becoming more and more of a problem. Recently laid off, he was moody and out of sorts. Gail hated Sam's drinking. It reminded her of Dad. Just the smell of alcohol brought back horrible memories. And Gail tried hard *not* to think about Dad.

As they pulled into the driveway, the kids jumped out of the car and met their cousins. Gail's daughter, Cindy, was fourteen years old. She was a cute kid with a lot of personality. Billy was quieter and going through that awkward age. Off the kids went to be with their cousins, and Gail made her way to the kitchen to help the women prepare the meal.

Sam was already pretty loaded when they arrived, and Jack was scolding him for drinking too much. Angered, Sam took a walk to the basement to cool down. He found Cindy alone playing a Nintendo game. As he approached her, Cindy smiled and asked if he wanted to play with the other joy stick. He declined but moved toward her and grabbed at her breast and thighs. Cindy pulled away, but he grabbed for her again. He pulled her down and was groping her all over. Cindy struggled free and ran upstairs. Visibly shaken, she asked her mom to take her home now. Gail tried to get her to say what was wrong, but Cindy wouldn't talk and was screaming she wanted to leave. In order to avoid a scene, Gail and Dave rounded up Billy and climbed into their car to leave.

At home, Gail tried to calm Cindy down again and get her to talk about what happened, but Cindy refused to speak. She just cried and rocked herself in her room. Cindy was mortified by Uncle Sam's actions. How could he do such a thing? Maybe she did something to provoke him? She was confused and ashamed and told no one about the incident.

For months Gail tried to get Cindy to tell her what happened that night at Uncle Sam's, but Cindy insisted it was over, and she didn't want to talk about it. Maybe Gail had overreacted. Months went by, and Cindy was gaining weight. This concerned Gail. Something was wrong with Cindy, and she knew the extra weight would bring her more problems.

Cindy's weight kept climbing up. Gail's cute, outgoing teen had become isolated and withdrawn. Teased relentlessly about her weight in high school, Cindy finally broke her silence and told her mom what happened the night they were at Uncle Sam's. Cindy cried, and Gail tried to comfort her. Gail struggled to keep her anger from exploding. Cindy figured her "fat" would protect her against future sexual advances from Uncle Sam. It seemed to be working, because he left her alone at family dinners. But Cindy was miserable and could no longer carry the secret.

Gail left Cindy's room and was livid. She wanted to wring her brother's neck. First, she had to help Cindy, but how? Like Cindy, she used food to hide her pain.

Gail sat on her bed and immediately flashed back to her childhood. Unlike Cindy, Gail *always* had a weight problem. Ever since she was little, her father repeatedly called her names and said crude things about her weight.

Dad was an angry man, always in and out of a job. Whenever he was angry about anything, Gail was the target. Dad rarely picked on Gail's brothers because they would hit him back. He beat Gail every time he came home from a drunken rage. He told her what a disappointment she was to him. After slapping her around, he would tell her no one would want such a "fat pig." Gail was beaten and demeaned weekly, sometimes daily, for years growing up.

Gail's mom was also beaten by her dad and felt powerless to help Gail. Scared and dependent on her husband to pay the bills, she wouldn't leave. In the evenings, Gail's mother worked a part-time job to make ends meet. She hoped some day it would turn into a full-time job so she could leave her husband and take the children. Gail was beaten in the evenings when Mom was at work.

Food became Gail's comfort and friend. The food was always available to make her feel good. It was one of the few things in her life that brought pleasure. She often hid food under her bed and binged after her father beat her. Food could soothe and calm her down. As she binged, she would become numb to the abuse.

Gail's weight steadily increased in high school, especially when faced with dating and socializing. Men could be hurtful, and food was safe. So she continued to eat and distance herself from men. So she understood Cindy's comment about fat protecting her. She too believed that staying heavy would keep men at a distance.

The beatings seemed to lessen the older and bigger she became. She didn't know why, but during her senior year, her father resorted more to verbal abuse—calling her names, telling her no one would ever want her and making derogatory comments about her body.

At the first chance, Gail left home. By the time she left home, her oldest brother, Jack, was long gone and had escaped from the family madness by going to college. Sam joined the military at the first opportunity, and Gail just moved out and looked for a job. At eighteen, Gail met Dave, who was in the military and treated her kindly. He was an insecure guy who had a stuttering problem, but Gail saw kindness and stability. Eventually they married and had two children.

Gail's husband never said anything derogatory about her weight. In fact he had little to say about a lot of things, but he was a sweet and gentle man. To Gail, that meant a lot.

Gail was tired of being a prisoner to food. On the one hand, it calmed her down and provided comfort from the stress of life. On the other hand, it consumed too much of her time and thoughts. She felt more and more out of control and started to worry about her decreasing capacity to function in everyday life. She had to do something to get control because she was feeling more depressed. She was also teaching her daughter to use food to soothe her troubles.

Gail saw her doctor, who yelled at her, handed her a twelve-hundred-calorie diet and told her she wouldn't live long if she didn't get control of her eating. Gail was caught up in a cycle of overeating she couldn't stop. Daily she binged on a variety of foods. She skipped breakfast and then tried to eat a "diet" lunch. By afternoon she was famished and started bingeing. Her choice of binge foods usually included submarine sandwiches, chips, pizza and cheese. After stuffing herself, she washed it down with a liter or two of soda.

Hours later she started on sweets—ice cream, cookies or whatever else she could find in the house or at the 7–11. Then she would "try to be good" at dinner and eat a regular meal. Evening was the toughest time, however. As her daughter and husband brought out the snacks, she joined in and munched on food all night long until bedtime.

In bed, she determined that tomorrow she would be "good." No more bingeing. She would get control and start a diet. Tomorrow never came, and Gail continued to feel out of control.

Gail become depressed with her inability to control the bingeing. She felt trapped in a cycle that was making her feel more and more uncomfortable with her body. Walking her dog left her winded and short of breath. Climbing the stairs to clean took effort and hurt her joints. She was constantly tired. She found herself agitated and irritable with people. She was spending too much money on food. She was too young to be feeling this old.

Gail wanted help. She had been on every fad diet you could imagine—grapefruit, soup, protein and others. She always lost a few pounds but never maintained the weight loss, and she usually gained back more than she lost. She tried commercial diet programs like Weight Watchers, Jenny Craig and Diet Center, but again she wasn't able to stay with the eating plan long term.

Her friend suggested she take diet drugs, but the news of serious side effects and complications ruled out this option. She was desperate to find a way to stop bingeing. If she could stop bingeing, she knew she would lose weight.

As long as she was sending Cindy to a therapist for sexual abuse, she decided she needed a therapist to tackle her eating problem. She never tried therapy, but she knew both she and her daughter used food to deal with past abuse. It was time to stop avoiding the abuse and get control of the eating.

I had no interest in helping Gail start another diet. Instead, Gail needed to learn to eat in a healthy way. First she had to stop depriving herself of food for long periods of time. When she skipped breakfast and ate only a little at lunch, she set herself up for a binge. The long period of food restricting left her physically hungry. Then she would overindulge to make up for feelings of deprivation.

I referred her to a registered dietitian who would establish a regular eating schedule with her and help her choose foods. No foods were forbidden or "bad." Skipping meals had to stop. "Diet" was not in our vocabulary. We were interested in lifelong changes, not short-term fixes.

Gail's bingeing was bigger than a will power issue. Bingeing was a stress reducer and a way to cope with bad feelings. Gail's father had been physically and verbally abusive. To cover up her hurt, she numbed herself with food. Food was a reliable distraction from her pain.

Gail needed new ways to deal with stress. I gave her a list of about a hundred things she could do when she was upset. Eating was *not* on the list. She could listen to soothing music, take deep breaths, pray, walk outside, read a book, take a hot bath or dig in her garden. She had to pick twenty items off the list and place them on her refrigerator. When she felt the urge to binge, she had to pick one thing from the list and do it.

We practiced stress management in which she learned to relax her body and tune into body sensations such as tension, anxiety and true physical hunger. She was asked to write down situations that led to bingeing so we could identify what set her off, and work on those cues or responses.

We learned that most of Gail's binges occurred in the evenings, the time of day when her dad used to beat her. Even though she experienced no abuse from her husband, evenings made her tense and anxious. All those years of being beaten made it difficult for her to relax and enjoy her family.

She was tense in the evenings but wanted to be with her family. Unfortunately the family's main way to relax and spend time together was eating. So the family needed tips on activities that would bring them together that weren't food related.

Gail's father was dead but she knew she was holding onto feelings of bitterness and anger toward him. She needed to let go of those feelings and free herself from carrying that weight. In a letter to Dad (she obviously couldn't send), she articulated her thoughts about how he hurt and abused her. It was an emotional letter for Gail to write and read, but put her in touch with the intensity of her pain. Gail had to forgive her father. As she did, a tremendous weight was lifted.

Next she had to deal with her brother Sam. She decided to confront him. He claimed he didn't remember fondling Cindy and that Cindy probably made it up. But Gail took control and protected her daughter. Sam would not be allowed alone with Cindy again. If he ever tried to abuse her in the future, she'd report him to the police. Again, Gail had to forgive a man who didn't ask for forgiveness. Sam was harder to forgive than Dad. He was still alive, hurt her daughter and refused to take responsibility.

Although she attended church, Gail was skeptical about God. She understood her need to forgive her dad and Sam but wondered why God allowed these men to hurt her and her daughter. What did she or Cindy do to deserve abuse?

The truth was they did nothing to deserve abuse. Men are abusive because evil abounds in their hearts. Dad and Sam were not walking according to God's ways and allowed sin to control their lives. They were weak men who didn't control their rage and lashed out on those around them who were vulnerable. What they did was wrong and sinful. But God doesn't force Himself on men who have no interest in Him. If they choose to live in disobedience, they will hurt themselves and others. They invite evil into their hearts through sin.

251

Physical abuse was generational in Gail's family. Her father was beaten by an alcoholic dad and her mother by a mean and harsh father. The sins of the father were evident in Gail's house growing up.

Gail prayed the sinner's prayer with a friend of the family when she was eighteen years of age after moving out of the house. The same lady prayed for the generational curse of physical abuse to be broken in Gail's family. Gail never understood what this meant.

I explained that generational curses are broken by the shed blood of Jesus Christ. When Gail asked Jesus into her heart, the sins of her father no longer had influence over her. She had the power to heal and be free because of Jesus. As a Christian, she had the power to overcome the evil that was inflicted on her.

She married a man who was not abusive.

Jesus also told her in Matthew 5:38–42 that she had to love her persecutors and pray for her enemies. For Gail's healing to be complete, she not only had to forgive her abusers but also get to the point that she could pray for them. In Gail's case, this applied only to Sam because her father was dead.

Gail's husband was more the example of Christ. He submitted himself to God's Word and evidenced the fruit of the spirit. He saw beyond Gail's body and loved who she was—kind, giving, caring, intelligent and a good wife and mother. He treated her with respect because he loved her and was obedient to God's Word. Her husband, like Christ, accepted her unconditionally and saw her good heart.

Gail had to recognize evil when she saw it and not fear it. She had the right to protect herself and her daughter from future attacks but couldn't lead her life bitter and fearful because of the past. When she chose to forgive those her hurt her and could pray for Sam, she was free to experience God's love in a new way. She no longer needed food to comfort and soothe her. That was God's job, and He was waiting to fill her up full with good things.

Overeating is a way of coping with discomfort. It's a way to numb yourself from emotional pain. It is a way to protect yourself. It's a way to find comfort. It is not an intentional self-destructive behavior or simply a lack of self-control. Overeating is a way to gratify yourself without having to experience painful emotions that may be present. In Gail's case, food medicated her from the intense pain she felt from abuse.

Tolerating negative feelings is something all women with eating disorders must work to do. Instead, they try to ignore or numb out the feelings with food. When food is not used to self-medicate, the pain of losses and hurts is felt more acutely. You must learn to work your way through pain and loss so you can get to other side—a new spiritual body transformed by Christ.

No More Diets Please

Food obsessions keep us stuck. Instead of dealing with life's losses directly, we are distracted with food and dieting. There are many ways to be distracted when it comes to losing weight. We try them all. The belief is that once the weight is lost, life will improve and all of our problems will be solved. So dieting becomes the focus of life. If you are overweight, you have probably been like every other woman and tried a million diets.

You know the diets—eating grapefruit, special soups, high protein-low carbohydrates, the popcorn diet, the Beverly Hills diet, the Scarsdale diet, Weight Watchers, Jenny Craig, Diet Center...the list is long. The word *diet* should be stricken from your vocabulary. When you diet, you do lose weight. The problem is when you stop dieting, you gain weight back. Stop dieting and learn to eat sensibly. Learn to handle your emotions without using food.

Where are the magic pills?

Dieting is something you do for a period of time. Eating healthy is a life change. But there are other tempting options to losing weight besides dieting. One of those is drugs. Drugs are not the magic pills people believe them to be when it comes to sustaining weight loss. At least not yet. The side effects can be serious. Long-term results are not yet promising. Remember the phenfen (phentermine and fenfluramine) scare? These anorexiants were tauted as the new magic pills to solve the problem of obesity. We later discovered serious potential medical complications for some people using these drugs. You need to be careful not to jump on the band wagon craze of medication cures until there is clear data indicating their safety and long-term effectiveness.

VLCDs

Very low calorie diets (VLCD) were hot in the 1980s. Remember Oprah's stint with Optifast? VLCDs are supposed to be used for those who are at least 30 percent above their ideal weight. They need to be medically supervised by a doctor who understands how to monitor your health. There should also be a multidisciplinary treatment team involved. Typically these diets involve twelve to sixteen weeks of drinking a special liquid, followed by a refeeding phase and weight maintenance with behavioral strategies to help you eat and live differently. In the short term, you lose weight. The problem is most regain their weight after a few years. The other problem is we can all lose weight on liquids, but eventually we have to face food again.

I was asked to be the behavioral consultant to one of the well-known liquid fasting programs. I ran a number of groups but soon ditched the group format the program suggested. It was not meeting people where they were emotionally. A few people were successful over the long haul, but most steadily gained back the weight after two years of eating solid food again.

VLCDs must be carefully supervised by a physician. In my opinion, that's the minimum requirement. Someone needs to work with you on the other issues we've discussed and care about all of you for true success to happen.

Surgery

Surgical options are usually reserved for the very obese (at least one hundred pounds overweight) who have failed at most other treatment approaches. Usually, surgery is only considered when there are medical dangers caused by the obesity. For example, one of my clients had surgical weight reduction because her weight was contributing to congestive heart failure. Her internist and the surgeon believed there was less risk having surgery than doing nothing. You need to find surgeons who are knowledgeable about obesity surgery, up on the latest techniques and experienced with a good track record of success.

There are various forms of gastric restrictive procedures used by surgeons. Assessing who will benefit from surgery is still tricky business. A few patients never survive the surgery. Surgery always carries a risk. And the post surgical complications can be serious for some patients.

No short cuts

All in all, weight-loss efforts are still up for grabs when it comes to keeping weight off long term. You need to work with someone who is up on the latest research regarding all the options so you know the risks and aren't responding to fads. New developments in the field of obesity are happening all the time, which is encouraging but should not be our only hope.

The psychological issues have to be treated no matter what you do to lose weight. Sometimes, dealing with the emotional component of overeating is what leads to success. My advice is this. It's going to sound simple again, but of course it is incredibly hard to do—learn to eat sensibly, begin to exercise and stop using food as your emotional nurturer. Spiritually, fill yourself up so that food takes on less power in your life. You do not need to be a slave to food; food should serve you in a way that is truly nourishing. You may have to work with a therapist to make this happen.

GOD'S SELF-CONTROL

Our hope is in God who promised that we can have self-control. Galatians 5:22 says, "But the fruit of the Spirit is love, joy, peace, longsuffering, kindness, goodness, faithfulness, gentleness, self-control." Love is the fruit. Fruit comes from a seed. The seed is the Word of God. You plant the seed (the Word) in your heart first. The result of knowing and believing God's Word is love, or, said another way, the result of planting the seed is fruit (love). God's love then produces self-control.

Because we love God, we want to please Him and keep His commands. As we bring ourselves into obedience to His plan, His way of living and His will, these things produce self-discipline. Self-discipline entails practicing self-control in all areas of our lives. This may mean changing your behavior and addressing areas you have previously denied or numbed by food. As we practice self-control and please God with our lifestyles, He gives us supernatural control. Then it is possible to be self-disciplined with food. Remember, when we are weak, He makes us strong.

The idea here is that in the natural it is hard to exercise self-control over many things in our lives. We try, but it is a struggle. As we understand all the issues involved with overeating, it helps us understand why self-control is so hard. Without God to help us, failure is predictable. When we bring all our behavior and motivations into alignment with God's Word and let Him drive the car, we get to the destination, which is self-control in all things.

So work on all your "stuff" associated with overeating but don't neglect filling yourself up with God's Word. It produces love, which produces self-control. God's love is the secret ingredient. It's what changes us from striving to overcoming.

15

Overcoming Eating Disorders

There is hope for overcoming eating disorders. You don't have to live with these problems for the rest of your life. You will hear from some professionals that recovery is only possible—that you will always struggle with the disorder, trying not to engage in the eating behaviors. There are women like this. They are *better,* though not *healed.* There are also girls and women who don't get better.

I believe you can be completely free from these disorders if you allow God to be part of the recovery. Jesus came to free people from mental health problems, not just help improve their symptoms. There are no instances in the Bible in which Jesus helped people *a little.* When He touched them, they were *completely healed.*

Your goals should be freedom from the problematic eating behaviors, renewal of your mind, emotional health and restoration of your physical body so you can move on with your life to experience the fullness God has for you. So how do you get to that place? Let's begin with practical steps you can take. Some of these will sound very basic but are necessary. Others will be harder to do but also necessary for your healing.

ANOREXIA

Stop denying the seriousness of your problem and that you have an eating disorder.

Typically, you forcefully deny the problem and plead with family members to give you one more chance to put on weight. Too often, you only want to put on weight to please others and get them off your back. If you don't see the need for help, you will bargain with those who care about you and be manipulative. It's only when you stop denying the seriousness of your weight loss that healing begins. If you are a family member of a girl or women with anorexia, you may have to be adamant about the need for help. You will be resisted. Be firm and loving.

Get help.

This is a problem that gets worse without intervention. You need to find someone you trust who specializes in the treatment of eating disorders and start working with that person. An eating disorder specialist knows how to connect food problems with underlying emotional issues. I can't stress enough the importance of working with a therapist with experience and knowledge about eating disorders. The sooner you get help, the better.

Get a physical exam from a physician who understands eating disorders.

The medical complications of this disorder can be severe, so you need medical supervision. Women die from anorexia. You need a doctor who will work with you on monitoring lab work and weight. He or she needs to be family friendly and sign a release to work with the therapist. Personally I work with internists, endocrinologist, knowledgeable pediatricians and well-trained family practice doctors.

You must gain weight.

There is no way around this. You won't *feel* like gaining weight. You will feel like losing weight, but you can't give in to that feeling. Instead you must trust the person you are working with to help you gain to a healthy weight.

There are two weights to work with in treatment.

The first is called a *target* weight. This is the absolutely lowest weight you can maintain to be medically safe. This weight is determined by the treatment team. The second weight is called an *ideal* weight, which is based on your body frame and height. The ideal weight is usually given as a weight range and is a goal to work toward. The first step in healing is to reach your target weight and maintain it. Then work toward gaining closer to the ideal range.

The greatest fear is that you will get fat.

No one wants you fat, they just want you healthy. Most of my clients have to accept this by faith. Everything in you resists gaining weight, so it's a matter of trusting the people who care about you.

Work with a registered dietitian as well as a therapist and medical doctor.

You need to learn how to gain weight slowly and safely and develop good eating patterns. Healthy eating is the goal. There are no "bad" foods. How to eat sensibly and in moderation has to be learned. A dietitian will work with you and introduce calories and foods gradually into your diet. She's your coach, not the enemy. She is not the wicked witch in *Hansel and Gretel,* trying to fatten you up to eat you for dinner!

Involve the entire family in treatment.

Self-starvation is something you have to change, but family is a part of the solution. I won't see a girl or woman with an eating disorder unless the family is involved. There is too much research supporting the notion that family involvement helps long term. My clinical experience also bears this out.

This disorder is about growing up and finding a voice in the family system. You have to learn to be connected to the family and also be a separate person. Starving yourself in an effort to stay childlike helps you avoid growing up, but is life threatening and undermines your sense of competency. You can't face your continuing self-development when you are obsessed with food and refusing to eat. Self-starvation is not the way to approach your quest for independence. The way family members relate and react to emotional issues has much to do with your choice of symptoms (anorexia). All family members have to make changes, not just you.

Learn to identify and express feelings.

You don't know what you feel and how to express feelings. Consequently you are tense in your body and hold feelings inside. I frequently tell my clients that they have so many feelings stuffed in their stomachs there is no room for food. The first step is to learn to put a name on a feeling and then get it out of your stomach.

Learn to deal with conflict.

Anorexics are usually conflict avoidant. Sometimes they lack good models of conflict resolution because family members don't deal well with conflict. Instead family members hold upsets inside and put on agreeable fronts. Compliance is highly valued in these families.

Conflict is a part of adolescent development and needs to be dealt with directly so that you learn how to resolve conflict. An eating disorder is an indirect way to deal with conflict.

Change your thinking.

Your thoughts need renewing. Self-denial is not a virtue when it is taken to an extreme. Even Jesus rested and went away from the crowds for periods of time. You do not have to be perfect to be loved. Self-control is important but is hard to maintain at all times when you are growing up. People won't hate you when they know how you really feel and think. Conflict is not bad. You need to share your thoughts so they can be challenged and corrected if necessary. The correction comes from the Word of God and how He thinks about you and what He has to say about you. When you learn what God has to say, you'll be pleasantly surprised.

Face your emerging sexuality.

Although sexual feelings can feel scary and uncontrollable at times, they have to be acknowledged and expressed. The way you feel about your developing body is important. If it has been violated, you need help working through the violation. If not, you may need to learn to accept the changes and feel comfortable with your changing physical body.

Fill yourself up with love.

You must learn to love God and consequently yourself. When you understand how God thinks of you, esteems you and cares about you, you have to feel good about yourself. He unconditionally accepts you, made an unbreakable promise to you and wants to bless you. This is the basis for good self-esteem.

Be willing to face tough issues.

You must be committed to the process of healing. You will get mad at your therapist a lot because she is pushing you to eat and deal with issues you have avoided that are uncomfortable. Therapy is the place to practice identifying and expressing your upsets. Therapy is the place to learn how to connect feelings to your self-starvation. Then you practice facing tough issues in your family and out in the world. Eventually you will feel more competent. What feels unfamiliar at first will become easier with practice.

BULIMIA

Stop bingeing and purging.

Seems obvious enough! The first order of business is to get the bingeing and purging under control. The longer you have been involved in this cycle, the more difficult it is to break. Many women talk about bingeing and purging like a habit. Habits are tough to break, but can be broken. A qualified counselor can give you tips on how to resist a binge and purge. Prayer and the power of the Holy Spirit can help you overcome temptation.

Recognize the cues that set off a binge.

I often have my clients keep track of what happened right before and after a binge. Was there anything about the situation that set it off? Can you identify a place, person, feeling that led to bingeing? If so, you may need to change that cue or learn to deal with it differently. For example, many clients binge when they are bored, so it would be important to plan activities so boredom doesn't become a cue for bingeing. Other cues are things like having an argument with a boss, being rejected by a boyfriend, being put down by a friend, a loss, anniversary or a death, a financial pressure. If you write down the cues, you may see a pattern. You can then work on handling specific situations differently so as to prevent bingeing.

Establish a regular eating schedule.

Skipping breakfast sets you up for a binge. Skipping any meal and eating at irregular periods does the same. You have to learn to eat at regular intervals and eat balanced meals. This sounds so simple, but so many of you don't do it. The lack of disciplined eating also carries over to sleep, activities and self-care. There is usually a lack of balance in other areas of your life as well.

Change your thoughts.

Like anorexics, bulimics usually have distorted thoughts. You tend to think in all or nothing terms—it's all bad or all good. You tend to think things are a catastrophe or can't be managed. Your thinking can be negative and self-critical.

Learn to say no.

You can't do everything. If you try, you will fail so you must set limits and learn to say no to an overload of activity and food. You can't please everyone or impress them so don't try. (There's a thought that needs renewing!) Do what is reasonable, not extreme.

Tolerate frustration.

Dealing with life is hard work emotionally, and you must learn to accept and tolerate frustration. You tend to act impulsively or panic when presented with frustration. You need to learn to tolerate negative feelings, not give in to them or avoid them. Be patient with yourself as well.

Face up to your shortcomings.

Look, we all have them. You might as well take a good inventory and start to work on them now instead of later when the damage is done. Eventually women in therapy have to face where they fall short. I hope you are also thinking about the spiritual significance of this step. When we admit that we all fall short of the glory of God, we have hope. When we pridefully believe we can be perfect, we don't need God. We take things on in our own power, which usually leads to a vomited mess.

You may have other areas of impulse problems.

Many of you are out of control in areas other than food. You may be sexually impulsive or have addiction problems. For example, you may drive impulsively, react too intensely to situations or binge on alcohol. Bingeing applies to more than just food. Sexual impulsivity is often a wish for nuturance and a desire for connection with another person. It is a confusion of sex with caring, and thus engaged in to meet nuturing needs. Take a look to see if you binge in other areas of your life, and work on those areas as well.

Manage stress.

Stress is a part of life and should not be handled by eating. Learn other ways to manage stress like relaxation techniques, taking time outs and walking. There are a number of good resources on stress management. The Bible tells us to give our cares to God.

Express negative feelings directly.

Negative feelings (anger, hurt, frustration) are hard to admit and express directly because people may get upset, not like you or come back at you in some negative way. You must learn to express those negative feelings in appropriate ways and not use food to medicate them. It is not weak to admit to feeling bad. There are productive and destructive ways to deal with negative feelings. Learn the productive ones.

You don't have to be perfect to be loved.

We don't *earn* love, we just *are* loved. This is a simple but revolutionary concept to most. If you don't feel loved, then look to God. He freely gives you love and doesn't expect anything in return. It is not how good you are, what you do, how many awards you earn, how successful you are that earns you God's love. Love is His unbreakable promise to you. Accept it on the unconditional terms with which it is offered.

COMPULSIVE OVEREATING AND OBESITY

Lose the word diet *from your vocabulary.*

I'm talking to you straight again. We don't diet. We learn to eat healthy for life. Sorry there is no short cut or magic pill. You must change your eating habits for good. Losing weight is not that hard. Keeping it off is. Many women make the mistake of eating well for only a period of time and then go back to old habits. If you are overweight, chances are you can't diet and then go back to old habits. A lower metabolism and other factors we talked about in the previous chapter are no doubt affecting you.

Exercise.

I know this is basic, but most of us don't do it. It is clear that exercise helps maintain weight loss and is good for your health. Don't wait to get motivated. It may never happen. Instead, think of exercise like getting out of bed—you do it because you have to face the day. Start with something you enjoy or can tolerate. Walk and gradually increase the time you do it. Walking is a good place to begin, because it is less painful than other types of exercise and can gradually be built up. Swimming is also good, because your weight is lifted in the water and causes less stress on your bones and joints.

Make simple lifestyle changes.

Anything you can do to get moving and more active helps. So make small changes like these examples—park farther from the door of the mall so you have to walk more, take the stairs instead of the elevator, dump the remote and get up to change the TV channel. Small changes, over time, make a difference.

Learn the difference between physical hunger and psychological hunger.

Overweight women often mistake emotional emptiness for hunger. You need to learn the physical sensations associated with hunger so you can tell the difference. You will have to distinguish true physical hunger from the need to soothe yourself emotionally.

Stop waiting to be thin.

Your life won't dramatically change when you lose weight. Many clients have been disappointed that weight loss didn't bring more dates, more happiness and more attention. The reason weight doesn't solve all your problems is because it didn't cause all your problems. Maybe you need to be more assertive, initiate conversation and learn how to show interest in others. The point is—losing weight doesn't change your personality. It may give you a boost or added confidence, but it won't make interpersonal skills magically appear.

Don't hide behind the fat.

When you are overweight, you can use the extra weight as a protective layer. You may secretly wish to stay overweight, feeling there is less pressure to deal with your sexuality. Interestingly enough, a study at Michael Reese Hospital in Chicago found that heavier women desired sexual intercourse more than their thinner counterparts. (Hey, finally some good news.)

Even so, you may be afraid to feel sexy, worry about controlling your impulses or worry that men will be more attracted to you and make advances if you lose weight. If you don't feel prepared to handle your sexual feelings, you may try to hide in lots of ways.

Learn to be assertive.

You may be passive and allow others to rule your life. Then you build up anger and resentment. You have to speak up to get your needs met. People can't read your mind. Instead of getting mad because no one is responsive to you, make sure you are being direct with your needs. Take lessons, and practice assertiveness skills.

Find your talents and abilities.

You may be dependent and feel you can't do things because of feelings of low self-esteem. You have more potential in you than you realize. We all have talents and abilities. You may need to find them and start using them rather than rely on others to meet your needs. If you rely on people too much to take care of you, start evaluating if that is necessary. In others words, give less control to other people and start trying to do for yourself. You may be amazed at your hidden capabilities. The less dependent you are on others to meet your needs, the more you can trust God to supply all that He has promised. As you place your dependence on the right person (God), your urge to overeat will be less.

Take charge of impulses.

Overeating is an act of immediate gratification. It is the inability to deny the immediate pleasure of food. You have to learn to deny the immediate pleasure for the long-term goal of health. Eating is delightful. Food is good, and you may not find anything else at the moment that will make you feel as good as food. That's OK, because your behavior should not be based on doing only what feels good at the moment. You can admit that food is delicious and tempting—so is premarital sex, the high of drugs and pornography, but we don't give in to these temptations. Submit to God, resist the devil and he will flee from you (James 4:7).

Resolve relationship conflicts.

Relationship conflicts tend to get avoided, and the pain gets pushed down deep inside. Why? Because you don't want to rock the boat. Food is used to cover over hurts and wounds. You have to commit to resolving problems with the people involved rather than eating your way through them.

Find food substitutes.

I usually ask my clients to list enjoyable activities other than eating. It's hard to top food, but there are other things we do that are enjoyable and must be substituted for eating. When you have the urge to eat, try to do one of the things on your list instead. Over time, the habit of reaching for food will lessen.

THE SPIRITUAL SIDE

Overall, the idea is to find new ways to deal with old problems. Food has become the accepted way to solve dilemmas. You eat because you are upset, happy, bored, lonely, angry or rejected. You must learn new ways to cope and not have food become the outlet for stress. Remember that food obsessions are about the loss of control. Anorexics feel out of control, so they take extreme control over their bodies and diet. Bulimics binge out of control, then purge to regain control. Bingers and overeaters lose control and overeat because they feel out of control in other areas of their lives.

How should we view eating disorders from a spiritual perspective?

The Bible does talk about eating. I can't say I've heard many sermons on the topic, but eating is discussed in the Bible. Proverbs 23 talks about gluttony and ties it to poverty. Matthew 6:25 tells us not to worry about what we eat or drink or worry about our bodies. That's pretty direct, wouldn't you say?

We are also told God wants to feed us both spiritually and physically (Matt. 25:35). Jesus is described as the bread of life. If we come to Him, we will never thirst or hunger (John 4:14; 6:35). Great scriptures, but how do we apply them? How do we stop from worrying about what we eat and let God supply all our needs?

Let go of pride.

First, let's admit what the apostle Paul so wisely pointed out. (See Romans 7:15–25.) We often do what we hate. So even though we want to trust God to help us, we still put our trust in our own power. That becomes a problem. To help you overcome an eating disorder, you must first want help. You have to give up fear, pride or whatever is telling you that you can do this on your own. If you could, you would have!

Recognize deception.

We have to recognize the deception involved in these disorders. I'm convinced there is spiritual deception. So far, no one has really explained why women with eating disorders have a distorted image of their bodies. But the distortion explains why a ninety-pound woman looks in the mirror and see herself as "fat." Anything that is not representative of the truth is a lie. If the enemy can keep us deceived, it fits into his plan to destroy us. Eating disorders qualify because they are destructive to the body.

So the action you take is to choose not to believe the distortion you see. How do you do that? By having faith in someone you trust who is trying to help you get well. If that's a therapist, then believe she is telling the truth even though you can't see it. Whether you have a therapist or not, you have God. He's worthy of our trust. Remember faith is the evidence of things not seen, so you must have faith that God and people who want to help you wouldn't lie to you.

Have faith.

God tells you that the truth sets you free. So for example, if you know that weighing one hundred twenty-five pounds puts you at a medically safe weight, believe you need get there. Don't wait to feel good about it. Just have faith. Feeling OK with your body may take a while. Some of us never get there! Healing involves applying faith at many different levels.

Pray against the deception, and ask for your spiritual eyes to be opened.

Ask God to bring to the surface the deeper issues involved in the fear of weight gain so you can begin to address those issues. When He does, be willing to address those issues. This usually involves confronting emotional pain, but remember He gives you nothing you can't handle.

Ask God to heal you.

As I said, you need to ask for total healing—not just recovery. There is a difference. Recovery implies a regaining of something lost. When we lose something, we try to recover or retrieve it. But the time you spend struggling with an eating disorder rather than facing the challenges of development can't be recovered. You must grieve the lost time and ask God for something new. He restores what was lost with something better and new.

Discover who you are in Christ.

You are in the process of forming a firm and corrected identity in Christ. You are facing issues previously avoided. You are asking for the courage to confront life without hiding. Be assured that the One who raised people from the dead can heal you. What's a big deal to us is small potatoes for God. He's the same yesterday, today and forever. Continue to read your Bible and fill yourself up with His Word. Your body is fertile ground, and God wants to grow beautiful women with His seeds (the Word).

The path to healing is unique for each person. But there are enough common threads to which we can all relate. The one common thread is that we all need God, must accept His love, be obedient to His Word and walk in faith.

There is hope if you or someone you know struggles with an eating disorder. Be encouraged that you are not a disappointment to God. He accepts you as you are. Your weight doesn't matter to Him, but your body is His temple and should be honored. Honor God with your body. Do all you can to be more conformed to the image of Christ. Deal with your problems directly and with courage. Most of all accept God's love for you. He wants you whole.

EPILOGUE

More Thoughts on Transforming Loss to Newness

For the past twenty years I have listened to hundreds of stories of peoples' lives. I have learned a great deal as they have graciously allowed me into their most intimate conversations. I have cried, laughed and steadfastly held onto the belief that change is possible for all.

I hope you have seen that my optimism for change is not because I am well studied or trained. It's not because people have within them the power to heal. It is because of the hope of Jesus Christ in us. He is the fulfillment of all He intended us to be. The healing power of Jesus transcends the natural in a way that is hard to explain unless you have witnessed or experienced it.

Loss is not something we have to fear. It's not depressing to face the reality that living is about facing dying. Dying, as you have learned, involves more than physical death. It involves facing the loss of relationships, things, dreams, control, giving up childhood, structure, the perfect body and more. Successfully navigating loss requires dying to self and putting your trust in God. When we die to self, we are no longer controlled by people and the circumstances of life. We are surrendered to God and His plan. His plan for us is always good.

Any problem you face can be overcome by the power of God in you. There is nothing that is hopeless or cause for despair. You may wonder how you can walk in that confidence when so much of living seems to be a struggle. Most of you reading this have been frustrated with a life that doesn't feel very victorious.

My intent is to help you move to a place where you are not stuck in the muck of life. Rather I want you living a victorious life overcoming depression, anxiety and eating disorders. You can do it; don't let anyone convince you that you can't. You don't have to be recovered from anything; you can be free, transformed. There is nothing too great for my God to do.

I should tell you that much of my growth in this area has come from four sources—reading my Bible while sitting under an anointed pastor who knows and preaches the Word of God; being schooled and trained by people who have mentored me in the professional and academic worlds; talking to hundreds of clients throughout the past twenty years; and working through my own losses and life experiences. Everything we do and experience has to ultimately measure up against the Word of God.

Most of us are unfamiliar with the true nature of God. Our ideas about God have been shaped by Sunday school teachers, books, preachers, self-help manuals, testimonies, seminars and relationships with other people. People give us a distorted view of God if they are not grounded in God's Word. And let's admit it, most people aren't. There are a lot of well-meaning people giving their opinions and putting hope and trust in the wrong things. We are so desperate for truth, we'll listen to anything, anyone, rather than check what they are saying against the ultimate authority of Scripture.

Our families are also a basic source of learning about God. You have learned in this book that families can be a major source of distortion when it comes to understanding God. Our parents are the prototype for who God is. They are supposed to love us unconditionally. They are supposed to protect us and never let us down. In reality, they fail us at times. Then we look toward other people to love us unconditionally. We hope marriage, our friends or even the church will give us love, but we are often let down in those relationships as well. When this happens, we tend to transfer our views of failed love onto God. God gets all the negative attributes and then doesn't look so appealing either.

Our culture preaches a message opposite from the love of Jesus, which is why Jesus isn't a popular figure to emulate. The culture tells you we are inherently good. Jesus says we are all sinners in need of redemption. The culture says we can heal ourselves—that we have the healing power within us and just need to find it. Watch any talk show, and you will see guest after guest promoting the *power of you,* not the *power of the gospel.* Why is this? Because we don't want to admit our need for Jesus. We don't want to surrender our will to His and be conformed to His image. Why? Because we don't trust that what He wants to do with us will be better than anything we could possibly dream or think ourselves. We are arrogant and prideful.

The culture tells us to get what we need at the expense of others. Jesus says it is better to give then receive; not to store up treasures here; not to love money; not to covet and envy things. The culture tells us marriage is a contract; Jesus says it is a covenant. The culture says giving and taking life should be our decision. Jesus is the Creator and has a time for each one to live and die.

The culture says get revenge when someone wrongs you. Jesus says love them, pray for them and bless them. The gospel is a radical gospel of love.

It seems we are more interested in seeking God our own way then going to the direct source—the Bible. The Bible is God speaking to us. The Bible tells us God's will and gives direct counsel for how to live our lives. Yet, even well-meaning Christians don't go to the Bible for answers. And when they do, they don't do what it says.

Here's an example from just the other day. I was confronted with a situation in which someone was upset at her inability to mend the relationship with her grown son. She had fasted and prayed but reported there was no change. When asked if she talked with her son, she said he won't listen. Her despair was that she earnestly sought God and there was no movement.

I was puzzled by her decision to fast and pray over what to do. God already told her what to do in His Word, "Be ye reconciled one to another." Go do it. Make amends in whatever way it takes. God has already spoken to the situation. She needed to act.

The point of this example is help you understand that we don't need to plead with God or beg God to help us. We don't always need a special word or an audible voice. He has already helped. The answers are written in a Book to help you. We need to do what He says. When we don't, we get into problems. *Knowing* and *doing* are two separate things, which brings me back to my initial point about getting unstuck.

How do you get to the place where losses are transformed to growth? How do you move out of the feelings of grief and into true joy? The answer is really quite simple and taken out of a sermon from my pastor. Here it is: YOU HAVE TO KNOW AND BELIEVE GOD LOVES YOU. Remember this simple point?

I know what you are thinking, *Yeah, yeah, we've heard that before. Nice try, Dr. Mintle, but that is hardly a new thought. Is this the best you can do with a Ph.D. and all your therapy training? We know God loves us. We've sung the song, and we've heard this a few times before in our lives.*

You're right, it's hardly a new thought. But it's a thought that has not penetrated your psyche or soul, or you wouldn't be in the place you are. It's the bottom line of all problems—not feeling loved.

I want you to understand God's love the way I have come to know it.

This is so important because if you really *knew* God loved you and really *believed* it, you'd get unstuck.

Love is not a feeling, a relationship or an emotion, although we often define love these ways. Love is an unbreakable promise from God. Go back to when God gave that unbreakable promise to Abraham. When He instructed Abraham to bring the sacrifice, God established His covenant with him. The sun was setting, it was dark (as is often the case in our lives) and a torch appeared. The torch represented Jesus. Smoke (representing God) also appeared, and God passed through the equally divided pieces of the animal sacrifice and established His covenant. The division of the pieces represented God being split in two—a promise to send Jesus to establish the blood covenant with us.

God so loved the world that He gave His only Son. According to John 11:32, Jesus saw us in our dead condition, had compassion on us and was moved to do something for us. Because of His great love for us, He gave up His place in heaven, surrendered to the will of the Father, came to earth and suffered a horrible death on the cross, just so we could be saved. He made good on His promise. When we were lost, He found us. He had nothing to gain for doing this. His motivation to find us had to be out of His deep compassion for us. He was willing to give up everything for us—*that* is love.

Luke 6:17 says Jesus came down and stood on a level place. He became flesh and equal to man and woman. Jesus who was God came to earth to bring us a taste of His love. Love made Him willing to sacrifice all. Nothing we did earned His love. (This is a powerful thought to keep reminded yourself of over and over.) Nothing can overtake the love of God. God is love, and He is more powerful than anything or anyone.

When God sent Jesus, He sent the provision for all our needs. He gave us a taste of heaven, of the glory that is found in Jesus. What did Jesus do? He felt compassion for the multitude and fed them. He went about healing the sick. He delivered people from all kinds of affliction. He did what they needed to be whole. And Jesus is the same yesterday, today and forever, so He wants to do the same for you and me.

No matter how upset God was with the children of Israel, He didn't break His covenant with them. This should tell you that nothing you do will break His promise to love you unconditionally. You don't have to perform or measure up. God chose you as one of Abraham's descendants. When we accept Jesus into our hearts, we are grafted into the blood covenant. He gave you an oath not based on your behavior but based on His promise. You don't have to earn His acceptance. You are unconditionally loved by someone who will never let you down.

On the cross, Jesus took your grief. He took your rejection, hurts, pain, abuse, grief—all of it. For a moment He was divided from the Father. But Jesus was not forsaken. He rose again. Love was stronger than death. That's what God's love can do—conquer even death. What more could you need Him to do for you?

We have to know His love, but we also have to believe He loves us (1 John 4:16). Unlike people, God will never let us down. We can depend on God's love. Did you know that there are over seven thousand promises in the Bible? Here are only a few related to God's love.

- God does not break His promise (Judg. 2:1). He made a covenant with us and will not reverse it.

- He will never leave us (Heb. 13:5). Our behavior doesn't push God away.

- He will never forsake us. Nothing we can do will separate us from His love.

- God delights in mercy (Mic. 7:18). He shows us His mercy daily.

- He never remembers our sin (Mic. 7:19). His blood covered our sin.

- Our sins are forgiven and forgotten, and we are presented clean to the Father.

We often feel this is all too good to be true. We don't deserve such love. That is exactly the point. We don't deserve such love, but He gave it anyway. Once you understand this and believe it, it will change your life. Why? Because your self-esteem, your security rests on being loved. No matter what your past or what your circumstances, you are loved. You are a part of God's family. A daughter of great esteem.

The Bible is a love letter from God to you. It is full of God's promises of love and goodness. You need to receive it and believe it. Jesus faced the ultimate loss—death on the cross, and He conquered it. This gives us hope to conquer any loss as well.

When we accept the love of God, we will want to give His love to others. Having God's love equips us to act in love. Without it, we act in human ways that are often the opposite of God's ways. When you are secure in God's promises, you can freely give love.

When I heard the following news account read from the pulpit one Sunday, I was moved to tears. It was such a vivid picture of God's love for us. Do you recall the Northwest Airlines crash in Detroit in 1987? All the passengers on that flight were killed except one four-year-old little girl. It was inconceivable to many how that little girl could ever have survived the fire, smoke and impact of the crash. Everyone around her was dead. But she survived.

How was that possible? Her mother, knowing the plane was going down and that her child could die, got down on the floor, wrapped her body around that child and never let go. Nothing could separate her from loving and protecting that little girl—not even her own death. That is love, and that is how God loves you. He has His arms wrapped around you, wants to protect you and won't relax His hold. He will provide. He will supply. He will meet your every need. Let Him wrap His arms around you and hold you close.

Love is the fruit of the Spirit. The seed of the fruit is God's Word. We plant it in our heart, and it grows to a beautiful fruit of love. Out of love comes the expression of joy.

Because we are loved, we also have the promise that we will be more than a conqueror (Rom. 8:37). We have victory over trials, tribulation, negative circumstances and people because we have God's strength, which is the joy of the Lord. With God's strength (joy), I can move any mountain in my way. The enemy is already defeated because of the cross. That's why James tells us to count it all joy. We are loved. The trial is only a test to see if we will stand firm in His love. Don't let the trial move you from His love. Don't let depression, anxiety and eating disorders have a grip on your life. Don't stay stuck. Let God's love pull you out. Let God's love transform you from loss to growth. Just let God do what only He is so capable of doing—loving us unconditionally.

NOTES

CHAPTER 4
FACING THE LOSS OF RELATIONSHIPS

1. Holmes, T. & Rahe, R. The social readjustment rating scale. *Journal of Psychomatic Research,* (1967) 11.
2. Ahrons, C. R., "Redefining the divorced family: A conceptual framework," *Social Work,* November 1980.
3. Kelly, Jr., Gigy, L. & Hausman S., "Mediated and adversarial divorce: Initial findings from the divorce and Mediation Project." In J. Folberg & A. Milne, Eds., *Divorce Mediation: Theory and Practice* (New York: Guildford Press, 1986).
4. Chiriboga, D.A., Robert J. & Stein, J. A., "Divorce, stress and social supports: A study in help seeking," *Journal of Divorce 2,* 1978.

CHAPTER 6
FACING THE LOSS OF DREAMS

1. "I Will Listen" by Twila Paris. Copyright © 1996 by Sparrow Communications Co. All rights reserved. Used by permission.

You can experience more of *God's grace & love!*

*I*f you would like free information on how you can know God more deeply and experience His grace, love and power more fully in your life, simply write or e-mail us. We'll be delighted to send you information that will be a blessing to you.

To check out other titles from **Creation House** that will impact your life, be sure to visit your local Christian bookstore, or call this toll-free number:

1-800-599-5750

For free information from Creation House:

CREATION HOUSE
600 Rinehart Rd.
Lake Mary, FL 32746
www.creationhouse.com